FRESNO
California's *Heartland*
BY ELI SETENCICH

FRESNO
California's Heartland

BY ELI SETENCICH

PHOTO CREDITS:

Backgound-texture photo with pistachios, rainbows, and spheres, and bordered inset photo (page 2) by Keith Seaman/CAMERAD, INC

Sculpture of William Saroyan (page 2) and bordered inset photo (page 1) by Point Anderson

Irrigation water and grapes (page 1) by Paul Rutigliano

Fresno Water Tower (page 1) by Tamela Ryatt

Elecronic image editing by Paul W. Ringger, Jr.

CORPORATE PROFILES BY ROBERT TORRES

ART DIRECTOR BRIAN GROPPE

PHOTOGRAPHY EDITOR TIMOTHY A. FLEMING

SPONSORED BY THE FRESNO CHAMBER OF COMMERCE

TOWERY PUBLISHING, INC.

Preceding pages:
The arch was a sign of
the times when it was
erected in 1925, for
Fresno indeed was a lit-
tle city with a population
of around 80,000. Fresno
is now a metropolitan
area of some 500,000
people, and the arch is
no longer at the entrance
to the city, but the same
pride exists.
Photo by Point Anderson

Library of Congress Cataloging-in-Publication Data

Setencich, Eli, 1924-
     Fresno : California's heartland / by Eli Setencich ; corporate profiles by Robert
Torres ; art director, Brian Groppe ; photography editor, Timothy A. Fleming.
       p.   cm. — (Urban tapestry series)
    Includes index.
    ISBN 0-9628128-8-9 : $39.50
     1. Fresno (Calif.) 2. Fresno (Calif.)—Pictorial works.
3. Fresno (Calif.)—Industries.   I. Torres, Robert.   II. Title.
III. Series.
F869.F8S47   1993
979.4'83—dc20   92-53587
                                                      CIP

Acknowledgments

The publisher wishes to thank the Fresno Chamber of Commerce, without whose
support this book would not have been published.

TOWERY Publishing, Inc.
1835 Union Avenue, Suite 142
Memphis, Tennessee 38104

Publisher: J. Robert Towery
Editor: Patricia M. Towery
Managing Editor: Michael C. James
Assistant Editor: Allison Jones Simonton
Profile Art Director: Anne Castrodale
Editorial Assistant: Karen L. Bedscle
Editorial Consultant: Jerry Bier
    Editorial Contributors: Lloyd G. Carter
                                   Judy House

**URBAN
TAPESTRY
SERIES**
TOWERY
PUBLISHING, INC.

FRESNO
California's Heartland

C O N T E N T S

Following pages: There is beauty by a dam site east of Fresno in the springtime when the High Sierra snow begins its melt, filling reservoirs like Pine Flat on the Kings River and Millerton Lake behind Friant Dam on the San Joaquin. Construction of the two major dams in Central California assured a more reliable supply of water for the fields below. (Photo by Paul Rutigliano)

A mayor, no less, once called it the gateway to Bakersfield. Funny about Fresno, though it's not a laughing matter anymore. And not just because Johnny Carson has said goodnight for the last time, although that definitely was progress. ♦ For longer than its citizens like to remember, Fresno has been a punch line. Nobody can explain exactly why. Put it down to the name.

Fresno stands for "ash tree." Now, is that funny or what?

After a 1984 national survey purporting to measure livability ranked Fresno 226 among major cities, an upstate New York geography professor went for the jugular by proclaiming Fresno the worst place to live in the country, period—a conclusion he reached, it should be noted, without ever visiting.

Before that, a study in 1980 had come right out and said that among perceptive observers in salons and saloons from coast to coast, Fresno was viewed simply as "The Pits."

Predictably, it wasn't long before all this caught the eyes and ears of the trendsetters and social arbiters of television, who proceeded in 1986 to produce, at no small expense and effort, a week-long, prime-time spectacle titled, surprisingly enough, "Fresno"—as in "Dallas." Except for the raisins and the historic Water Tower, it had about as much to do with reality.

As might be expected, bashings of this nature do little for a city's self-esteem, not to mention its dignity. But the people of Fresno are not without humor, a sense based on the supreme confidence that they will have the last laugh. They held heads high and took the television spoof in stride, if not to their hearts. To show the stuff of which their leaders are made, no less a personage than the then mayor himself made a cameo appearance, showing up as the King of Siam at a masquerade ball and dancing a turn with Carol Burnett, the series' star.

But that is history. No joke, Fresno is beginning to be taken seriously, and not only by locals, most of whom will invite you to step outside the bowling alley over the city's good name. *Time* magazine, whose agent, unlike the geography professor, actually spent a few days in the Hilton Hotel downtown, found Fresno to be on the brink of something. No longer a hot dusty bump on Highway 99, Fresno, he told the reading world, was growing up.

Instead of water, all the old Fresno Water Tower holds anymore are memories. A downtown architectural symbol, it went out of operation in 1963, nearly 70 years after it was constructed. The tower's last role was as a backdrop in "Fresno," the 1986 television mini-series.

Well, maybe not so much up as out, far out, across the valley landscape to the horizon, visible in recent years only after the sky is washed by a passing storm. What once was a farming village is becoming more urbanized with each new arrival fleeing the gridlock and maddening crowds of the mighty metropolises. People who used to drive through Fresno on their way to somewhere else are driving to it and staying, settling in, buying homes, raising families.

The attraction is probably not its attractiveness, for Fresno will never win any beauty contests. Fresno draws people because, in many ways, it is still a down-home, country kind of town. There's a freeway, but it doesn't go too far. The trains still run through town. People still know their neighbors.

Fresno is attractive because it is reasonable. The cost of living is sensible. Housing is affordable. In Fresno, a new home in a new suburb still goes for under $125,000. While it is going through the trauma that every expanding city goes through, Fresno continues to be a place where the quality of life remains high. And the price is right. In Fresno, the embattled dollar goes further.

For big city folk seeking the simpler life, Fresno is a place where people can start anew, whether it's financial value, family values, or, in the case of the immigrants, a whole way of life they seek.

How did Fresno go from being the butt of the "Tonight Show" monologue to the envy of other cities in the overburdened state of California? Fresno stuck to what it knows best: hard work, economy, family, faith. The attempt to enshrine "family values" may have been a hot topic in the 1992 national political campaigns, but in Fresno the old-fashioned virtues never went out of style.

Fresno's particular kind of down-to-earth living seems to assure its continued growth—new faces, new industries, new demands, new problems. But Fresno, as always, will take things in stride and, with good humor, welcome the challenge of the '90s.

Following pages: From the snow-capped Sierra flows the water that is the lifeblood of the San Joaquin Valley— downward and westward through rivers, ditches, and canals onto the orchards and fields. (Photo by Brent Oliphant)

SACRAMENTO

SAN FRANCISCO
YOSEMITE

FRESNO COUNTY

FRESNO
KINGS CANYON
SEQUOIA

LOS ANGELES

SAN DIEGO

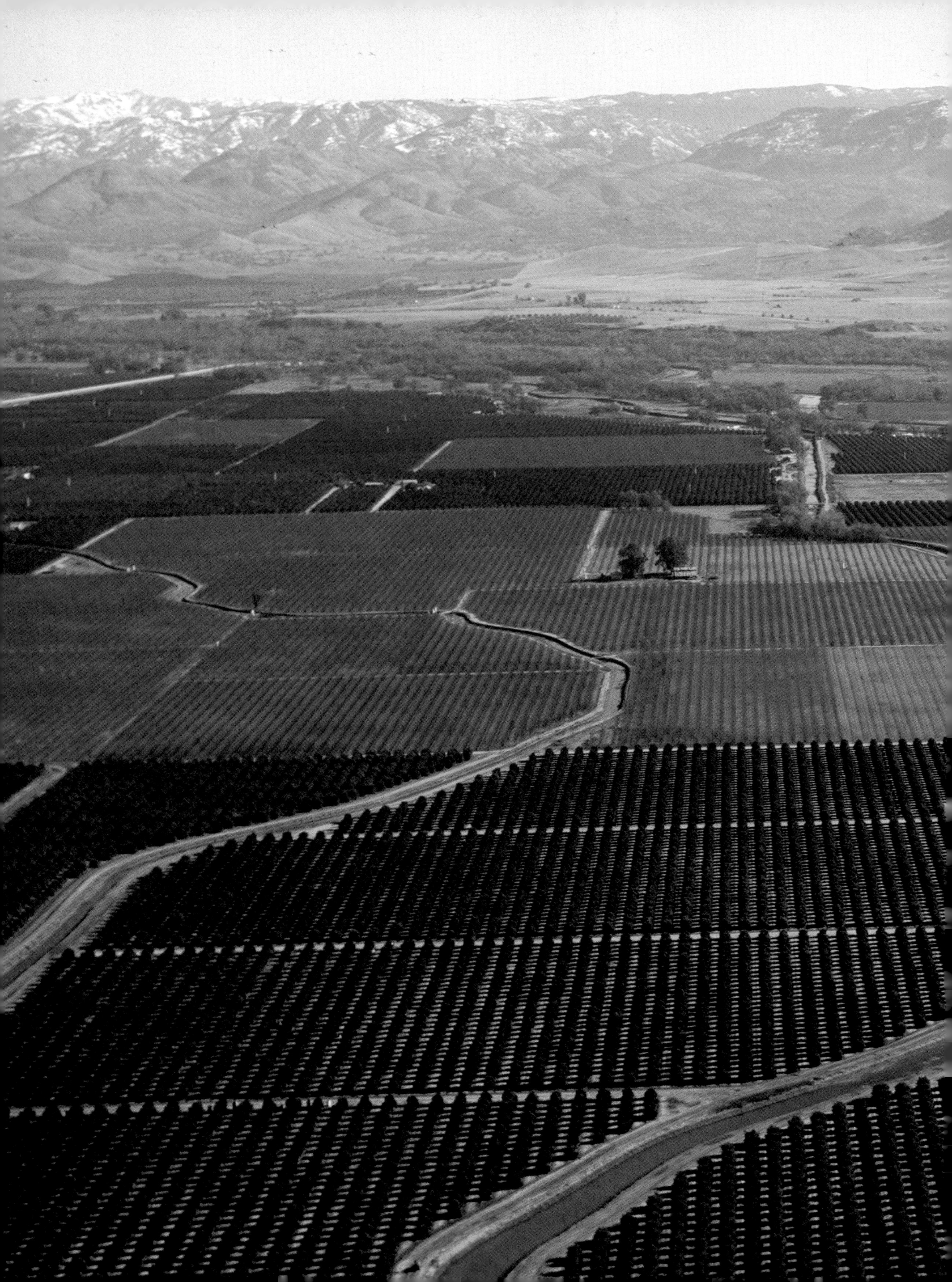

On a clear day in Fresno you can see forever, from the Sierra on the east to the Coast Range on the west. Fresno is at the heart of the San Joaquin Valley, the most productive agricultural area on earth, halfway between San Francisco to the north and Los Angeles to the south, and flanked by two once-great rivers, the Kings and the San Joaquin. ♦ It's become a cliche, but no less a truth, that the irrigation from the rivers is the lifeblood of the Valley. Each spring the thawed snows of the Sierra flow down to the farms of the Valley floor, making the harvest of abundance possible.

In the middle of all this is Fresno, a sort of regional capital, growing as it never has before, mostly northward to the San Joaquin River's edge.

While a stranger may never mistake Fresno for a Garden of Eden, it does lie in the shadow of some of the natural wonders of the world, from the Sierra Nevada, Yosemite National Park, and Huntington Lake down to the lush river bottoms of the Valley and across the westside plains to the Pacific. Only minutes away are rolling foothills, emerald green in spring, dotted with oaks and lakes, and, increasingly, with homesites. Another hour and Yosemite, a paradise of towering granite walls and waterfalls and light and shadow, unfolds in an image never to be forgotten.

To the south and east are the Sequoia and Kings Canyon national parks, wonderlands in their own right and living quarters of the largest of all living things, the Giant Sequoias, nearly as high as a football field on end and as wide as your living room. In the wintertime, it is all downhill in the snowy Sierra, standing-room-only for the skiers on the slopes of venerable Badger Pass in Yosemite, where Nic Fiore, almost as old as the park, gives lessons and still beats his best pupils to the finish line. Farther south along the Sierra is the newer Sierra Summit, a winter playground that beckons skiers from far and wide.

But it is incomparable, unbelievable Yosemite that is the shining star of the region. Hundreds of feet above the valley floor, a visitor is lost in time and space, as was explorer John Muir in 1868. He wrote about standing on a narrow ledge and peering at the moon through the cascade named Yosemite Falls:

"The effect was enchanting, fine, savage music sounding above, beneath and around me; while the moon, apparently in the very midst of the rushing waters, seemed to be struggling to keep her place ... I was in a fairyland between the dark wall and the wild throng of illuminated waters, but...'in an instant all was dark.' Down came a dash of spent comets, thin and harmless-looking in the distance, but they felt desperately solid and stony when they struck my shoulders like a mixture of choking spray and gravel and big hailstones. Instinctively dropping to my knees, I gripped an angle of the rock, curled up like a young fern frond with my face pressed against my breast, and...submitted as best I could to my thundering bath....I was weighing chances of escape ....My fate seemed to depend on a breath of the 'idle wind.' ..."

Today, the adventurous visitor can share the experience, though he will have a little more company than John Muir had a century or so ago.

Closer are the foothills, brown in summer but green as clover in spring—places like Squaw Valley, Tivy Valley, and Wonder Valley, where on a clear and sunny morning everything clops along at a slow trot at the dude ranch, quietly as the wind in the oaks. Little has changed since the days when all the fancy dudes moseyed up from Hollywood and other backwaters to hunker down for some hayriding or whatever under the stars. Among them were movieland cowpokes like Tom Mix and Hoot Gibson, and stars like Victor McLaglen and Betty Hutton. Before them, gunslingers from the notorious Dalton Gang used the Valley as their hideout after riding back into the hills from another train robbery. Nowadays, it's regular dudes, more often than not, riding into the sunset on a bicycle rather than a horse.

All is next to the city, a clod's throw, minutes away down country roads or over highways. The neighboring towns that are a part of Fresno County extend the down-home feeling, throwbacks like Selma and Reedley with downtowns that turn back the clock; Kingsburg with its Swedish traditions, down to the pancakes; Sanger, the Christmas Tree City, on the road to the Sequoias.

And then there's Clovis, wild and wooly Clovis, the feistiest of them all, coltish and kicking. The signs say, "A Way of Life." Better believe it, pardner. It is cowboy down to its boots and spurs, a horse-in-every-garage kind of town. The big event is the weekend Clovis Rodeo, an annual spring hoopdedoo that pulls in the toughest bronc busters and calf wrestlers that ever sat a saddle. If you don't believe it, step into Jim's Place and say your piece.

There used to be gold in these here hills northeast of town. Now they are covered with scrub oak and used mostly as grazing land, but, sure as rain, the hills will eventually yield a pot of gold for developers who keep building farther out for the growing population.

The irrigation from the rivers is the lifeblood of the Valley. Each spring the thawed snows of the Sierra flow down to the farms of the Valley floor, making the harvest of abundance possible.

Then don't let the door hit you on the way out.

They are all Fresno, places like Fowler on old 99 and Orange Cove among the orange groves, Kerman in the vineyards, Firebaugh and Mendota among the melon patches, Coalinga in the cotton fields down west, all part of what makes this the heartland.

◆

AS THE SEASONS COME AND GO IN FRESNO, the transition can be missed if you're not paying attention. Nobody misses summertime, which is hot, which is good because heat makes the grapes and peaches and cotton grow, which makes the economy go.

Back in the '40s, '50s, and '60s, when Miss Eleanor McClatchy was alive and setting the tone for *The Fresno Bee*, the only and thus leading daily journal of essential information in town, "heat" was a four-letter word, never to see the light of day in her newspaper. Same for the three-letter version; "hot" got very little play. Fair and warm was as bad as a day ever got in summer. Under her policy, when temperatures climbed into the 100s—not an uncommon occurrence even now—the paper informed its readers that the Valley was in the grip of a warmth wave.

It wasn't that Miss McClatchy had trouble coming to grips with the truth or that she single-handedly managed the news. It was simply a matter of semantics. Hot, she decreed, was just too extreme a word to describe the weather that made all those good things grow and ripen. Sunshine was as right as rain. Besides, she assumed most folks can pretty much tell for themselves when it's hot without having to read about it. Since her departure, the policy of the paper has changed; unfortunately, the summertime weather hasn't.

It is still hot, mostly in July and August—not clammy, but hot, crazy-making weather that can make the old underwear scoot up and stick like plastic wrap. It's endurable, particularly in the evenings after the heat waves go down and the breezes come up. What makes it even more comfortable is the absence of tornadoes, and there isn't a geezer around who can remember the last time a hurricane plowed through Fresno.

Winter is mostly cold, frequently foggy. Tule fog, it's called, clinging low and hard to the ground, but hardly ever keeping a person from going about his or her duties. Snow? Maybe once in a generation or two. It falls mainly in the high country, stacking and packing, everyone hopes, until spring, when it thaws and rushes down the big rivers into the reservoirs behind Pine Flat and Friant dams, stored there until needed.

In the spring, the blossoms in peach, plum, nectarine, and almond orchards grow so profusely that now there is a Blossom Trail, a leisurely 18-mile drive through the pink and white countryside. No cherry blossoms, but who needs them? It is still a sight for tired winter eyes. As is autumn, especially in the vineyards and orchards near the river bottoms where the deep reds, yellows, and oranges against a sky full of clouds bring the finest out of local watercolorists like Rollin Pickford, or local writers like William Saroyan: "I like all that about Fresno. I like the geometry, the precise geometry of setting out vines and orchards...and the total freedom and independence of the lifestyle....Fresno is a good place. It's a world...."

It's best of all, right after a storm, on a morning when the Sierra come up with the sun, rising in glory across the horizon as far as the eye can see. And white, from the dusting of frost by the river bottom to the wispy clouds, residues from the storm, creeping along the crest of the foothills to the crown of snow above it all.

"This Valley after the storms can be beautiful beyond the telling," is how poet William Everson, another local boy, from Selma down Highway 99, began his "San Joaquin." He knew the Valley all right.

▲ PAUL RUTIGLIANO

In the spring, the blossoms in peach, plum, nectarine, and almond orchards grow so profusely that now there is a Blossom Trail, a leisurely 18-mile drive through the pink and white countryside.

When it's springtime in the Valley, a normally sensible soul is likely to be transformed into a blooming idiot by the explosion of color and perfume in the orchards.

Following pages: "As high as an elephant's eye," row after row of ears will go mostly for livestock feed. Compared with cotton, grapes and a cornucopia of other crops, corn represents a mere fraction of the produce grown in the Valley. (Photo by Tamela Ryatt)

*H*istorically speaking, Fresno is a kid, a puppy, a babe in the vineyard compared to cities in much of the nation. Given a second choice, it is probably not where you would think to build a city in the first place. But it happened to be where Leland Stanford ran his railroad. ◆ Stanford was the founder and director of the Central Pacific Railroad. Upon seeing a wheat-

Like the rest of the Valley's wondrous bounty, the nectarines are something to crow about, tree-ripened and fresh as a June morning.

field thriving in the middle of the California prairie, he declared, "Wonderful! Here we must build a town!" Had it not been for that decision by Stanford, Fresno might today be a river town nestled by the oaks and cottonwoods and spanning the banks of the mighty Kings or San Joaquin—a Paris in the Valley of the Sun. Instead, it is between them, spanning neither river but rather the Southern Pacific and Santa Fe tracks.

It was in 1871 that Stanford and friends, chugging through, caught a glimpse of A.Y. Easterby's 2,000-acre ranch, lush and green with grain that had been irrigated by water from the Kings River. The diverted river water flowed through a stretch of ditches and canals engineered by Moses Church, an early leader in irrigation and one of the first ranchers in the area to raise sheep. So taken was Stanford with the sight of that bounty, he decided then and there that this would be the site of the Valley station on the new Central Pacific (now Southern Pacific) Railroad line. He wanted a place on the middle of the route, and this was to be it.

But Stanford and his business cohorts were not the only ones to get Fresno on track. Plentiful water from the Kings and San Joaquin flowed onto the Valley floor season after season, attracting farmers mostly, as if they knew in their bones that somewhere down the line this would become the richest agricultural region on God's green earth. Gradually, cattle ranching and wheat farming gave way to more diverse agricultural pursuits, the large spreads reduced to smaller farms that produced fruit crops—grapes, peaches, plums. By 1885, enough schools, businesses, churches, and homes had sprung up alongside the tracks to call the place a city. Well, a town.

Martin Theodore Kearney, known in some circles as the Belted Baron because of his continental connections and bearing, arrived on the scene in the early 1880s when land was dirt cheap. Brimming over with both self-confidence and cash, Kearney proceeded to buy up 10,000 acres. In his hands it did not lie fallow long, the Baron being a man with an irresistible urge to plant, be it palms or eucalypti or grapes—especially grapes, which under the Valley's hot summer sun would evolve into raisins.

So taken was Leland Stanford with the sight of that bounty, he decided then and there that this would be the site of the Valley station on the new Central Pacific (now Southern Pacific) Railroad line.

Following the lead of men like Francis Eisen (believed to be the first vineyardist to turn a sunburned grape into a delicacy), A.B. Butler, and other pioneer growers, Kearney became the original California Raisin, dancing all the way to the bank and into the San Joaquin history books. Kearney died in 1906, leaving his carefully tended garden to the University of California to be used as a working farm devoted to the advancement of agricultural science. He also left behind a fledgling industry whose practitioners were as gnarly and tough as a century-old grapevine. Little wonder they drew mention in his epitaph: "WARNING: Here lies the body of M. Theo Kearney, a visionary who thought he could teach the average farmer, and particularly, the raisin grower, some of the rudiments of sound business management. For eight years he worked strenuously at his task, and at the end of that time, he was no farther ahead than at the beginning. The effort killed him."

It did not, however, kill Fresno. Over the next decade, the town grew and prospered, and its population nearly tripled to nearly 35,000 souls, nourished by the area's productive agriculture. By the turn of the century, Fresno had become the fourth richest farm county in the country. As California grew, so did Fresno, flourishing like the fields surrounding it. Before long, there were the Courthouse and Courthouse Park, hotels and office buildings, a hospital, and even a zoo, thanks to a donation of park land from nurseryman Frederick Roeding. Rooted in agriculture, primarily the grape and raisin industry—and gradually cotton—Fresno bloomed. M. Theo Kearney, the visionary, saw it about right.

On another note, the same tracks that brought Kearney and the speculators and settlers to early day Fresno were also the way out for the less desirable as time went by. Though on the fringe of a Bible Belt transplanted by various migrations from civilization, Fresno was not without its share of wickedness. From Chinese number tickets in dens across the tracks to high-stakes roulette and green-shade poker in posh downtown parlors, gambling was part of the city's fabric until sent packing out of town by its reform-minded mayors.

Before television took over, the place to be was in line for the Saturday matinee. The old theaters—Warnors (formerly Warner's) and the Tower—remain, restored venues for comics and organists still. The Warnors Theater came by the name change when it changed hands in 1967. The movie house did not undergo renovation, however, until acquired by local businessman and philanthropist Frank Caglia in 1973.

One of them was the estimable Parker Lyon, a man of grit and action. In the aftermath of the 1906 San Francisco earthquake, the professional ladies of the Barbary Coast, suddenly bounced out of work, sought employment elsewhere around the state, including ripe and growing Fresno. After enduring a couple of days of spitting and hair-pulling between the newcomers and the locals, the mayor and police chief settled matters by rounding up the carpetbaggers, packing them onto a special Southern Pacific train, and dispatching the whole gaggle to Los Angeles. That, clearly, was in the days of a strong mayor form of government in Fresno.

Perhaps an even bolder mayor was Gordon E. Dunn, who came along a few generations later—and not just because he was nearly six-feet, five-inches tall, 250 pounds, and an Olympic medalist in the discus throw in the 1934 games in old Berlin. Slinger Dunn not only liked to throw his weight around, but also that of anybody else who tried to muscle in on his racket-busting agenda—a character trait that earned him a reputation as the toughest civic leader in the nation.

Dunn had hardly gotten comfortable in the mayor's chair in 1949 when he demonstrated that toughness to an unfortunate visitor from Los Angeles, a sharp-faced, sharply dressed hood packing $35,000 in bills from Mickey Cohen's bookie syndicate. Before the mug could slap the bribe on the desk of the $8,500-a-year prince of the city, the fixer was flying backward through the mayor's office door and into the street. "No Fun Dunn,"

they called the mayor after that.

While they may not have been as colorful, other city leaders have put their stamp on Fresno, from Chester H. Rowell, who became a reform mayor at the turn of the century, to Arthur L. Selland some 60 years later, after whom the city's Convention Center Arena is named. Art Selland, who upon losing a bid for a seat in Congress expressed relief and happiness because it meant he could continue living in Fresno, died in an automobile accident during his second term as mayor.

Other notables include Floyd Hyde, who presided as mayor during the 1960s, an era when the city's renewal efforts earned worldwide acclaim. Declared a "Model City" by the Department of Housing and Urban Development, Fresno in 1968 was one of only 11 cities in the nation that year to be designated an "All American City" by the National Municipal League and *Look* magazine, which called it "a city with heart that cares about people."

The city's growth and progress continued under the stewardship of subsequent leaders, among them Daniel K. Whitehurst, who at 28 became the city's youngest mayor ever in 1977, and Karen Humphrey, who in 1989 became the first woman elected mayor of Fresno.

Colorful—perhaps crazy at times—Fresno grew and prospered, surviving gamblers and other rascals in the beginning, and, later in 1985, its centennial year, refusing to declare itself a nuclear free zone.

Following pages: Downtown was uptown in the black-and-white '50s, before the noble experiment to give the streets to the people in the form of a mall. For a while it worked. Businesses prospered on the Fulton Mall, and Fresnans and other pedestrians flocked to enjoy the fountains, the trees, and the artwork. But as in many communities, when the new wore off, the exodus to the city outskirts resumed. Ever optimistic, Fresno is trying anew to reinvigorate downtown with plans for a stadium, farmers market, and an education and medical complex. (Photo from the collection of Oscar Deleon)

*Following pages:
It's a city on the move in
more ways than one as
these early risers demon-
strate. Crowds of Fres-
nans participate in
numerous marathons
and walkathons, this one
in conjunction with the
annual Fresno Fair.
(Photo by Dave Fultz)*

heroes, all of them, like the Levys—Joe, the department store magnate, and Sharon, his wife, the first woman member of the Fresno County Board of Supervisors; Roger Tatarian, who went on to head United Press International, then returned home to teach and goad and needle with his column in the daily sheet; Sam Iacobellis, another product of Fresno schools, now president of Rockwell International's North American Aircraft division and coordinator of its BIB project; Gilbert Khachadourian, all the way from Turkey, through Fresno State, and now district manager for the Social Security Administration; John Krebs, a native of Germany who came to represent Fresno in the halls of the United States Congress.

And Barbara Morgan, the school teacher from Fresno who became an astronaut and was part of the backup crew on that ill-fated January morning in 1986 when the *Challenger* exploded after liftoff. These are only a few of the people who grew with Fresno. Who will achieve greatness next? The pupil in Manchester GATE School who could barely speak English when he started? The farm worker's daughter working her way through California State University, Fresno? Is there another astronaut in the crowd, another jet engineer, another poet, another bishop?

Indeed, Fresno's most famous son was the son of immigrants from Armenia. While it's true he did not spend a great deal of his time in his birthplace after seeing Broadway and success in the '30s, novelist and playwright William Saroyan always came back. Fresno, he said more than once, was his favorite town: "I discovered the human race there. I discovered art there. And where you discover helpless man and his hopes, that is your place, favorite or not.... Who was the human race I discovered in Fresno? It was my family, my neighbors, my friends, the teachers at the school, the classmates, the strangers in the streets, and myself."

he Indians were the first Fresnans, Yokuts and Monaches mostly, who lived in the Valley and the Sierra foothills. They lived by the bow and arrow and the trap and harpoon, and on pine nuts, berries, wild oats, and wild grapes until the Spanish arrived in the late 1760s, bringing with them a foreign agriculture and architecture—and Christianity. ◆ The Spanish were followed by more outsiders, the trappers and fur traders who worked the San Joaquin River for otter and beaver, and prospectors and miners from China, South America, and Australia, who worked the streams and veins of the eastern foothills.

From across the border came other settlers from Mexico, ranchers with their herds who put down stakes in the grasslands. They were followed by people from even farther away, all seeking a better life in the New World—Chinese, Armenians, Volga Germans, Japanese, Italians, Portuguese, Scandinavians, Dalmatians, and Basques, then by the Okies and the Arkies blown west by the Dust Bowl, and most recently by the boat people and their families from Southeast Asia.

In and around Fresno, they have put down roots again and again, at least 70 ethnic groups, each with its own language, religion, and cultural heritage. What was a melting pot in the early 1900s has become a melting kettle, a vat, brimming and simmering with variety. With the population of metropolitan Fresno now edging toward the half-million mark, nearly half the population is made up of Hispanics, Asians, and other ethnic groups.

To no one's surprise, this quilt is not without tears, problems brought on by its very diversity. Assimilation of so many languages and cultures has not been easy. It wasn't for the Armenians barred from membership in the country club, or for the Chinese who could only find employment in a laundry. It wasn't easy for the Japanese, many of whom lost farms and businesses and spent the duration of World War II in far-away detention camps. It's difficult even now for the newly arrived Hmong seeking a better life.

The Okies and the Arkies and the homeless from Texas who moved west ahead of the Dust Bowl in the 1930s to work in the orchards and vineyards were not welcomed with open arms. Along Route 66 they went, and then up Highway 99 and into the big Valley. In the words of their chronicler Woody Guthrie: "We rattled down that highway/To never come back again. . ."

Like the others before them, they persisted and became latter day leaders; Bernie Sisk, who arrived with the dust of Texas on his boots, wound up representing Fresno in the U.S. House of Representatives for a quarter of a century, retiring in 1978.

It was Clayton Turner, quadriplegic artist from Fresno who paints by holding the brush in his teeth, who said: "I am an Okie, yes. I say it without any self-consciousness. Among older people, the word expresses pride. Those who use it without any sense of our history are wrong. Okies came here from the Middle West and helped put California together."

Pretty true, those words, especially when it comes to politics. Unknown numbers of voters are descendants of the pilgrims chronicled by John Steinbeck in *The Grapes of Wrath*. New Deal Democrats gave their hearts to Franklin D. Roosevelt and left steamy migrant camps to prosper as farmers and businessmen. They remained registered Democrats for the most part, but, ironically, tended often to vote otherwise on election day.

Another irony of local politics is that a loser went on to hold the highest government post ever to be occupied by a Fresnan. Phillip V. Sanchez, former farm worker and ex-county administrative officer, lost in a bid to depose veteran B.F. Sisk in Congress, but was awarded the top job in the U.S. Office of Economic Opportunity in 1971. Sanchez was later named ambassador to Honduras by President Nixon, illustrating what a bright, young Republican of Mexican descent can achieve in a democratic society.

It took a little longer, however, for Spanish-speaking Democrats, requiring the greater part of a century for a Hispanic—lawyer Al Villa—to be elected to the Fresno City Council in 1971. One year later lawyer Armando Rodriguez was elected to the Fresno County Board of Supervisors.

Nor has it been easy for African-Americans, but they succeeded, too. Joe Williams was the first black elected to the city council in 1975; Jim Aldredge became Fresno city manager in 1986; and Joe Samuels became the city's first black police chief in 1991.

So this is Fresno, one generation to the next, growing in diversity, but growing together as well. In spite of snubs and rejection, determined immigrants gradually have found Fresno a neighborly place to live and let live. You see it in the names. Soon there will be more Vangs than Smiths in the telephone book, more Villas than Browns. Local

The faces of Fresno are many, as are the festivals like Cinco de Mayo, when young and old celebrate the independence of Mexico in costume and on horseback.

In and around Fresno, they have put down roots again and again, at least 70 ethnic groups, each with its own language, religion, and cultural heritage.

*S*ome of William Saroyan's old Fresno still lives, but most is gone, replaced by freeways and garages, a hotel and convention center. Gone are the houses downtown that Saroyan grew up in and wrote about, the schools where he learned to love the written word, the seedy bars and hangouts, the bordellos alongside the Southern Pacific tracks, the movie houses on Fulton Street downtown, the fine Greek and Yugoslav restaurants on Broadway next to the card rooms, and Young Corbett's tavern, named after the prize fighter who became champ in 1933 and, for a while, made Fresno as famous as Saroyan did.

Fresno has undergone many changes since the early 1900s. A look around the city will reveal monuments to the city's past that remain intact, like the Water Tower, a symbol nearly as old as the city and a centerpiece in the never-to-be-forgotten television series. These comforting reminders of Fresno's heritage are rightly juxtaposed with the sometimes controversial symbols of the city's optimism about the future. For instance, the "New Age" City Hall, which opened in early 1992, inspired opinions from every quarter, from those who look upon it with pride as a $31 million, 21st-century statement about a city on the move, to others convinced it is an unidentified flying object unable to get airborne, to the truly imaginative who see it as an elaborate takeoff on Madonna's notorious bra.

Next to City Hall is the Santa Fe depot, built at the turn of the century and still in operation serving Amtrak travelers. On one side of town sits Chandler Field, where pilots have been taking off and landing since the days of helmets and goggles and barnstorming Jennies, and, on the other side of town, the Fresno Air Terminal with connections to the four corners of the globe and a baggage label recognized worldwide as FAT.

There's old Chinatown across the tracks, where Okie Yokomi has been peddling fish ever since he and his Japanese brothers and sisters departed the World War II internment camps, and Dick's Men's Wear, where Richard Avakian fishes around for just the right hat or pair of work boots while reliving the days when his father ran the store, one of the oldest running retail establishments in the city.

There's the beery gregariousness of the Tower District, a neighborhood on the fringe of downtown for the thirtysomethings with its eclectic restaurants, antique shops, theaters, restored homes, and the Tower Theatre, a monument to art deco lovingly renovated in 1989 by Dotty Abbate, film buff. The theater is now a performance hall for visitors the likes of Eartha Kitt, Ray Charles, The Limeliters, and the Smothers Brothers.

Van Ness Avenue, heading out of town and flanked by old trees and grand homes, is where, in days gone by, trolleys clanged from all parts of town. Nearby stands Old Fig Garden, shady and cool, where acres of fig orchards have given way since the turn of the century to one of the city's most gracious residential districts.

Farther out as the city spreads forth is Fresno's newest park, Woodward, a legacy of Fresno businessman Ralph W. Woodward, who left a $1 million estate to the city for the creation of a park and bird refuge. Since its completion in the early '70s, Woodward Park has been ringed by glossy new homes and man-made lakes.

Farther north to the edge of the county are the serene bluffs of the San Joaquin River, the highest of the high rent districts, with its tennis courts and, needless to say, a swimming pool in every backyard.

Back in town, codgers in Courthouse Park playing checkers under the trees remember the old Courthouse building—the one with the dome and cupola and rickety stairs and Justice with her scales balanced. Deemed a hazard by the experts of the day, the stately old structure grudgingly gave way to the wrecker's ball in 1965 and was replaced by an unimaginative office building, a square, hulking honeycomb.

The Meux family home, built by Dr. Thomas R. Meux in 1889 and bought by the city in 1970, stands as a symbol of Fresno's early architectural taste. Saved, also, was M. Theo Kearney's mansion in the park west of town bearing the old baron's name. Gone, though is the brooding, brick-and-mortar Sun-Maid Raisin plant, a massive symbol of the nature of the place that sat at the edge of town, not far from the equally old Fresno Brewery building, still standing atop one of Fresno's rare knolls and serving now as a carpet warehouse. Still cooking is the Valley Bakery nearby, where Jan Saghatelian turns out the same kind of peda bread infused with sesame seeds that her father and mother baked when they arrived from Armenia and opened the bakery in 1922.

Gone is old Fulton Street, the main drag that was dragged mainly by the American Graffiti-ites.

The tracks which brought the city's founding fathers into the Valley still provide passenger service to Fresno, these days through Amtrak's San Joaquin. Amtrak reports that ridership keeps climbing year after year on the San Joaquin, which travels from Oakland to Bakersfield. In the fog of winter, it's the only way to go.

Farther north to the edge of the county are the serene bluffs of the San Joaquin River, the highest of the high rent districts, with its tennis courts and, needless to say, a swimming pool in every backyard.

In the fall when the Fresno State Bulldogs are in town, everybody wants a seat with a view in Bulldog Stadium. Coach Jim Sweeney's popular team finished the 1992 season with a stunning victory over the University of Southern California Trojans in the Freedom Bowl.

▼ MEGAN A. MICKEL

Fresno's main street was replaced in the '60s by the downtown mall, an ambitious four-block experiment of sculptures and benches, fountains and gardens. For a time—before it was evident that shoppers were determined to stick to the suburbs—the mall was the talk of towns across the country and beyond, widely seen in the 1960s as the future of urban planning. An outdoor gallery, the mall features works which range from the classic *LaGrande Laveuse* by Pierre Auguste Renoir to the simple poignancy of *Mother and Child* by Ramondo Puccinelli to Claire Falkenstein's non-objective *Three Fires*, branded rubble and worse by some of Fresno's pedestrian critics because the flames don't look like real flames.

No less controversial was the city's decision to buy for the Convention Center a 10-foot tall, crouching, thrusting hunk of welded steel plate titled *Bucephalus*, after Alexander the Great's famous steed. The sculpture was created by one of America's most honored and imitated artists, Alexander Calder, and, at $30,000, it was also no doubt one of the best deals the city will ever make.

Not to be left behind, Courthouse Park sports an epic sculpture, this one called *David of Sassoon*, the Armenian folk hero, wrought by Varaz Samuelian, local artist and erstwhile skirt-chasing pal of Saroyan's.

While in his lifetime Saroyan got his hackles up anytime someone suggested it would be nice to name a building after him, he couldn't do anything about it after he died. So now, appropriately, the Convention Center has a William Saroyan Theater, an elegant environment for a wide array of performers over the years: Isaac Stern, Mikhail Baryshnikov, Mary Martin, Van Cliburn. The theater also is the venue of the Fresno Philharmonic Orchestra, a first-rate symphony whose repertoire ranges from Bach to Stravinsky.

The play's the thing at Roger Rocka's Music Hall where Broadway comes to the Tower District and local talent gets a chance to strut in front of packed houses, performing everything from *Pirates of Penzance* and *Gigi* to *Oklahoma!* and *Ain't Misbehavin'*—and as nicely as you're going to see anywhere.

The house is usually packed at the Fresno Metropolitan Museum, the newest of the city's museums, especially when the dinosaur exhibit rumbles into town. The museum building used to house *The Fresno Bee*, before the newspaper moved into its new plant. The building was about to be razed when the late Lewis S. Eaton, a banker with the soul of a poet, stepped in and led a move to convert it into a museum. The Met has been making news ever since, scoring first-time exhibitions like the 3,000-piece jade collection from the government of Taiwan. And of all things, it also has a gallery devoted to the life and works of Bill Saroyan.

A quarter of a century older is the Fresno Art Museum, founded by Florence Vanderburgh, whose vision and perseverance culminated in the establishment of the city's first art museum. The Art Museum provides a setting for the works of artists ranging from Ansel Adams to Edouard Manet, B.J. McCoon to Georgia O'Keefe.

For livelier, noisier art, there is the Chaffee Zoological Gardens, named after the late Paul Chaffee, the director who nurtured the place as he would an orphaned lion cub. The popular zoo is a kingdom for more than 400 specimens of mammals, birds, and reptiles. Set in Roeding Park not too far

from downtown, the zoo's paths lead adventurers through rain forests and monkey houses, from flamingos to baboons, from bathing pools for the elephants to love nests for the birds. It is one of the few zoos to have a breeding colony of American flamingos, and its reproductive research on endangered species of reptiles has earned national recognition.

Animals of a more domesticated variety make their home on the campus of California State University, Fresno, also known as Fresno State, to the chagrin of perfectionists among alumni and faculty. The campus is as big as a farm, which most of it is, with nearly 2,000 acres of vines, orchards, and livestock, not to mention a dairy and a winery. While justifiably recognized for its agricultural programs, the university's schools of business and nursing are also of the highest rank. The Henry Madden Library, named after the school's late librarian, is considered one of the finest in the California State University system, with more than 700,000 volumes. In addition, the university boasts the Sid Craig School of Business and Administrative Sciences, named after the husband of weight-loss heavyweight Jenny Craig. Sid Craig, a Fresno State student in the early '50s, was so grateful to the institution that in November 1992 he repaid it with a $10 million grant, the largest gift in the history of the school and the Cal State system.

Now situated in what used to be Fresno's boonies, the university dates back to 1911, when it

With the irrepressible Jim Sweeney as the ringmaster, football has become an autumnal circus, a Saturday night special of almost 40,000 screaming, red-clad fans in Bulldog Stadium, the home team against the infidels.

started out as Fresno State Normal School, a teachers' training college, making it one of the oldest campuses in the state university system. Before moving to new ground north of the city, it was barely a football throw from the center of town, a site now occupied by Fresno Community College, founded in 1910, the oldest two-year college in the state.

Fresno is a sporting kind of town, from softball and bowling to soccer and football, especially Fresno State Bulldogs football. With the irrepressible Jim Sweeney as the ringmaster, football has become an autumnal circus, a Saturday night special of 40,000 screaming, red-clad fans in Bulldog Stadium, the home team against the infidels.

Bulldog Stadium, still expanding and with luxury boxes no less, is another monument to civic pride. It is the legacy of leaders like Mr. Eaton, the late Leon S. Peters, philanthropist and president of Valley Foundry and Machine Works, and Russell Giffen, the late agribusiness giant known in his heyday as California's Cotton King.

When the Bulldogs are in the home these men built, you don't need a schedule to tell you so. You can smell it in the wind, in the hundreds of barbecues that are a part of one of the biggest tailgate parties this side of the University of Nebraska. Win or lose, when the season finally ends—sometimes not until a bowl game, if the Bulldogs play it right—there's a lot of crying in one's beer. But only up until the start of basketball

The time to celebrate in Fresno is any time of year. In spring the large Hispanic population sings and dances in honor of Cinco de Mayo, and in winter the growing number of Hmong, newer arrivals from Southeast Asia, observe their New Year. Those with hot-air balloons dance with the clouds over Clovis during the California Balloon Race on Labor Day weekend. And mid-summer, Fresnans help themselves to chicken and rice at the International Food Festival.

MICHAEL PENN / FRESNO BEE

DONN WESTMORELAND

season, another major attraction, when the cheering starts all over again.

Rare is the winter night that Selland Arena in the Convention Center isn't piled to the rafters with rooters, most of them in bright red. This is the Red Wave, the Bulldog loyalists who follow the teams like star-struck groupies, both at home and on the road. You can't miss them: a barrel of boiled lobsters isn't as colorful.

For the dedicated, no game is too far when the Bulldogs are playing, even if it's in Madison Square Garden. In 1983, when CSUF made it to the final four of the National Invitational Tournament, a goodly hunk of Fresno's population, decked in the team color naturally, went to New York to watch the home boys blow away the Eastern effetes and win the championship. And as if that weren't enough, when they got back home again they held a parade that wouldn't stop till the end, which was a long time coming.

Maybe it's the air around Fresno, or the water, that makes the young men and women run faster, jump higher, hit the ball farther, put it in the hole better. It is a fact that Fresno has produced two baseball Hall of Famers, the most recent being terrific Tom Seaver, a giant of a pitcher who reigned mainly with the Mets of New York in the early '70s. The other was Frank Chance, arguably the most famous of all Chicago Cubs, whose time in the limelight goes back a little further, all the way back to the celebrated Tinker to Evers to Chance double play combo early this century.

Good sports, all of them, going back to high flyers like Dutch Warmerdam, pole vaulter extraordinaire, and Walter Marty, high jump champion. From Clovis next door came Darryl Lamonica, the

Raider's mad bomber of the mid-1960s. And further back, Bill Vukovich, the man who died on the track at the Indianapolis brickyard trying for another title. For as long as they've been keeping statistics, Fresno has been a home of champions, on one field or another, from the days of the Fresno Rockets to today's Fresno State Lady Dogs, softballers supreme.

Sometimes, even the horses can be champs. But don't bet on it. Not on the ones that run at the Big Fresno Fair, previously known as the Fresno District Fair. Some of the entries are a step ahead of the tallow works, not that that keeps aficionados of the sport away from the track. In Fresno, you can always tell the nags are running when you can't find a lawyer or a judge or a doctor till after the ninth race.

But parimutuel betting is just one of the reasons hundreds of thousands come to the fair, more of them each year. Some come to see the rodeo, others the tractor pull. Mostly, though, they're here to show off and see the bounty of the Valley, the grapes and melons, the figs and squash, not to mention the jellies and jams, cakes and pies. For more than a century, communities throughout the county have competed for bragging rights and ribbons, as have young Future Farmers of America and younger 4-H Clubbers, with their homegrown and fattened pigs, cows, and sheep. Started in 1884, the fair is as constant as the Valley seasons. When it's October in Fresno, it's Big Fair time—that's big, as in the largest agricultural show in the nation.

Given the many cultures represented in Fresno, the city is a natural for festivals. The celebrations abound, from Cinco de Mayo to Hmong New Year, from the California Balloon Race to the Interna-

▲ TIM FLEMING/FLASH FOTO

▲ SHAWN JEZERINAC

tional Food Festival. And there is a restaurant for every taste: Korean, Basque, Thai, Italian, French, Mexican, and Armenian.

Even more remarkable, there seems to be a church for every denomination, from the Cross Church founded by the Volga Germans in 1892, to the mighty Peoples Church on the northside, whose Bible teachings regularly draw standing-room-only congregations, to the Buddhist Temple across the tracks on the other side of town, to the Carter Memorial African Methodist Episcopal Church, founded in 1882 and believed to be one of the oldest churches in the state established by African-Americans.

> The celebrations abound, from Cinco de Mayo to Hmong New Year, from the California Balloon Race to the International Food Festival. And there is a restaurant for every taste: Korean, Basque, Thai, Italian, French, Mexican, and Armenian.

In a recent count, Fresno had more than 400 houses of worship. New Temple Beth Israel, old Holy Trinity Armenian Apostolic downtown, St. Peter's Serbian and St. George's Greek midtown, and historic St. John's Catholic, where the baby Jesus in the stained glass windows has red hair, reflecting the early day Irish flock that sang Mass there—all represent the variety of ways Fresnans express their faith.

The Roman Catholic presence is as old as the city, its leaders including Roger Mahony, who has gone on to Los Angeles and to a higher calling as cardinal, and Msgr. James G. Dowling, pastor of the shrine of St. Therese. Together with Rabbi David L. Greenberg of Temple Beth Israel and Dean James M. Malloch of St. James Episcopal,

Dowling created the Forum of Better Understanding in the late 1930s, a radio program that achieved nationwide recognition. They were preaching ecumenism before most souls could spell the word. For nearly two decades they gathered to discuss the events of the day as they related to their religions. A bronze sculpture of the forum members by local artist Clement Renzi is in Courthouse Park.

Behind the facades, behind the stone, steel, and stained glass of Fresno's houses of worship is concern for those less fortunate—within the halls of Northwest Church, which hosts hundreds of youngsters in church school during summer, and Wesley United Methodist, whose parishioners minister to the needs of refugees from other lands. With the help from other congregations throughout the city, the Fresno Metropolitan Ministry fights the good fight against the problems of unemployment, inadequate health care, racism, and old age. Poverello House, a non-sectarian haven supported by the community, remains a beacon of care and hope for those without shelter.

Altogether, it's Fresno, a kaleidoscope in which sometimes all the pieces do not fall into place. A changing city, with joys and despair, failures and good deeds, a young city headed into a new century for better or worse. For Fresno, there is only one way to head. Up and out.

*S*o what do we have here in the heartland? While the good earth and what it produces will continue to be the reason for its being, Fresno is changing. Gradually, fewer and fewer of its inhabitants are going home from work with dirt beneath their fingernails. Data from the 1990 United States Census show that the area has become increasingly urbanized and

The future is rosy in Fresno where the palaces are pink and the new City Hall is a picture to behold.

white-collar in the past decade. As companies move from the larger metropolitan areas to the Valley, more people are likely to be employed as business executives, sales representatives, and clerical workers, and in professions that require special expertise, like education, medicine, and law.

As *Time* magazine discovered, Fresno is "the last real California" and proudly so—one of the few places in the state where housing is affordable and you can still catch a breath of fresh air or cross town on less than a full tank of gas. Unless the rivers it lies between dry up and disappear, Fresno will continue to grow and prosper. The test will be whether it can do so for the good of all.

A beginning is the blueprint offered by the Little Hoover Commission, a group of civic-minded Fresnans who laid out a list of priorities. More parks, more trees, the study says—more of what has made the quality of life in Fresno so fine all along. Among other recommendations, the commission calls for a long-range redevelopment plan for low- and moderate-income housing, assessment of property owners to pay for new parks, elimination of the police and fire department pay formula based on that of other cities in the state, combination of the police and sheriff's departments by 2004, and consideration of change to a strong mayor form of government.

Also in the works is a plan to rejuvenate a stagnant downtown district. The plan by Southern California consultant Wayne Ratkovich calls for a bustling central district joined with rehabilitated residential neighborhoods—an area that would include a farmers market, an expanded entertainment area, a mall with an ethnic theme, and possibly a downtown stadium. The City Council was serious enough to budget $365,000 for the study.

Another plan for downtown is the proposed $300 million medical complex that would include the present Fresno Community Hospital, the county's Valley Medical Center, and the Fresno unit of the University of California at San Francisco School of Medicine. Housing and commercial development are seen as part and parcel of the complex that, if successful, could lure a University of California medical school, and serve as a catalyst for other central area growth.

"There are good signs out there that Fresno is emerging as the capital city of the region, the commercial and cultural center," says former mayor Daniel K. Whitehurst.

A University of California college campus early in the 21st century is a distinct possibility provided all the blocks fall into place, such as an improved state economy. Among the projected sites for what would be the tenth UC campus is a plot of rolling hills east of the city. So, too, on the wish list is a river parkway along the San Joaquin, a lasting piece of nature for future generations. As envisioned, the parkway would extend 22 miles along the river, from Friant Dam in the foothills down to Highway 99 north of Fresno, and include a series of parks, wildlife preserves, recreational and educational settings, hiking and biking trails amid wildflowers and trees, canoeing and picnic areas.

All are the kinds of additions to the Fresno scene that Lew Eaton dreamed about for the city he lived and died in. If anyone had a feel for Fresno, both past and future, it was Lewis S. Eaton, banker, civic leader, visionary. Before his untimely death in late 1992, Eaton talked about growing up in Fresno, when he could ride the trolley car from his home near downtown out to the San Joaquin River for an afternoon swim. That was not too far from where the 18th tee on the San Joaquin Country Club golf course is now and only a couple of long 3 irons from where his office was.

"And all for a nickel," he said. "You could ride to the river, to the fairground, to the dentist downtown."

He loved Fresno in those carefree, uncomplicated days, hawking magazines like *The Saturday Evening Post* and the *Pictorial Review.* Years later, he still expressed love for the city. "I do, I love it," he said. "I may get a little distressed about it, but never discouraged."

Though he would beg to demur, Lewis S. Eaton was "Mr. Fresno," if anybody deserved the title. Without him there would be no Fresno Metropolitan Museum and possibly no Bulldog Stadium at California State University, Fresno. Thanks to his vision there may someday be a San Joaquin River Parkway. He was a civic leader in every sense of the term.

Lew Eaton was a man born to serve. A third generation Fresnan, he almost became a Clevelander after his discharge from the Army following World War II. But he declined the job offer. "No way I was going to work in Cleveland when I could come back to Fresno. It was an easy choice," Eaton said. It was a choice he never regretted, largely because of Fresno's quality of life. "People who live here may sometimes lose track of that," he said, "but those who relocate here recognize it."

Eaton liked the small-town feel of the place, he said, its rural underpinnings and sense of community bound by mutual interests. A multifaceted area, he called it, with a truckload of selling features, large enough to support a wide range of commercial and cultural interests, yet small enough to provide a comfortable and affordable quality of life.

"Where else," he liked to ask, "can you get across town to work in a matter of minutes?"

The driving force in the campaign to transform the old *Fresno Bee* newspaper building into a state-of-the-art museum, Eaton visualized other successes in Fresno's future, notably the river parkway: "It can be a great attribute for this community for generations to come. If we don't do it, there's no second chance."

David of Sassoon, a statue of the Armenian folk hero by Fresno sculptor and artist Varaz Samuelian, stands in Courthouse Park, where it was dedicated in 1971. A gift of Fresnans of Armenian descent, the statue depicts King David of Sassoon astride his horse, Gallal, as he charges the king of Egypt.

LOUISE STULL.

Eaton had no doubt it will happen once all resources are focused on the goal. "It's like World War II, when we had a common goal, something that brought us together," he said. "On a smaller scale in Fresno we had the museum, and now we have the river parkway to make all our lives richer. That's when people perform the best, when they have something to work for."

The city, he predicted, is on the threshold of greater growth and prosperity. "Outside businesses see the attractions: a lot of open land, a good labor force, an attractive cost of living. Compared to other cities, we have a lot going for us," said Eaton. "Sometimes we tend to dwell on the negative. You can always find things you don't like. But we have so much to like."

If there was any single trend that caused him

concern, it was the influx of newcomers who do not speak English. He found the problem puzzling and frustrating, but one that must be solved by mobilizing people through education.

"We need a tremendous emphasis on strengthening our education system. It's our future," Eaton said. "Maybe I'm nuts, but I take the optimistic view. We can make Fresno better with more people to help us do it. The idea is to focus on the carrot."

Dan Whitehurst couldn't agree more. Only 28 years old when he was elected mayor in 1977, he had the brashness of youth to go along with a finely tuned wry sense of humor—just what a mayor needs when the city he heads is deemed the least livable from sea to shining sea.

During his second term, at the height—or more correctly, the depth—of the World's Worst City Crisis, the mayor did his best to put a happy face on matters, including keeping his constituents up past midnight to watch him turn the charm on David Letterman.

When he called his town the gateway to Bakersfield, Whitehurst was only making another little Fresno joke. But that was then. The mortician-turned-mayor-turned-mortician is not quite ready to bury Fresno.

"What I said then I said jokingly," explains the ex-mayor. Against the wall of his second floor office overlooking the upscale north end of the city is a five-foot high stack of cardboard boxes containing personal papers from his mayoral tour of duty. Uncertain about any plans he has for them, he grins when it's suggested that the university might be interested.

"Yeah? Which one?"

For one, there's St. Mary's in Northern California, where he did his undergraduate studies, or maybe Hastings College of the Law at University of California, Berkeley, where he earned his law degree, or even the John F. Kennedy School of

Government at Harvard which he attended as a fellow following his stint as mayor.

Unfortunately for Whitehurst, he also came along during the Great Tax Revolt in California, the dreaded Proposition 13, which limited property taxes and cut 20 percent of all state and local revenues. "It was the start of planned neglect of our problems," he says. "We held off on new parks, on landscaping." As a result, he thinks, Fresno isn't all that it might have been.

"But there's a lot to like about Fresno," Whitehurst insists. "I actually like the weather here. Summers should be hot and dry and clean the way they are here. It's not right to live in a city where you can't go barefoot."

All right, be serious. "I am serious. It's the whole environment about Fresno and about the Valley," he goes on. "I do think there is something about the mix of people here that makes it special, a climate of tolerance for races and cultures and religions that has a beneficial impact on the community."

The former mayor thinks it goes back to the agrarian nature of the place. "Most people came here to be farmers, and many still do," he says. "Farming sets a tone for people of diverse backgrounds to pursue their ambitions. We have a nice foundation to deal with diversity that other cities might not have. This is what makes Fresno special.

"But Fresno shouldn't be compared to big cities. If you want a big city lifestyle, don't come here. You won't find it. What Fresno should strive to be is not a big city but a regional center."

It has the ingredients, he believes. "There are good signs out there that Fresno is emerging as the capital city of the region, the commercial and cultural center," says Whitehurst. "And the region itself is becoming more prominent as the population keeps growing and the economy becomes more diversified. So Fresno's role is enhanced."

Noting a survey that showed Fresno becoming a popular destination for manufacturers and distributors, Whitehurst predicts a steady increase in the range and type of employment in the area: "There will be more of a corporate presence, health care and professional jobs, especially health care if the downtown medical center takes shape."

A man of guarded optimism, Whitehurst is not without concerns: "At the moment, our drawing power is unrelated to economic expansion. The unemployment rate is a negative, although from an economic development standpoint it could be a positive. A large pool of workers is an attractive feature to people who want to go into business."

The prospect of a University of California campus is a real boon to the Fresno area. A major player in the campaign to convince the Board of Regents to select the Fresno County site in the Sierra piedmont east of the city, Whitehurst has no doubts about what it would mean to Fresno: "That would have a most dramatic effect on the future here, economically, culturally, and educationally. It would provide the missing link in the economy."

Until then, what Fresno must keep in mind is that it is not a San Francisco, a Portland, or even a Sacramento. "We're not quite there, not yet," says Whitehurst. "You know there will be steady growth, year in and year out. Take that for granted. A city's like a tree: Plant it and it grows. Here the potential is extraordinary, I think. The challenge is to get better as we get bigger."

Dan Whitehurst, former mayor, glances out the window toward the Sierra on a clear day. "There's something about this place," he says, "the feel of the place, a way of life here that's attractive and comfortable." You almost expect him to reach down and remove his shoes. He starts to laugh. The way Fresno may someday have the last laugh.

TIM FLEMING/FLASH FOTO

As perplexing as it is colorful, the sculpture is appropriately named Balanced & Unbalanced. *The work by artist Fletcher Benton stands at the front entrance to the Fresno Art Museum.*

Following pages: Like the jewel in the crown, Fresno's new City Hall reflects the brilliance of a summer's night. Even some of those who fought City Hall and its 21st century architecture are beginning to fall under its shining spell. (Photo by Shawn Jezerinac)

Preceding pages: As precise and delicate as the etched glass in the restored Tower Theatre, agriculture no longer is just dirt farming, but painstaking laboratory work leading to better preserving techniques for fruit and vegetables. *Page 44 photo by Keith Seaman/Camerad, Inc Page 45 photo by Point Anderson*

They could have danced all night for the spectators attending an exhibition of ballroom dancing staged by a Fresno school of dance (below). If the night's entertainment doesn't entice you inside, it is nevertheless a treat to take in the architectural detail on the outside of the old Warnors Theater downtown (opposite).

SHAWN JEZERINAC

SHAWN JEZERINAC

KEITH SEAMAN/CAMERAD INC

The Tower Theatre, restored to all its art deco charm, is a beacon to the stars—also to dancers, singers, and entertainers of all kinds. (right)

It's hard to beat an evening with the Fresno Philharmonic Orchestra in the cozy Saroyan Theater. Featured here are the fast hands of Rick Shiine at the timpani (opposite).

It can be a wonderful whirl around Fresno, whether taking a chance on a ride at the Big Fresno Fair or doing a spin at the Horned Toad Derby in Coalinga, whether turning the wheels of industry in Fresno's downtown industrial park or watching World War II biplanes in the sky over Madera at the annual Gathering of Warbirds Air Show.

Above the crowds and congestion coming and going into downtown, Capt. Scotty Sample calls out the pitfalls and potholes to commuters tuned in to radio KMJ. The lunch crowd gathers early at one of the many popular restaurants in and around downtown (bottom left), where the cuisine ranges from Armenian to Mexican to Cambodian to Thai.

TIM FLEMING / FLASH FOTO

52

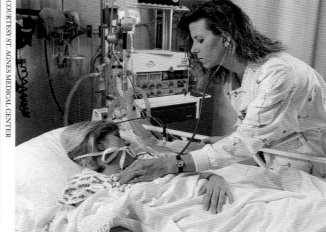

Farther north on the outskirts of the city are the new high-rise buildings, including a reflective Sierra Community Hospital (bottom left) and the venerable St. Agnes Medical Center (bottom right), where the care is tender and loving.

Water, precious water everywhere: in recharging basins where it will replenish the underground supply; in Millerton Lake behind Friant Dam on the San Joaquin River, where the hang gliding is easy on a summer afternoon; and in the man-made lakes ringed by new homes near Woodward Park north of the city. From the control tower at the Fresno Air Terminal, the view can be busy with small aircraft coming and going.

As the crow flies it's not too far from the new City Hall and the hum of computers in office buildings to the other side of the city limits, where family farmers keep a close watch on finances.

After the passage of another Pacific storm from out of the Northwest, the High Sierra stand covered with snow that in spring will feed the great rivers that flow into the Valley.

Each year the water becomes more precious as demand for it rises. Dotted among the peaks are the lakes and reservoirs, as blue as the sky and just cold enough for the fattest trout.

A walk in the sun can get a bit grueling in the High Sierra (opposite), and it's not recommended for the tenderfoot. In Yosemite National Park, the granite walls create their own weather, and the waterfalls their own rainbows. It is worth the hike.

The water is fine, what-ever level of excitement you choose, from a lei-surely canoe ride on the San Joaquin just outside Fresno to kayaking the rapids of the Kings River. The really laid back may prefer a rubber raft on the placid waters of the Merced River in Yosemite.

SHAWN JEZERINAC

DAVE FULTZ

Following pages:
Built following World War II by the Army Corps of Engineers, Pine Flat Dam provides flood protection down-stream and recreation upstream in its massive reservoir, while supply-ing irrigation water to farmers in the Valley. The reservoir holds a million acre-feet of water when full, a rarity in recent years of drought.
Photo by Keith Seaman/ Camerad, Inc

Dry seasons or wet, the flora finds a way to root, even among rocks of the Sierra.
Photo by Tim Fleming/ Flash Foto

Pages 66-67:
From the piedmont of the Sierra strewn with boulders as old as the hills, the vista is orange grove after orange grove to the city limits of the aptly named Orange Cove, just west of Fresno.
Photo by Tim Fleming/ Flash Foto

The fruit of the Valley grows in abundance, in this case Chinese apples nurtured to ripeness by the good earth, the warm sun, and the clear water flowing through irrigation systems.

When the blush is on them, they're good enough to eat, the grapes and plums, the fat strawberries, and the pomegranates, as crunchy and juicy as they are sweet.

Under the hot sun the pace in the Valley quickens, both in the vineyards and orchards where the fruit is harvested and in the packing houses where it is boxed, put in cold storage, and shipped to market.

Following pages:
When the shadows are long in the peach orchards, it's easy picking on the Wawona farms outside Clovis.
Photo by Brent Oliphant

Then as the day heats up, there's nothing like a cold one out of the old icebox.
Photo by Keith Seaman / Camerad, Inc

Mechanical monsters do their jobs, on the one hand the harvester plowing through fields of grain, and on the other, the pump extracting oil from deep below the ground near Coalinga on Fresno County's far west side.

PAUL RUTIGLIANO

PAUL RUTIGLIANO

The natural fibers of Fresno on the hoof and in the field—take your pick, wool or cotton. At Wonder Valley to the east (bottom and opposite), a dude lands at the ranch airport, while another hand kicks up dust in the orchard.

Plums in the Valley are something to cackle about, but the really big deal is king cotton, gathered here by a giant green harvester, up one row and down the next before the rain sets in.

The blessing of the earth, a tradition of Southeast Asia carried on by the immigrant Hmong, assures a fruitful harvest, like the peaches and grapes drying in the Valley sun.

▲ LOUISE STULL

An itinerant sidewalk artist kneels on the Fulton Mall to produce a chalk drawing that one can look up to.

DONN WESTMORELAND

83

On a summer evening, it's concert time at Woodward Park, where someday soon, if the Rotary Club has its way, an amphitheater will rise, a venue for song and dance and Shakespeare under the stars.

The California Raisins (opposite), in their quest to spread the word about the goodness of dried grapes, have achieved the kind of instant recognition that most singing groups and ad campaign managers would kill for.

In terraced gardens and in high-tech hydroponic plots, the vegetables grow like weeds, some into jolly green giants.

For those who don't grow their own, there's the Farmers Market, where the picking is as fresh as the morning dew, and the price is right, too.

▲ GEORGE FLINT, JR.

Following pages: Above the rocks along the hillside, the storm has passed, leaving in its wake nature's spectral work of arc, the rainbow. *Photo by Point Anderson*

A distant ancestor of western cattle hangs in stony silence, now a piece of decorative art. Older are the ceremonial dances and costumes of the Native Americans whose ancestors hunted the Valley and ground their corn and nuts on the hard Sierra stone.

▲ SHAWN JEZERINAC

▲ KEITH SEAMAN / CAMERA5, INC.

Ride 'em, dude, ride 'em, cowboy. The greeting depends on where the ride is happening— out east in Wonder Valley or at the Clovis Rodeo for a weekend of bronc busting. For the more adventurous, there are opportunities for pack trips aboard horse and donkey in the Sierra.

TIM FLEMING / FLASH FOTO

Old Festus stands tall in Clovis' Old Town. The statue is a memorial to Ken Curtis, who played the amusing character for so long on the television series "Gunsmoke." Curtis lived in nearby Clovis from 1980 until his death in 1991.

TIM FLEMING/FLASH FOTO

At the Clovis Rodeo, it takes a firm grip to hold on, particularly if one of those spurs happens to rile the bronc some.

North of the border, the old ways continue with the young, who take pride in their heritage through brightly painted murals and through festivals celebrating Mexican independence.

TIM FLEMING/FLASH FOTO

It's so peaceful and quiet in the Shin Zen Friendship Garden in Woodward Park, you can hear fish flap in the pond. The reenactment of rituals as old as Japan takes place in a serene setting of waterfalls and wooden bridges bright with maple leaves and dragonflies.

TIM FLEMING/FLASH FOTO

RICHARD HAAS

Ancient and ceremonial arts of the Far East and Southeast Asia are displayed on the downtown mall during the International Festival and practiced in the nearby foothills.

The flags come in all colors at the annual downtown International Festival, their brilliance matched only by the smiles of the folks behind them.

News anchor Pedro Santos (right) and Lupita Lomeli interview Gabriel Garcia Perez of the Mexican Consulate on Fresno's KFTV, the Spanish language television station whose signal reaches nearly 700,000 households in the Valley.

There is dancing in the streets with a swirl of native costumes and headdresses when the International Festival hits its stride mid-summer on the downtown mall.

RICHARD HAAS

Too much of a good thing can poop a body out, as in the case of one little reveler, who seems to be in good hands (bottom left).

Like a beacon in a storm, the historic Holy Trinity Armenian Apostolic Church downtown has drawn thousands upon thousands of worshippers over the years to pray, to visit with old friends from across the sea, to sit down at banquets and weddings, and to listen to the words and teachings of holy men like Father Sassoon Zumrookhdian. In a recent count Fresno had over 400 houses of worship where the myriad cultures and ethnic groups that have made Fresno home honor their faith.

Did somebody say send in the clowns? They come from all over, smiling and drawing smiles, especially when the circus comes to town, a laugh a minute.

Fresno City College, the state's oldest two-year community college, does not shy away from the arts. In 1992 it mounted a well-attended production of Shakespeare's *Taming of the Shrew*, complete with Renaissance regalia and fanfare.

▲ BOB KEMPEN

The only way to fly over the river is in a lazy hot air balloon, drifting along with the breeze—although in this case, gently down the stream might be a more appropriate description.

Balloons are getting big in Fresno, as evident in the California Balloon Race, which attracts nearly 100 enthusiasts from the western states during the Labor Day weekend.

RICHARD DARBY / FRESNO BEE

In 1889, *The Fresno Weekly Expositor* called the home of Dr. Thomas R. Meux, a surgeon for the Confederacy, probably the most elaborate residence in town. Thanks to the dedication of preservationists and work of volunteers, it still stands, owned now by the city and serving as a lovely reminder of Christmas and other days past in Fresno. Farther out, amidst the great trees is M. Theo Kearney's mansion (opposite), where he hosted the rich and famous of the day and drew up plans for the region's agricultural future.

POINT ANDERSON

▲ FROM THE COLLECTION OF OSCAR DELEON

Some street scenes of Fresno show the changes that time has wrought. The modern Fresno City College campus (top left) lies down the road from lovingly cared for homes in the old neighborhoods. Across town lies the entrance to tree-lined Kearney Boulevard (top right), one of the oldest farm-to-market thoroughfares in the city, a street which stretches to Kearney Park and its historic mansion. Blackstone Avenue (bottom), site of one of the first McDonald's, isn't quite what it used to be, a jungle now of fast-fooderies, car lots, and billboards.

▲ POINT ANDERSON

DAVE FULTZ

DAVE FULTZ

POINT ANDERSON

Art being in the eye of the beholder, there is much to behold in Fresno. Above (clockwise from bottom left) are three stunning examples of the work of Fresno artist Clement Renzi: *The Visit*, a Yokut Indian on the Fulton Mall, and *The Three Graces*, which graces the entrance to a local bank. The Tulu Atlantean sculpture (right), located in Courthouse Park, was a gift from the people and government of the Mexican state of Hidalgo. For razzle-dazzle, there are the creations (opposite) of Fresno artist Varaz Samuelian, whose sculptures of his old pal William Saroyan are on display at the Saroyan Theater and the Fresno Art Museum. On hot summer days Samuelian prefers working in straw hat and cutoffs.

It is not a flock of Canadian geese headed south for the winter but a flight of speeding planes showing off for the groundlings at an air show over Madera north of Fresno.

Honoring the 50th anniversary of Gen. Jimmy Doolittle's raid on Tokyo, a pair of B-25s, the type that flew the daring mission, rumble over the Fresno Air Terminal after a flight that took them over the general's Carmel home on the California coast.

TIM FLEMING/FLASH FOTO

TIM FLEMING/FLASH FOTO

Vintage warplanes looking as good as new share the stage with aerobatic formation flights trailing smoke at the Gathering of Warbirds annual air show.

From Buicks to Thunderbirds of every color, the dear old things sparkle at automobile shows like the Concourse d' Elegance. The older the better.

From the Southern Pacific shop in Sacramento, locomotives like the 1863 C.P. Huntingdon (left) and newer models hauled passengers and freight through the San Joaquin Valley and beyond.

What really keeps things on the right track in the Valley is the local hardware store (bottom), with everything from hammers to nails, screws to nuts.

The iron horse, not to mention a lot of other contraptions on four wheels, helped put this mode of transportation out to pasture for good.

Even the toughest old tractors can't pull their load forever, like this one that finally gave out in the green foothills.

The brew was fine in times past. Joe Dale, a staunch Bulldogs fan, produced the Dale Bros. grind for 50 years until his death in 1972. The coffee company shut down in 1973. Suds were cooked up in the old Fresno Brewery (opposite) until the mid-'40s. In the brewery's heyday its Sierra Brew and Bohemian Beer sold for a refreshing five cents a glass. The building now serves as a carpet warehouse.

Industrial plants create their own startling artwork, while a four-legged creature (opposite) ignores one of society's most popular signs.

Following pages:
Across the bridge and
through the palm trees is
the lower San Joaquin
River, a seemingly
exotic setting for one of
the oldest mobile home
parks in the area.
*Photo by Keith Seaman/
Camerad, Inc*

▲ MICHAEL KARIBIAN

Fun is where you find it on a Valley summer day, whether sand-sculpting on the beach at Lake Millerton, basking on a mattress in a backyard pool, or surfing down a city street.

▲ E.Z. SMITH

Deep as the ocean, Huntington Lake is the summer scene of the annual High Sierra Regatta, with scores and scores of eager sailors tacking and backing. On the shores of Millerton (opposite), the water runs knee deep, just right for folks who run a little better than knee high.

A fearless threesome, laughing all the way, zoom along the Sierra slopes, downhill all the way. Cross-country and downhill skiing are popular from Thanksgiving through April in the Sierra National Forest northeast of Fresno.

Youthful bike riders pump their way skyward in a pretty rousing imitation of ET and his earthling friends.

Come vacation time, it's a small world around the pool. Before you know it, you're out of the pool and back to school, the lifeguards giving way to crossing guards.

When it rains at Beiden Field, named after legendary teacher of the game Pete Beiden, everybody pitches in and pulls his weight, from Fresno State Bulldogs stars to the coach. Tomorrow, when the sun returns, they'll play two.

It used to be the West Coast Relays, the place "Where World Records Are Broken" by local heroes of long ago, like pole vaulter Dutch Warmerdam and high jumper Walter Marty. Now it's called the Fresno Relays, but only the name has changed. The hurdles—for university and college participants down to the kids from elementary schools—are just as high and difficult to cross.

Meet the Bulldogs, the Fresno State Bulldogs, as they scoot through the band on another full-house fall evening in Bulldog Stadium.

By playing in summer, the semi-pro Bandits (opposite) capture the attention that falls to the Bulldogs and high school teams in autumn.

Some people just can't help playing dirty, especially when the soccer field is muddy. Soccer is a big draw for amateur sportspersons on weekends, as is soft-ball on summer nights and, in the winter, city league basketball. There are a dozen golf courses within short driving range in the city as well, and tennis courts to a fault.

MEGAN A. MICKEL.

MEGAN A. MICKEL.

The pride of Clovis, football great Darryl Lamonica (top), used to throw them. Passes, that is. Now he catches them. Basses and other fishes, that is.

Another certain smile is on another champ, this one in the Horned Toad Derby. The Memorial Day weekend Derby in Coalinga has been an annual tradition for 58 years, interrupted only by the 1983 earthquake.

Before this little princess kissed him this was just another silly old prince.

▲ GEORGE FLINT, JR.

▲ GEORGE FLINT, JR.

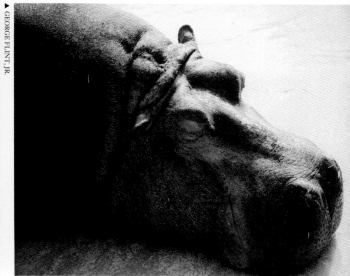

At the petting zoo at the
Fresno Fair, a boy has a
rhino by the tail.
Actually, it's just a
piggy, which the
llama knows.

Birds of many feathers gather at Chaffee Zoological Gardens in Fresno's venerable Roeding Park. Even the hummingbird (bottom) may show up for a look around before slipping away to find something to sink its beak into.

A flamingo on the rocks and
the next thing you know,
you're seeing pink birds
flapping away. Around the
park (bottom), there's
always a soft spot for the
family if you look hard
enough.

Pogonip the Indians called the fog that clings to the high ground and the canyon walls of Yosemite. The thick mist floats and rolls until the sun climbs over the rim and warms the granite.

Yosemite the beautiful was formed millions of years ago by glaciers etching and polishing the rock as they moved, leaving in their wake a tableau of breathtaking grandeur.

Following pages: The Giant Sequoias, the world's largest and among the oldest of all living things, rise into the sky over 300 feet, inspiring more than a million visitors a year. *Photo by Point Anderson*

For all their appearance of ruggedness, the evergreens can be delicate and, thus, are at the mercy of National Park management, including control burning to help maintain the forest's vigor. *Photo by David B. Ashcraft*

Over hill and over dale
go the bicycle racers,
pumping away through
the rolling back country
east of Fresno.

Stretching out below the hills at the foot of the Sierra are the orange groves and beyond them the peach orchards and the vineyards.

Out east, there's a red
and blue and green and
yellow rainbow 'round
an old oak tree.

The blue sky is
reflected in clear water
by a granite outcropping
in the lower Sierra
(opposite).

FRESNO
California's Heartland

Profiles in Excellence

BY ROBERT TORRES

A LOOK AT THE CORPORATIONS, BUSINESSES,

PROFESSIONAL GROUPS, AND COMMUNITY

SERVICE ORGANIZATIONS THAT HAVE

MADE THIS BOOK POSSIBLE.

Looming above the water fountain is the steel and glass Fresno City Hall, facing the future.

Downtown Fresno in 1912 was scene of the annual Raisin Festival and Parade up Mariposa Street. Fresno was formerly known as "Queen of the Valley" for its fanciful architecture. In the far background the cupola of old the County Courthouse is visible.

With Glenn Luther Martin at the wheel, the *Fresno Morning Republican* got delivered to Madera on time. Martin, who went on to fame and fortune as an aircraft designer and manufacturer, ran one of the first air express services in history in 1912.

FRESNO
California's Heartland

1 8 5 0 - 1 9 2 5

1850	VALLEY MEDICAL CENTER
1884	THE BIG FRESNO FAIR
1886	FRESNO BUSINESS JOURNAL
1889	SHEPHERD KNAPP APPLETON, INC.
1891	CENTRAL CALIFORNIA COMMERCIAL COLLEGE
1895	FRESNO CHAMBER OF COMMERCE
1897	COMMUNITY HOSPITALS OF CENTRAL CALIFORNIA
1898	THE TWINING LABORATORIES, INC.
1901	UNITED ASSOCIATION OF PLUMBERS, PIPE AND REFRIGERATION FITTERS
1903	BAKER, MANOCK & JENSEN
1911	CALIFORNIA STATE UNIVERSITY, FRESNO
1912	SUN-MAID GROWERS OF CALIFORNIA
1913	ELECTRIC MOTOR SHOP, INC.
1916	STAMMER, McKNIGHT, BARNUM & BAILEY
1920	NEW ENGLAND SHEET METAL WORKS, INC.
1922	THE FRESNO BEE
1922	THE UNISOURCE CORPORATION

Before the California Raisins became the singing and dancing spokesmen for one of the mainstays of Fresno agriculture, there were Fresno Raisin Day Parade girls, like this lovely bunch who were honored in 1920.

The day after Thanksgiving, 1991, one of the worst traffic disasters in American history occurred 60 miles from Fresno. A severe sandstorm hindering the vision of drivers traveling on Interstate 5 resulted in a chain of collisions involving more than 100 vehicles. ♦ California Highway Patrol officers rushed to the site where they assessed the tragedy: there were 15 on-site

deaths and 103 injuries, ranging from abrasions and broken bones to critical burns. Valley Medical Center, the Coordinating Hospital Command Center for Central California, was notified to mobilize area hospitals for an immediate influx of emergency room patients.

Valley Medical Center had prepared itself for large numbers of the severely injured. As the only Level I Trauma Center in the San Joaquin Valley, the hospital remains prepared to deal with major disaster situations such as earthquakes and aircraft crashes. The hospital's designation as a trauma center also requires that it have a full surgical team on-site 24 hours a day.

Valley Medical Center's north and south towers were joined together in 1977 to form one complex.

"Fortunately, we were in the middle of a shift change and had plenty of staff on hand for the Interstate 5 emergency," says Tom Stoeckel, emergency department manager. "We treated about half of the 90 people who needed emergency care,

although we could have handled more. Our excellent training and experience saw us through it."

Among the I-5 crash victims treated at Valley Medical Center were those who suffered severe burns. Valley Medical Burn Center is the only facility of its kind in Central California, an area roughly the size of the state of Alabama. Opened in 1974, the burn center features such state-of-the-art equipment as a Hyperbaric Chamber, a pressurized, oxygenated tube that enhances the wound-healing process.

A LEADING REGIONAL HEALTH CARE PROVIDER

Fresno County's oldest hospital, Valley Medical Center is licensed for 417 beds. Each year, the facility admits approximately 13,500 patients, delivers over 4,000 babies, conducts 5,000 surgical procedures, and logs 200,000 outpatient and emergency room visits. The hospital is operated by the county of Fresno and is one of the state's premier teaching hospitals. With a staff of 2,000, Valley Medical Center is one of the county's major employers.

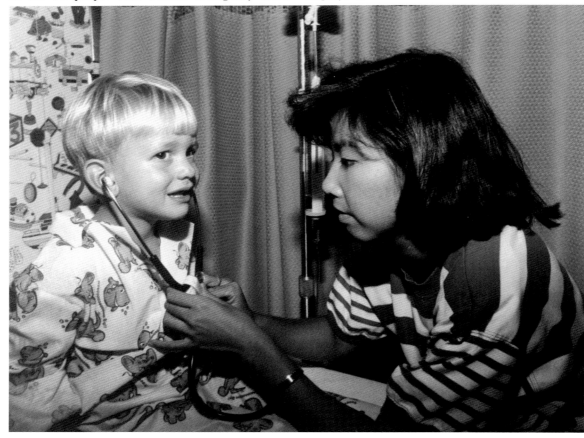

In 1986, a children's health center, with full X-ray services and a laboratory, was added to the hospital complex.

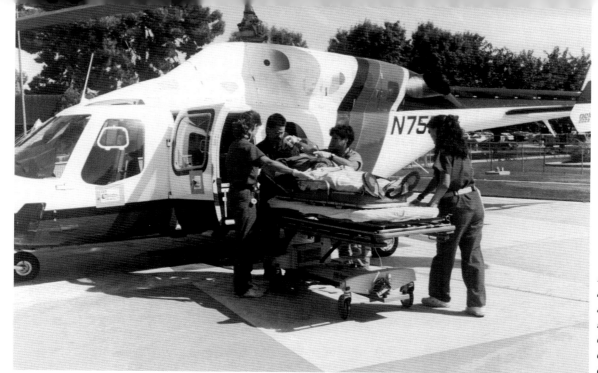

The hospital traces its beginnings to the medical practice of Dr. Lewis Leach, who arrived in Fresno County in 1850, not long after gold was discovered in the foothills northeast of Fresno. Dr. Leach began his medical career in the Valley by treating local soldiers and Indians who were fighting one another at a site near Millerton Lake, about 20 miles north of what is today downtown Fresno.

In 1865, Dr. Leach was appointed county physician, but lacking a hospital facility, he housed patients in private homes. In January of 1870, Leach leased a building to treat the indigent sick, and by the end of that year the building was purchased by Fresno County to serve as the region's first hospital.

By 1877, the county Hospital Board of Supervisors had purchased 80 acres on Ventura Avenue near the present site of the fairgrounds, and in 1889 the hospital's first permanent facility was built there. The hospital received accreditation by 1921 and was officially named The General Hospital of Fresno County.

The present North Building of the hospital was constructed in 1955, and the parallel South Building was added in 1959; the two structures were joined together in 1977 to form a complex, which today serves as the center of the hospital's services. In 1986, a children's health center, with full X-ray services and a laboratory, was added to the hospital complex.

A TEACHING AND RESEARCH HOSPITAL

In 1921, Valley Medical Center began its outstanding teaching program, which during its first 60 years trained over 1,500 physicians. From 1923 to 1958, a nursing school was also operated on the hospital grounds. Today, the hospital has nine residency programs with approximately 160 physicians in training.

"Students from all over the United States and across the globe attend our program because of our large variety of medical specialties and unique services," says Jack Voice, president of the Valley

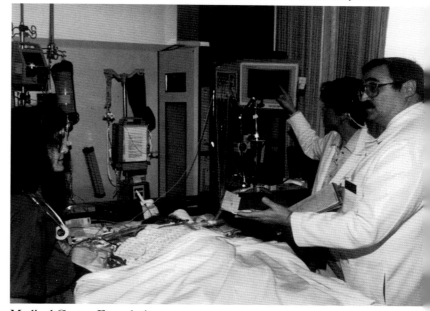

Medical Center Foundation.

During the 1992-93 term, students from as far away as India, Novosobrisk (formerly part of the USSR), Egypt, and Taiwan did internships and residencies in internal medicine, family practice, surgery, pediatrics, emergency medicine, obstetrics, and gynecology, among other programs. The hospital also has training positions in dentistry and oral surgery through its affiliation with the University of California at Los Angeles. About half of the physicians stay in the San Joaquin Valley to practice after completion of their training at Valley Medical Center.

Over the course of more than a century, the hospital has provided outstanding medical care to the Fresno area and has served as a leader in medical education and research. As the Coordinating Hospital Command Center for Central California, a Level I Trauma Center, and the site of the regional burn center, Valley Medical Center is a leader among medical institutions in the state of California.

In 1884, the first Fresno Fair featured a five-day horse racing meet, a few small produce displays, and a couple of livestock exhibits. Today, as the fourth largest fair in the state, The Big Fresno Fair attracts approximately 700,000 visitors each year from throughout the bountiful state of California. ◆ People from all walks of life congregate at the fairgrounds for 17

days in the fall to compete for coveted blue ribbons in their areas of expertise, enjoy free nightly world-class entertainment, experience the thrill of the rides and games at Butler Amusement's spectacular carnival, wager bets during 14 full days of live horse racing, and view the unique agricultural and livestock exhibits.

The Big Fresno Fair offers 14 days of live horse racing at the fairgrounds.

"The main idea behind the fair is to provide fabulous fun for the whole family," says Brian Tatarian, president of The Big Fresno Fair. "We are indeed Fresno County's largest event, and you just can't find a better buy for your entertainment dollar."

The Big Fresno Fair is run by a nonprofit organization, the 21st District Agricultural Association, and regulated at the state level by the Department of Food & Agriculture, Division of Fairs & Expositions. This self-supporting agency is governed by nine prestigious voluntary members of the Board of Directors, each appointed by the governor of California. Every member is allowed to serve two four-year terms. This executive team in conjunction with a 50-member staff works year-round to make the fairgrounds come alive each October.

SOMETHING FOR EVERYONE

More than 1 million people, including fairgoers, visit the fairgrounds each year. Besides the fair itself, four primary interim events are held there as an integral part of The Big Fresno Fair.

Fiesta Days is Fresno's spring fair designed to recognize and honor the local Hispanic community, which comprises 35 percent of the city's population. The three-day Cinco de Mayo festival includes local, national, and world-renowned entertainment, traditional Mexican foods, and displays by local artists, photographers, and native Mexican artisans.

The Cross-City Race, traditionally held the Sunday prior to the fair, is the re-creation of the Fresno Republican Cross City Race conducted on September 29, 1914. The race provides an opportunity for everyone from the recreational amateur walker to the competitive runner to participate in the 10K run,

Recognized as the "Valley's Biggest Show," the Fresno Fair has an average daily attendance of approximately 40,000 people.

two-mile run, or two-mile walk. In 1992, 10,000 runners came out, making this event one of the largest racing events in Central California and certainly the largest participatory event in Fresno.

AgFRESNO, an agricultural exhibitors show, commemorated its 10th year with The Big Fresno Fair in 1992. This agribusiness supermarket is a showcase of the latest in farm equipment and services, including seminars, exhibits, speakers, and recreational and educational activities.

ach year, people in resno and beyond look rward to a day at e fair.

Satellite wagering occurs daily at the fairgrounds. The facility receives satellite transmissions from notable California racetracks such as Santa Anita, Hollywood Park, and Los Alamitos in the south, and Golden Gate and Bay Meadows in the north. The Big Fresno Fair also takes part in the live horse racing circuit for the duration of the fair under the auspices of the California Authority of Racing Fairs.

Many other events take place year-round, ranging from home and garden shows to health fairs. The fairgrounds operates 365 days a year with an annual budget in excess of $9 million. The facility, located on 165 acres, boasts 430 commercial exhibit spots in 780,750 square feet of maintained building space, as well as 90 food concession spots.

BECOMING THE VALLEY'S BIGGEST SHOW

In its pioneer days, The Big Fresno Fair stood on shaky ground. A series of management changes and financial predicaments came to an end in 1910 when Clyde Eberhart became the general manager. His innovation and direction paved the way to the success the fair enjoys today. Eberhart was responsible for organizing spectacular events such as the "Great Train Wreck," which involved two locomo-

tives slamming into each other while hundreds of fairgoers watched.

The Fresno Chamber of Commerce took over the fair in 1920, but dropped its support in 1931 when the fair was rescued by the Fresno County Junior Farm Bureau. With the then grand sum of $300, the Farm Bureau introduced some events which continue today, such as the live broadcasts by Fresno radio station KMJ.

The fair continued to grow and was attracting approximately 100,000 visitors annually when World War II put a temporary halt to the event. Then in 1948, the fair emerged as a new entity and has grown by leaps and bounds ever since. Now recognized as the "Valley's Biggest Show," the Fresno Fair has an average daily attendance of approximately 40,000 people.

Combining the best of tradition with the best of new attractions, the inclusive event offers tractor pulls, live entertainment, and a petting zoo.

"We maintain a very solid agricultural base for the fair," says Tatarian, "but we are not afraid to try innovative ideas in order to keep the fair lively and contemporary. We look forward to bringing Fresnans the traditional events they expect each year along with new, exciting events for the future."

The fair celebrates the bountiful San Joaquin Valley through unique agricultural and livestock exhibits.

*G*ordon M. Webster Jr. may not be the maverick of the family, but he certainly is a maverick in the publishing industry. As owner and publisher of the Fresno Business Journal, Webster heads perhaps the most innovative business periodical in California. ♦ In its new tabloid format, the Journal offers a comprehensive list of features, including information about

new business, bankruptcies, and real estate leasing and sales, as well as profiles on local business people. In addition, the newspaper reports on breaking stories about mergers, real estate developments, health and social issues, and the changing economic and business climates in the Fresno area.

Since its founding in 1886 as the *Daily Real Estate Report*, the newspaper has undergone significant change. The periodical, later known as the *Fresno Daily Report*, gradually expanded from its original focus on local real estate issues to cover such areas as legal news, bankruptcies, and construction permits. On February 3, 1992, the newspaper was completely revamped in perhaps the most radical change in its century-long history.

After more than two years of intensive marketing research and personal soul-searching, Webster decided to transform the newspaper to a tabloid format, which now includes the use of color, photographs, and graphics. And for the first time in its history, the paper has moved beyond reporting strictly business data and transactions of record by establishing a full editorial staff.

"The decision to make the change was not an easy one," Webster says. "I had to consider the legacy of more than a century of Websters. My family has shown a deep dedication to the community, and I felt it was up to me to continue that commitment. I believe this new vehicle will make an important contribution to the Fresno business community, in an area where little has been done before. Our city had been crying out for this kind of publication for some time."

DEEP ROOTS IN FRESNO
The family legacy began in Fresno in 1876 when Webster's great-grandfather, Morris Shelby Webster, arrived in the Central Valley and took work as a sheepherder in the foothills northeast of the city. In 1888, he purchased the newspaper from founder H.C. Miller & Co. for the then princely sum of $180.

The Fresno Business Journal *offers a comprehensive list of features, including information about new business, bankruptcies, and real estate leasing and sales, as well as profiles on local business people.*

Family ownership continued when Norman A. Webster took charge in 1937 after his father's death. The business changed hands again in 1979 when Gordon M. Webster Sr. stepped to the helm after his father's retirement. Though Gordon Jr. joined the business in 1974 and became president in 1982, his father and grandfather still maintain an informal association with the *Journal*.

The newspaper has boosted its circulation at least 10-fold during the course of its 107-year history, surviving two world wars, two fires, and the Great Depression. "I'm very proud of what our family has accomplished," Webster says. "And we are all proud to be part of the community. Our Fresno roots are very deep."

The family's longtime commitment to the community is yet another example of the depth of the Webster roots in Fresno. In addition to a half-century of membership in Rotary International, the Websters boast 20 years of involvement with the Bulldog Foundation, which supports athletic programs at California State University, Fresno. The family has also devoted time and resources to the business community through long-standing membership in the Fresno Chamber of Commerce. Gordon Webster Jr. continues the family's public participation as president-elect of the American Court of Commercial Newspapers. He is also a member of the board of directors of the Fresno City and County Athletic Hall of Fame and president of Bullard High School Boosters.

Although Webster devotes much of his time to the community, he reserves a great deal of his enthusiasm and commitment for his business. His financial and emotional support of the *Journal's* staff has created a family atmosphere which employees acknowledge with a high degree of loyalty.

"I have been fortunate to have the support of such a great family, and I am very proud of my staff," Webster says. "We are a forward-looking organization, but despite our success, we don't lose sight of how we got here."

Gordon M. Webster Jr., owner and publisher of the Journal, *heads one of the most innovative business periodicals in California.*

tability, innovation, and community commitment have been the building blocks of success for Shepherd Knapp Appleton, Inc., an independent full-service insurance agency founded more than a century ago. Over the years, outstanding service to clients has remained the cornerstone that supports all other efforts at the agency, which today services more than 6,000 clients.

Founded in Fresno in 1889 by local businessmen and brothers William and Benjamin Franklin Shepherd, the agency has developed a reputation as an outstanding hometown company focused on serving Fresno area residents. "Throughout our history we have been committed to steady, manageable growth and building the best possible company to serve the Fresno area," says B. Franklin Knapp, who joined the firm in 1937 and today serves as chairman of the board.

Principals Knapp, Billie Balliet Knapp, and Robert H. Farmer, along with a dedicated staff of 25 employees, offer the full spectrum of personal and business insurance coverage. The agency also writes life insurance, IRAs, pension and profit sharing plans, and group and individual health insurance policies under SKA Life Agency, an in-house corporation. "As independent insurance brokers, our job is to determine the best insurer and coverage to meet the needs of our clients," says Billie Balliet Knapp, president. "Our customer service is superior, from the initial research phase to seeing that claims are properly handled."

STABILITY AND INNOVATION

The stability that has undergirded SKA goes beyond longevity in the local business community: Its leaders represent a continuum of commitment throughout the firm's history. The Shepherd family directed the company for 34 years until the current corporation was formed in 1923 by Benjamin Franklin Shepherd (one of the founders), Grover Cleveland Appleton, and Benjamin Franklin Knapp, the father of today's chairman of the board.

Innovation also has been a part of the company since its founding. The agency, which through the years has utilized the latest technology and industry advances to better serve clients, is particularly proud of an SKA innovation in 1936 that changed business insurance writing worldwide. Until that time, businesses wanting comprehensive liability coverage had to purchase five individual policies to insure every aspect of their operations, which often resulted in overlapping coverage and wasted financial resources.

In 1936, agency principal G.C. Appleton presented his vision for an all-inclusive policy to J.W. Reynolds, president of United Pacific Insurance Company. While meeting over drinks at the Hotel Fresno, the two developed the world's first comprehensive liability program on a cocktail napkin. Known as "the cocktail napkin policy," the first

of these groundbreaking policies was signed on August 25, 1936 and subsequently revolutionized the insurance business.

From left: Principals Robert H. Farmer, Billie Balliet Knapp, and B. Franklin Knapp, along with a dedicated staff of 25 employees, offer the full spectrum of personal and business insurance coverage.

COMPANY AND COMMUNITY LEADERSHIP

Shepherd Knapp Appleton today seeks out employees with innovative, progressive attitudes, an ideal typified by the company's president, Billie Balliet Knapp. Although she joined the firm in 1974, Ms. Knapp boasts 45 years of experience in the insurance industry. In 1983, she became the first woman president of the Independent Insurance Agents and Brokers Association of Fresno. Also included in her list of local honors are "Boss of the Year" in 1986 and "Woman of the Year" in 1970.

Chief Executive Officer Robert H. Farmer's involvement in the community ranges from being on the Fresno Grand Jury to serving as District Governor of Rotary International (1993-94). Farmer feels that through the ideals of Rotary, SKA is following the true commitment to community service on the local, national, and international levels.

As part of the firm's commitment to charitable and civic causes in Fresno, Franklin Knapp has contributed countless hours in leadership positions for nonprofit organizations, including the Fresno Convention and Visitors Bureau, the Chamber of Commerce, Fresno Insurance Association, Fresno School Bond Drive, and Fresno Metropolitan Museum. In 1987, he received the Chamber of Commerce's highest honor for business and civic leadership, the Leon Peters Award.

Knapp sees the firm moving into the 21st century with the same values, strengths, and commitments that have guided it for over a century. Billie Balliet Knapp concurs: "I expect a great future for Shepherd Knapp Appleton based on a sincere desire to provide the highest quality service to every client."

*T*he Unisource Corporation, the largest distributor of paper products in the United States, has Fresno roots tracing back to 1922 and corporate roots reaching back to the California Gold Rush days. ◆ As it exists today, the company was established in 1985 in Long Beach, California, through a merger of two West Coast paper companies: the venerable Blake, Moffitt &

Towne and the more youthful Carpenter-Offutt Company, both of which had distribution centers in Fresno at the time. Unisource's parent company is Alco Standard Corporation, based in Wayne, Pennsylvania, which in addition to a paper products group has copy machine divisions.

Located in a new 100,000-square-foot facility on Cedar Avenue, Unisource employs 90 people in Fresno.

Unisource Fresno is one of 45 distribution centers operated by the company in nine western states, and one of 17 in California. Located in a new 100,000-square-foot facility on Cedar Avenue, the Fresno center employs 90 people. Its distribution area encompasses a large portion of Central California, from Modesto in the north to Bakersfield in the south. Fresno sales exceed $50 million a year to customers ranging from school districts and military installations to food processors, agricultural packing houses, food service businesses, and printing companies.

Nationwide, Unisource is a distributor for more than 100 American firms, including such giants as 3M, Container Corporation of America, Boise Cascade, and Mobil. Among the more than 50,000 products distributed by Unisource are commercial printing paper, copy machine paper, publishing supplies, industrial paper supplies, paper towels, and tissue paper. The company also distributes wrapping paper for meat and bakery products, grocery bags, fast food wrapping materials, kitchen accessories, plastic eating utensils, disposable aprons, soaps, sanitary papers, health care products, and hotel and motel paper items. Many of its products are recyclable or made from recycled materials.

AN IMPRESSIVE CORPORATE ANCESTRY

Blake, Moffitt & Towne, the larger of the two entities that merged to form Unisource, had a long and distinguished corporate life. The company's founders, Francis Blake, James Moffitt, and James Towne, were Easterners with printing backgrounds who moved to California during the Gold Rush era to seek their fortunes in the precious metal. The hard work of the gold fields failed to yield much, so they joined forces in San Francisco in 1855 to open a printing company that also distributed fine printing papers.

In 1868, the partners closed the print shop and began concentrating solely on the distribution of paper products. The firm opened its first branch warehouse in Portland, Oregon in 1887. The following year, the company incorporated.

Blake, Moffitt & Towne established a Fresno distribution center in 1922, and from 1927 to 1973 its San Joaquin Valley operations were located in the Ventura Street building that today houses the Old Spaghetti Factory restaurant. In 1961, the company was acquired by Kimberly Clark and changed hands again when it was purchased by Saxon Industries in 1968.

Meanwhile, Carpenter-Offutt got its start in 1968, also in San Francisco. Just two years later, the fledgling operation was purchased by Alco Standard and became a part of its paper distribution network. Retaining its original name, Carpenter-Offutt added a distribution center in Fresno in 1974.

In early 1985, Alco Standard purchased Saxon Industries, and along with it, Blake, Moffitt & Towne. On April 1 of that year, Alco Standard merged its new paper distribution company with Carpenter-Offutt to form Unisource Corporation. Today, Unisource employs more than 1,350 people.

Although only six years old in its present-day form, Unisource enjoys a corporate ancestry that provides the foundation and impetus for the company's current success. With a parent as strong as Alco Standard, The Unisource Corporation is poised for further growth, and its thriving Fresno operations will continue to be an important part of the company's future.

rom telegraphy to computer literacy, Central California Commercial College has kept pace with the needs of the Fresno business community for more than 100 years. The college marked its centennial in 1991 by opening its doors to an estimated 50,000 past graduates. Hundreds attended the celebration, the two oldest proudly displaying their diplomas from the class of 1916. "It was really something to see," says John Swiger, college director. "Some of the stories we heard were fascinating."

Considered Fresno's oldest continuous post-secondary educational institution, Central California Commercial College was christened Chestnutwood Business College in 1891. Its founder, Edward Payson Heald, had already established Heald Business College in San Francisco in 1863. When he sold his interest in the Fresno campus in 1922, the name was changed to Central California Commercial College, or 4C's, the name it continues to use today. In 1964, 38 years after Heald's death, Heald Colleges incorporated 4C's into its curriculum once again as an expansion campus. Since then, the school's name has become a household word among San Joaquin Valley residents.

> "Our emphasis is on practical application rather than general education," says John Swiger, director, "and we encourage students to dive right into their fields of study."

A PRACTICAL APPROACH TO LEARNING

Recognition has not been unwarranted. Accredited by the Western Association of Schools and Colleges, the school's hands-on curriculum is designed to offer a focused and practical approach to learning. Many of the students move directly from high school into the program, but the college also has a significant number of older students. The average age of the 225 students enrolled in the day program is about 24 years old, while the 60 night-class participants average about 29 years of age.

"Many of our younger students are looking for the most direct path into the job market," Swiger says. "What could be referred to as our 'reentry' student population typically found college not to their liking and went to work instead. They are coming back now for more training."

After six quarters of full-time enrollment at an average expense of $1,500 per quarter, students can obtain Associate of Applied Science degrees in accounting, computer applications, secretarial studies, and word processing. Despite the school's diverse offerings, Swiger says that students interested in telegraphy today will have to seek services elsewhere; the college has not offered that program for several decades.

Thirty staff members and 20 classrooms housing five computer, three typing, and four accounting labs are available to students enrolled in all programs. "Our emphasis is on practical application rather than general education," Swiger explains, "and we encourage students to dive right into their fields of study. We feel that two purposes are served by this approach. One, the student finds out early on if he or she is on the right track; and two, students will receive a lot more training if they concentrate more on experience than on theory. We endorse a hands-on philosophy here."

A VALUABLE JOB PLACEMENT NETWORK

It's no secret that experience and training are in high demand today, but graduates of Central California Commercial College take with them another tool of incalculable value. The school offers a lifetime placement service which is good through-

out the Heald College system. Graduates can take their diplomas to any of 10 campuses in Central and Northern California and be assured much-needed assistance in the job search.

According to Swiger, searching for work with a 4C's diploma is not the anxious task graduates might expect with other academic degrees. "The people we place are demonstrating the quality of skills they receive from our program, which has enhanced our reputation," he says. "What we offer is an alternative educational opportunity, and we have had a tremendous impact on our community."

Central California Commercial College has been Fresno's number one business college since 1891.

*C*ommunity Hospitals of Central California is the most established and largest health care system in the San Joaquin Valley. Excelling in such diverse medical fields as genetics, prenatal care, and geriatrics, this not-for-profit group of facilities dedicates an annual budget of more than $225 million to deliver an impressive array of services to residents of Fresno

and surrounding communities.

A locally owned, 1,000-bed system, Community Hospitals of Central California operates six fully staffed hospitals in the Fresno area, employing nearly 4,000 people. Among the primary fields covered by the hospitals are obstetrics, cancer treatment, mental health services, heart care, hospice services, and diabetes, eye, and elderly/convalescent care. Also included are lung therapy, pain management, regional poison control, physical rehabilitation, and the most comprehensive array of surgical services in Central California.

The environment of the Maternity Center encourages family participation in the birthing process.

"We enjoy a long heritage of health care service to the community," says Chief Executive Officer Bruce Perry. "In some categories, we are the only service providers in Fresno. For example, we have the only inpatient dialysis and Alzheimer's centers in the area."

SIX AREA FACILITIES
Over the years, individual facilities within the system have developed reputations in their own areas of expertise. Licensed for 95 beds, Sierra Community Hospital is widely known for its specialized orthopedic procedures. The California Vascular Institute, housed at the hospital, coordinates an innovative type of laser surgery that combines state-of-the-art radiology and cardiology techniques to free blocked arteries. Sierra also features the Innerlink Collaborative Healthcare Unit, which offers a personalized hospital experience that involves the patient in his or her own care.

Clovis Community Hospital, the newest facility in the system, opened in 1988. Licensed for 120 beds, it houses the Family Birthing Center, where approximately 1,750 of the 7,500 babies born annually in the Community Hospitals system enter the world. "Our strong commitment to the highest quality obstetric services represents one of the most satisfying aspects of our diverse health care offerings," says Perry.

Fresno Community Hospital began in 1897 as Burnett Sanitarium.

Community Hospitals of Central California also maintains a comprehensive convalescent care program carried out at three separate facilities. Located in the north central part of the city, Fresno Convalescent Hospital dedicates its 116 beds to providing 24-hour long-term care. The Community Alzheimer's Living Center, a 110-bed unit in northern Fresno, specializes in comprehensive care for patients with Alzheimer's disease. In fact, Community Hospitals is among the few health care providers in the Valley committed to meeting the unique needs of such patients. Sierra Meadows Convalescent Hospital, located 45 miles north of Fresno, is licensed for 64 beds and provides long-term care to elderly patients who need 24-hour supervised nursing assistance.

"We are very proud of these specialized facilities," Perry says. "We feel our convalescent services are essential and place us on the leading edge of solving the problems of our aging society."

The centerpiece of the Community Hospitals system is Fresno Community Hospital and Medical Center. Established in downtown Fresno in 1897, this facility has been an invaluable health care provider for nearly a century. Licensed for 458 beds, the Medical Center is today the largest facility in the group, with 900 physicians on its staff. In addition to a 24-hour trauma center, it currently houses one of the most comprehensive cancer treatment centers in the city, including diagnostic, intensive care, chemotherapy, radiation therapy, 24-hour emergency cancer-dedicated care, and hospice capabilities.

The Medical Center's extensive obstetrics program and the largest maternity center in Central California are housed on the third floor of the facility. On average, a new baby is delivered at the Medical Center every hour and 20 minutes.

A LONG HISTORY OF PEOPLE WHO CARE

The system's current spirit of volunteerism can be traced back nearly 100 years to Mrs. Celia Burnett, who opened a boarding house on the corner of Fulton and Calaveras streets to accommodate single men traveling through Fresno in search of their own "El Dorados."

In those days, people fell victim to virtually every sickness imaginable, and few had the money to pay

for professional care, even when it was available. As a result, Mrs. Burnett found herself acting as both house-keeper and nurse to those who sought shelter under her roof.

As her reputation for successful nursing care spread, a group of local physicians approached Mrs. Burnett in 1897 in hopes of opening a for-profit hospital in her boarding house. The new hospital was dubbed the Burnett Sanitarium and was incorporated in the spring of 1900. Five years later, the practice moved to a new location on the corner of Fresno and "S" streets, where Community Hospital remains today.

In 1945, the sanitarium was sold to a nonprofit corporation and became Fresno Community Hospital. The building underwent a $4.5 million comprehensive remodeling project in 1959, and a fifth floor was added in 1963, bringing the hospital's total capacity to nearly 300 beds.

A 10-story tower was added in 1972 on the same grounds at a cost of another $16 million. In 1979, Fresno Community Hospital merged with Clovis Memorial Hospital and the two were renamed Fresno Community Hospital and Medical Center and Clovis Community Hospital. Three years later, they became affiliated with Sierra Hospital Foundation to form Community Hospitals of Central California.

A PERVASIVE SERVICE STRUCTURE

After decades of mergers, new construction, additions, and renovations, the system achieved the far-reaching service structure it enjoys today. "Community Hospitals of Central California is really owned by the members of the community," Perry says, "and all of our resources go back into the system as a way of continually serving the community that supports it."

The most recent example of reinvestment in the community is a 25,600-square-foot, two-story cancer center. Fresno's premier cancer treatment

facility, the California Cancer Center was completed in 1992 at a cost of $11 million. Among its state-of-the-art cancer-fighting equipment are two nuclear accelerators, which focus an electronically generated X-ray beam onto the cancerous area, thus maximizing the effectiveness of the treatment.

"For the first time in this city," Perry says, "we are able to offer patients access to all the treatment necessary for comprehensive cancer care."

Despite a solid reputation for the best in health care services, the Community Hospitals system is not resting on its laurels. In fact, the system's officials view its future in much the same light as they see its past: filled with continuous growth and progress.

"Our vision is to provide the area with the broadest, most unique array of services and programs for patients throughout Central California," Perry says. "The intention of this system is to maintain high-tech care without compromising our commitment to the individuals of our community."

Left: The Medical Center's Community Suites offer a unique luxury room option.

Below: The Innerlink Unit at Sierra Community Hospital features an open-chart policy that helps keep patients informed and included in their health care management.

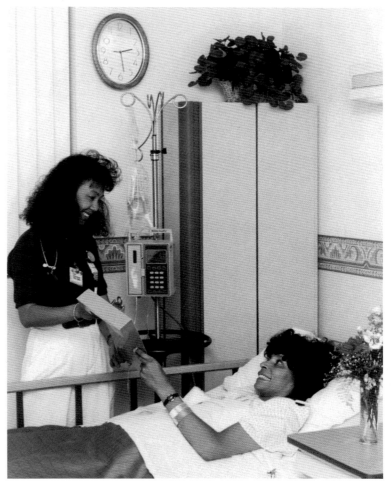

*S*ince 1898, The Twining Laboratories, Inc. and Fresno development have taken a hand-in-hand stroll through local history. Providing services through five operational divisions—Geotechnical Engineering, Construction Inspection and Materials Testing, Environmental Services, Analytical Chemistry, and Drilling Services—Twining has been an integral part of

Fresno's evolution into California's sixth largest and fastest growing city.

Owner and President Harry Moore is proud of the firm's legacy, which is why after 14 years as a company employee he purchased it in 1992. "Twining has played a significant role in Fresno's development," says Moore. "Until 25 years ago, we were the only firm in town supplying testing and chemistry services. We are very well established in the community and highly regarded for what we do."

Moore adds, "We consider ourselves a multi-disciplinary firm, and we have a highly qualified staff. Our mission is to provide unfailing delivery of excellent, prompt, and cost-effective professional services to every client. That focus is part of our history, and it will continue to be foremost in our goals for the coming years."

Through its Construction Inspection and Material Testing Division, Twining tests the strength of steel, concrete, and masonry.

The firm's Geotechnical Engineering Division provides a variety of site preparation and building foundation services.

COMPREHENSIVE SERVICES

Through the Geotechnical Engineering Division, Twining provides foundation investigations, geologic and seismic hazard studies, slope stability evaluations, pavement designs, and other services. Building-site preparation such as earth-work observations, field density testing, soil sampling and testing, and foundation failure analysis are also in the division's realm of expertise. "We basically form the very foundation for the buildings we work on," Moore explains.

Forming the foundation is just the initial phase of Twining's responsibilities at a construction site. Through its Construction Inspection and Materials Testing Division, Twining tests the strength of steel, concrete, and masonry. Other services include fireproofing, wood-truss inspection, and bolt tension testing. "Materials testing has been an essential part of the construction industry for a long time," Moore says. "Without the ability to assess the strength of construction materials, the building industry simply

would not be where it is today. I believe we have been a positive force behind the development of modern construction materials and methods."

Twining's Environmental Services Division offers environmental assessments, feasibility studies, risk assessments, remedial action plans, and the design and installation of groundwater monitoring wells. "Toxic liability is a serious area of litigation these days," Moore says. "People frequently contract us to provide an environmental assessment before they purchase land. On an old gas station site, for instance, we assess the extent of both vertical and horizontal contamination. Then we advise our clients on cleanup methods and how to restore the property."

Twining's Analytical Chemistry Division is certified by the State of California for the analysis of drinking water, wastewater, and hazardous waste under Certificate Number 1372. The laboratory performs confidential, unbiased testing in organic, inorganic, and microbiological chemistry. This division often assists the other divisions as the laboratory testing arm for water and soil analysis.

Twining's fifth division, Drilling Services, operates under State of California Well Drillers (C-57) Contractors License Number 506159. The division operates two fully equipped CME 75 drill rigs which are used to drill soil borings and collect soil samples for geotechnical engineering and environmental evaluations. In addition, Twining drills borings and installs monitoring wells for groundwater and soil vapor sampling and/or extraction.

The firm's extensive list of successful local projects includes providing services for schools, retail companies, hospitals, public utilities, government entities, and countless individuals. Over the years, Twining has played an integral role in the development of projects that affect every aspect of the lives of local residents. One of the firm's

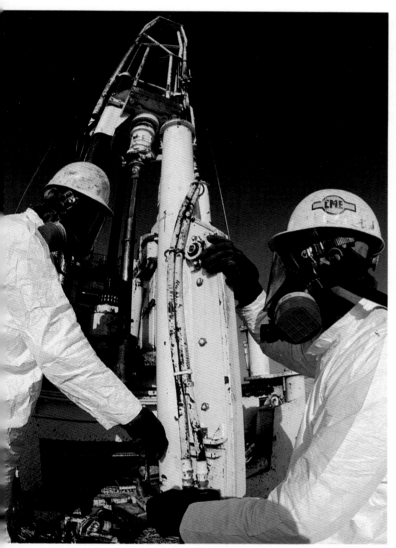

the standardization of drugs for local pharmacists. Dr. Twining also became widely known for his research in milk consumption safety.

In 1905, Dr. Twining moved his laboratory to Amador and I streets, where he added chemical testing to his portfolio of services. He broadened his horizons again in 1910 by purchasing equipment for the physical testing of materials—the foundation for the firm's Construction Inspection and Materials Testing Division. Today, Twining has more than $1 million invested in testing equipment.

As Fresno grew, so did the need for Twining's services. In 1912, the firm moved to a three-room facility in the Griffith-McKenzie Building. In 1930, Dr. Twining built a 22,000-square-foot, two-story office on Fresno Street to accommodate his growing staff of chemists and engineers. The company still maintains its corporate headquarters at that downtown Fresno site.

From humble beginnings, Twining today proudly boasts a work force of more than 120 people. Approximately 35 percent of the Twining staff hold college degrees in highly technical fields. "Although we have had our share of tough times, it has been the personal fortitude of the staff and owners of the firm which has contributed to the success and longevity of Twining," Moore says.

The Environmental Services Division offers environmental assessments, feasibility studies, risk assessments, remedial action plans, and the design and installation of groundwater monitoring wells.

Surviving two world wars and the Great Depression, Twining was well-prepared to meet a more recent challenge. In 1986, when the new City Hall was proposed for construction within a block of Twining's corporate headquarters, the firm's historic building was included in a plan to demolish several downtown structures and create new parking facilities. Unwilling to stand by and watch Twining's corporate office be sacrificed, company officials launched a campaign to save the old brick building. In 1991, it was placed on the National Register of Historic Places, saving for posterity a monument to Fresno's growth. Ironically, Twining has been instrumental in the later stages of the City Hall project.

The Analytical Chemistry Division analyzes drinking water, wastewater, and hazardous waste.

Today, Twining is taking on new challenges. Faced with added competition, soaring costs for changing technology, and skyrocketing potential for liability, the firm still manages to keep pace with growth in the San Joaquin Valley. Having added offices in Modesto (1963), Visalia (1973), and Bakersfield (1982), The Twining Laboratories plans to remain an integral part of California's future.

The Drilling Services Division specializes in drilling soil borings and collecting soil samples for geotechnical engineering and environmental evaluations.

latest accomplishments is Fresno's City Hall, a $30 million endeavor completed in 1992.

Another of its projects is Clovis Unified's Buchanan High School complex. Located in the neighboring city of Clovis, this facility is expected to carry a price tag of $48 million upon completion in the fall of 1993. The Buchanan project is one of the largest single school contracts of its kind in California's history.

The proposed $100 million Valley Children's Hospital, scheduled for completion in 1996, will also grace Twining's impressive resume. As in most other projects, the firm will be involved from start to finish. The groundwork has already been laid through geotechnical and seismic evaluation, as well as environmental assessment.

THE TWINING LEGACY

Twining Laboratories owes its legacy to founder Dr. Frederic E. Twining, a local bacteriologist who established the company nearly a century ago in a second story apartment above the Cutter Drug Store in Fresno. He spent much of his early career studying cattle diseases, primarily anthrax. Another of the early services provided by Dr. Twining was

The rigorously trained and highly skilled members of the United Association of Plumbers, Pipe and Refrigeration Fitters, UA Local 246, are part of the backbone of the Central Valley building industry. ♦ Organized in Fresno in 1901, roughly a generation after the city was founded in 1872, UA Local 246 has played a significant role in the bricks-and-mortar

construction of the area from its early days. "Few industrial or commercial buildings in this area have been built without our members on the job," says Robert D. Ward, union business manager since 1986.

The organization, founded at the turn of the century with just 10 members, has experienced a growth pattern that reflects the activity of the building industry in the area. In 1908, UA Local 246 had 25 members and sent its first delegate to the national organization's annual convention. By 1943, the Fresno group had grown to a solid 157 members. But over the next 17 years, the membership soared to a total of 573 in 1960 as the post-war years of prosperity brought new construction to the area. Today, UA Local 246, headquartered on East Shields Avenue in Fresno, has 670 members from four counties in the heart of the San Joaquin Valley—Fresno, Kings, Tulare, and Madera.

In 1924, members of UA Local 246 were hard at work on the Pacific Southwest building.

OUTSTANDING TRAINING PROGRAM

"Our members are highly sought after for their professionalism, experience, and expertise," says Ward. "We believe our comprehensive training program is the key to our success."

All members of the organization are required to complete a five-year apprenticeship program, which is recognized as one of the finest in the state. The program combines evening classroom study in building codes and methods, with on-the-job experience during the day. Members receive specialized training in welding, plumbing, pipefitting, and refrigeration, which enables them to work on a variety of jobs, from warehouses and manufacturing plants to hospitals and co-generation plants.

Ward is particularly proud of the important part UA Local 246 played in 1988 on the construction of the Balsam Meadows hydroelectric plant at the John S. Eastwood Power Station at Shaver Lake,

located 40 miles northeast of Fresno. The successful completion of this Southern California Edison facility, which required the construction team to work at a depth of 1,000 feet, is considered a monument to the talents of the area building industry. Edison publicly recognized UA Local 246 for the superior workmanship and outstanding performance of its members on the project.

Union members helped complete the Kaiser Permanente Medical Center in 1991-1992.

Membership in UA Local 246 also entitles workers to many other union benefits and services. As business manager, Ward acts on their behalf as arbiter for inter-local disputes, investigator of member complaints, and negotiator with area contractors on wage and benefit agreements. The organization also provides an active job placement service for its members.

A NEW HEADQUARTERS BUILDING

Throughout its history, UA Local 246 has leased office space and held membership meetings at numerous sites throughout the city, including the Union Labor Hall on K Street, the Boiler Tenders Hall, and the Moose Temple on Broadway. For the past two decades, the organization has operated from its current site on East Shields. But by spring of 1993, UA Local 246 expects to move into a facility of its own, a new 18,000-square-foot building on East Hedges Street in the Las Palmas Industrial Park. The union saved money to buy the land for cash, and the facility it is constructing will accommodate offices, apprenticeship classes, and union meetings. "This building has been a long time coming and will mean a lot to the members," says Ward. "It will be nice after all these years to finally have a home."

Ward believes a permanent home for UA Local 246 reflects the union's long and fruitful history and the organization's future place in the Fresno community. "We expect to remain a critical part of the San Joaquin Valley construction industry," he says. "We have had a long and successful history which we are determined to live up to."

*C*hairman of the Board Kendall Manock is proud of the diverse individuals at the law firm of Baker, Manock & Jensen. With backgrounds in engineering, urban planning, business, and government, 50 attorneys from all parts of the country make up a firm with perhaps the longest history of any in Fresno. ♦ One of Central California's largest law firms,

Baker, Manock & Jensen tackles complex issues in business and civil litigation; agriculture, farmer cooperatives, and water law; medical malpractice defense and personal injury; tax litigation and planning; mergers and acquisitions; real estate; international trade; estate planning; and employment law, including wrongful termination. One timely area of expertise is environmental law. "This is an important new field," says Manock. "There is increased public concern about air and water pollution and soil contamination. We are about the only firm in the area that has the horses to deal with the complexities involved."

Manock, John Baker, Douglas Jensen, and a dozen more of the firm's attorneys are San Joaquin Valley natives. Born in Hanford, California, 30 miles south of Fresno, Manock moved to Fresno as a child and delivered newspapers in the same neighborhood where the firm is now located. In 1951, he graduated from California State University, Fresno, and in 1954 received a law degree from Boalt Hall School of Law at the University of California, Berkeley. Born in Fresno, John Baker also graduated from CSU, Fresno and obtained a law degree in 1955 from Hastings College of Law at the University of California, San Francisco. Douglas Jensen, the youngest of the three name partners, also is a Fresno native. He received an undergraduate degree in 1964 and a law degree in 1967, both from Stanford University.

Today, the three share the responsibility of overseeing the firm with a diverse, but cohesive, group of shareholders. The practice is organized into a number of departments with the expertise to handle cases ranging from simple wills to multimillion-dollar transactions and complex litigation.

FOUNDED AT THE TURN OF THE CENTURY

The firm traces its roots to the turn of the century when William Sutherland formed a partnership with J.P. Bernard in 1903. Over the years, the firm has undergone several name changes as new partners have carried on the practice. Some historical names are Sutherland and Barbour; Sutherland, Dearing and Jertberg; Dearing and Avery; Avery, Meux & Gallagher; and Gallagher, Baker & Manock.

The firm's size remained relatively stable throughout much of its first half-century, with only three to four lawyers well into the 1950s. In the 1960s, the firm began growing in response to the community's increasing need for comprehensive legal services. Baker, Manock & Jensen now has more than 100 employees, including attorneys, paralegals, and support staff.

"In the early days, we were oriented toward general practice and business litigation and were strongly focused in the agricultural community," Manock says. "We are now also strong in the medical industry and other specialized businesses important to Fresno. One of the real advantages of adding more lawyers is the ability for individual attorneys to specialize and become recognized experts in their particular field."

▲ DAVID WAKELY

While Fresno's growth has increased demand for legal services, the firm recognizes another important local need—community service. Baker, Manock & Jensen donates funds, and its attorneys and staff volunteer countless hours to support social service organizations such as public television and radio, Valley Children's Hospital, Community Hospitals of Central California, the Fresno Philharmonic, the American Red Cross, and the Fresno Metropolitan Museum. Many attorneys are also active in state and local bar association activities to promote access to and understanding of the legal system.

Manock emphasizes that the firm's goals remain simple: "We want to contribute to the vitality of our community while practicing law with the highest possible standards."

From its headquarters in Fig Garden Financial Center, the firm is meeting the community's increasing need for comprehensive legal services.

For more than 80 years, California State University, Fresno has been a centerpiece of local economic growth, as well as one of the foremost contributors to cultural life in the San Joaquin Valley. Of the nearly 100,000 students who have graduated from the institution, an estimated 42 percent have remained to become Fresno's entrepreneurs, politicians, teachers, engineers, doctors, lawyers, social workers, human service professionals, and agricultural leaders.

Some 100,000 students have completed their degrees at CSU, Fresno in its 80-year history.

FILLING A VARIETY OF ROLES

"As we face the future," says President John Welty, "I believe that our fundamental mission is to create a university that is committed to developing productive global citizens and providing leadership for addressing regional problems through teaching, research, and pubic service."

The university also supports the region economically. CSU, Fresno's 1,000 faculty members and a support staff of another 1,000 make the school one of the city's leading employers. Each year, the university pumps over a half-billion dollars into the local economy through the combined disposable incomes of students, CSUF visitors, and employees, and through the school's direct purchase of goods and services.

Statewide studies have shown that for every job the university provides, 4.4 more are generated in the community, which means the school's annual expenditure helps provide another 8,800 Valley residents with jobs. "There is little doubt that we have a substantial economic impact on our community," Welty says.

But CSU, Fresno contributes a great deal more than money to the quality of life in Fresno. As part of its commitment to cultural enrichment, the university sponsors an annual lecture series, which brings speakers from all over the world to Fresno to discuss the events of the day. Among past speakers are nationally renowned authors and politicians, including former presidents Jimmy Carter and Gerald Ford.

The Phebe Conley Art Gallery and President's Gallery provide the community with a variety of exhibits featuring work by students and local and national artists.

The performing arts are also well-supported at the university. Students involved in music and drama have traveled abroad to perform at such notable events as the Montreaux Jazz Festival in Switzerland and the Edinburgh Festival of Performing Arts in Scotland. Most recently, "Passages," a university production tracing the experiences of Southeast Asian students, went on a performance tour to Hawaii and Japan.

"We make a major contribution to Fresno culture," Welty says. "Our music and theater programs provide local residents the opportunity to participate in, as well as attend, some of the finest examples of performing arts available."

CSU, Fresno also is enthusiastic about its thriving athletic program. Both men's and women's Bulldog teams have contributed to the school's acclaim: CSUF's basketball, softball, volleyball, baseball, soccer, and other programs have made their marks on the national sports scene. The Bulldog Foundation, a private organization formed by local citizens, has raised millions of dollars to support CSUF sports programs.

In the 1992-93 season, the university joined the Western Athletic Conference (WAC) to compete against other fine academic institutions such as the Air Force Academy, Brigham Young University, and the University of Hawaii. "Our athletic program has been well-recognized throughout California for some time," Welty says, "but our superior academic reputation also played a role in becoming part of the WAC. We see this as a significant step forward for our university."

The University Student Union and Free Speech Area at the center of the CSUF campus are focal points of student activities and forums.

PHENOMENAL GROWTH SINCE 1911

The friendly relationship between the university and the Fresno community—and the school's growing national recognition—have been developing for the past eight decades. Founded in 1911 as Fresno State Normal School, the institution had a primary focus to train qualified teachers for the Fresno area

Interaction with space-age technology, such as remote sensing by a NASA satellite, prepares students for tomorrow's world.

$22 million athletic complex, funded largely the community, has hanced the university's ercollegiate sports ograms.

and to provide practicing teachers continuing education opportunities.

In 1920, Fresno State Normal School led the western U.S. farming industry into a new era by establishing the region's first agriculture program. In 1935, the school changed its name to Fresno State College, and by 1936 it had become one of California's only comprehensive liberal arts colleges. The school broke ground in 1950 on a new 1,410-acre campus at Shaw and Cedar avenues. By 1957, operations were consolidated in that location, where CSUF remains today.

It was not until 1972 that the school's name was changed to California State University, Fresno. Today, a student enrollment of 20,000 mirrors Fresno's ethnically diverse demographic makeup. Minority enrollment over the last five years, for instance, has increased by 50 percent. Enriched by this diversity, CSUF offers 60 baccalaureate and 43 master's degrees in more than 100 fields of study. A joint doctorate with the University of California is offered in educational leadership.

The Henry Madden Library is one of the best in the 20-campus California State University system. It houses more than 830,000 volumes and includes an extensive music library, over 3,000 periodicals, a number of special collections, and a depository of U.S. government and state publications.

Business, teaching, engineering, sports—CSUF has built a reputation in many areas. But the school's location in the heart of the San Joaquin Valley, perhaps the most productive agricultural area in the world, has prompted a significant allocation of resources toward agricultural studies. With programs in animal science, viticulture, and agribusiness management leading the way, the university has solidified its place in the Valley's agricultural industry through a commitment to research. In fact, the school's California Agriculture Technology Institute (CATI) is among the best agricultural research programs in the state.

Since its founding more than 80 years ago, CSU, Fresno has made far-reaching contributions to the community, and its programs have evolved just as Fresno itself has grown and changed. But amid the constant evolution, one focus remains clear to Welty.

"The heart of the university is the commitment of our faculty to teaching," he says. "We see our primary objective as the education of our students, many of whom will remain to make a contribution to the Fresno area. It is fair to say the future economic growth of this region relies heavily on our ability to prepare students for that future.

"We are watching the development of a global community. Our students, even those who remain in the Valley, will need to be prepared to work and live in a global environment.

"The future will bring an increased dependence on technology, and we will need people who can apply technology creatively.

"Finally, we will need students who can work in teams. Working together we will solve problems.

"Therefore, the university will continue to expand its interactive relationship with the surrounding region to extend our partnership with the community in addressing the issues that confront all of us."

*W*ith one of the most widely recognized trademarks in the world—the familiar red box with the smiling girl in a bonnet—Sun-Maid raisins are known throughout the world for their natural goodness. ♦ In 1992, Sun-Maid Growers of California, which processes and sells half of all consumer-packaged raisins in the United States, reported net sales of $182 million.

Sun-Maid's Kingsburg plant, the largest and most modern raisin plant in the world, processes 100,000 tons of raisins each year, ranging from half-ounce miniature boxes to 1,100-pound bins of raisins shipped to cereal companies worldwide.

During a field trip to the Sun-Maid plant, elementary school students marvel at the "World's Biggest Raisin Box." Constructed by students at CSU, Fresno, the huge box was filled with 16,500 pounds of Sun-Maid raisins to establish a world record.

The history of Sun-Maid Growers of California, founded in 1912, is closely intertwined with the agricultural heritage of the San Joaquin Valley.

Grapes were being dried into raisins as early as 1860, but it was not until the 1870s that the crop showed any promise for commercial success. As one story goes, a heat wave hit Central Valley vineyards in 1873, drying the grapes on the vine and leaving farmers with a financial disaster on their hands. In desperation, enterprising growers took the dried grapes to San Francisco to sell as "Peruvian Delicacies." The new snack sold out immediately, and the raisin industry was born.

The next four decades saw tremendous, uncon-trolled growth with wide fluctuations in supply and demand. In 1912, a group of forward-looking raisin growers established a grower-owned cooperative called the California Associated Raisin Company. Searching for a more memorable identity, the co-op adopted a new brand name in 1915, "Sun-Maid."

In 1918, the co-op opened a 187,000-square-foot processing plant in Fresno, which served as its home for the next 46 years. The 1920s and 1930s was a period of over-production and depressed prices. To help stabilize the industry, Sun-Maid encouraged the formation of a federal marketing order, which became effective in 1949. Under the authority of the U.S. Department of Agriculture, the organization helps stabilize supply and demand through the strict management of all California raisin production.

In 1961, Sun-Maid Growers began construction on a new facility located on a 73-acre site between Kingsburg and Selma, an area where more than 75 percent of the California raisin crop was grown. The site has since been expanded to 130 acres.

STANDING THE TEST OF TIME
Despite growth and change, the basic structure of the co-op has remained consistent since its begin-ning. The association is today still owned and managed by its 1,500 grower-members, who deliver their raisin crops exclusively to Sun-Maid.

Innovative marketing strategies in the United States and abroad have allowed the co-op and the industry to succeed amid an ever-changing market. Sun-Maid raisins are stocked in pantries across the globe and are sold in more than 25 countries.

In 1980, Sun-Maid helped form a joint sales organization, Sun-Diamond Growers of California, to market its own products, as well as those of Diamond Walnut Growers, Sunsweet Prune Grow-ers, and Valley Fig Growers. This partnership created a comprehensive line of dried fruit and nuts that offers the same quality and natural goodness raisin lovers have come to expect from Sun-Maid.

In 1992, the cooperative marked a milestone with the celebration of its 80th anniversary. According to Gary Marshburn, assistant to the president, con-sumer confidence has played a big part in Sun-Maid's prosperous history. "We've been successful for eight decades because we have consistently provided a top quality product that the consumer can rely and depend on," he says. "When they buy the 'girl on the red box,' they know they are buying quality."

Community involvement, an appreciation of local heritage, and immigrant initiative are distinguishing qualities of Frank Caglia and his family, owners of Electric Motor Shop, Inc. ♦ In 1913, Central State Electric Co., the forerunner of Electric Motor Shop, opened its doors in Fresno under the ownership of Edmund Elmore Elzea, his wife, Mary, and two other

partners. That year, Frank Caglia was born in Italy. At age eight, he and his parents passed through Ellis Island federal immigration center in New York and headed for California.

In 1929, when he was a 10th grader in a Fresno parochial school, Frank Caglia was hired by the Elzeas to do billing, collecting, and sales for the company, along with some work in the repair shop. At that time, the firm employed just 15 people, and its primary customers were local dairies, packing houses, and other agriculture-related businesses needing electric motors or repairs.

Caglia worked hard, and in 1944, at age 31, he bought 10 percent of the business. He purchased another 20 percent in 1955 and two years later acquired the entire business, which by then had been renamed Electric Motor Shop, Inc. Today, the company employs 60 people and is a fully licensed electrical contracting firm located on the corner of Fulton and Monterey avenues in Fresno's downtown industrial district.

Frank Caglia, who came to America from Italy in 1921, remains active in the business after more than six decades of involvement.

A subsidiary company, Electric Motor & Supply Co., sells industrial electrical supplies, switchboards, and transformers. The Caglia family also operates two waste disposal companies, as well as glass and recycling centers near Fresno.

Electric Motor Shop [ha]s a vast inventory of [ele]ctrical equipment, new [an]d used motors, and [rel]ated supplies.

A FAMILY-RUN ENTERPRISE

Frank Caglia, still active in the business after more than six decades, enjoys plenty of family help in the management and operation of the firm. He and his wife, Florence, have seven children and many grandchildren, several of whom are involved in running Electric Motor Shop or other family enterprises. Frank's son, Richard "Dick" Caglia, serves as general manager of Electric Motor Shop. Dick's two sons, Richard and Rod, also work for the company. Frank's daughter, Sally, serves as executive secretary, and another son, Vince, maintains equipment for the company.

Electric Motor Shop can design and install virtually any type of electrical system for projects ranging from wiring for multi-story buildings to lighting for high school football stadiums. The firm has a vast inventory of electrical equipment, new and used motors, and related supplies. The company distributes products manufactured by General Electric Co., Emerson Electric Co., Browning Mfg., Appleton Electric Co., Baldor Electric Co., and Micro Switch Co. to customers throughout the San Joaquin Valley. The firm also offers a 24-hour repair service.

A HANDS-ON COMMITMENT TO THE COMMUNITY

While the Caglias are recognized as successful members of the business community, they are perhaps best known for their civic accomplishments. The old arch at the southern entrance to the downtown area, which proclaims Fresno "The best little city in the U.S.A.," was restored under Frank Caglia's direction and with his financial support.

In 1929, Caglia began his longtime devotion to the Warnors Theatre when he attended its reopening and fell in love with the big Robert Morgan organ in the orchestra pit. Decades later, when the theatre fell into decline, the family bought the property, and the building and organ were lovingly restored. Today, Caglia's daughter, Rose, is manager of the theatre, which provides a venue for a variety of productions and charitable events. Another daughter, Sally, is bookkeeper for the theatre.

Since their arrival in Fresno 72 years ago, the Caglia family has worked hard and prospered, making countless contributions to the economic, civic, and cultural well-being of the city. Today, as several generations strive to maintain that longtime commitment to the business and the community, the Caglias will undoubtedly continue to make their mark on Fresno.

STAMMER, McKNIGHT, BARNUM & BAILEY

*W*hen Walter Henry Stammer graduated Phi Beta Kappa from Stanford University and received a Juris Doctor degree in 1916, he probably did not envision the role he would play in Fresno's legal history. But the longtime local resident and founder of Stammer, McKnight, Barnum & Bailey set in motion a legacy of hard work and excellence that has continued

for eight decades. "We've been a general civil litigation firm from the outset," says Jan Biggs, managing partner. "We are trial lawyers. That's what we are, and that's what we do best."

Partners James N. Hays and Jerry D. Jones are members of the firm's team of 14 lawyers and 16 support personnel.

INVOLVED IN THE LOCAL LEGAL COMMUNITY SINCE 1916

Stammer first entered the field of law in May of 1916, when he began practicing in Fresno with W.B. Owens and L.L. Cory. But in 1929, he separated to establish his own practice and began building one of the finest litigation firms in the Valley. Along the way, Stammer compiled an impressive client list, including Southern Pacific Railroad, Chevron USA, Inc., John Deer Company, and Goodyear Tire and Rubber Co. "We have been representing essentially the same clients for the past 60 years," Biggs says. "When people think of quality law firms in Central California, they think of Stammer, McKnight, Barnum & Bailey."

Galen McKnight, also a Stanford graduate, joined the firm in 1931 after passing the bar exam and later became Stammer's first partner. Another Phi Beta Kappa Stanford graduate, James Barnum, became the third partner in 1950 following World War II. Dean Bailey, who is currently retired and the last living namesake partner, came on board in 1954.

"Dean Bailey was known as 'the professor,'" Biggs says, "because of his meticulous approach to his work. And McKnight and Barnum were, in their day, considered among the finest trial lawyers in the state. McKnight had a stretch of roughly 20 years when he didn't lose a case. As for Jim Barnum, he was probably one of the finest medical malpractice lawyers to be found anywhere in the country."

The original group of four all graduated from the Stanford University law program, which firm members today believe gave Stammer, McKnight,

Barnum & Bailey the foundation of legal knowledge that boosted it to statewide recognition. Jim Hays, the last of the "old guard" to remain active in the firm today, was invited to join his fellow Stanford graduates in 1969. A Fresno native, he got his start in the legal profession while in practice locally with his father. At age 67, Hays serves as the firm's senior partner.

"I guess you could describe us as the second generation," says Biggs, who joined the firm in 1974. "We are following in the footsteps of the original partners, and we work extremely hard to maintain their legacy of excellence."

"ONE OF THE FINEST TRIAL LAW FIRMS IN FRESNO"

Today's team of 14 lawyers and 16 support personnel serves essentially the same list of clients the firm has catered to for more than half a century. Although the current staff reflects a much broader representation of law schools, attorneys at Stammer, McKnight, Barnum & Bailey still maintain the same basic focus established by the first generation of partners. Negligence, medical malpractice, insurance coverage, products liability, hospital, and water law are today the firm's primary areas of concentration.

Another important aspect of the firm's legal practice is agriculture. Representing major railroad and oil companies in California is often not as cut and dry as it may seem. In fact, these industries are among the largest landowners in the state, a fact which has led Stammer, McKnight, Barnum & Bailey to develop an expertise in agricultural litigation. "Agriculture is perhaps the thread that joins all our areas of litigation together," Biggs says, "and it is certainly an important part of life in the Valley. If I had to pinpoint a theme in our legal representation, it would be that we have become an integral part of the agricultural community."

Since its founding more than seven decades ago, Stammer, McKnight, Barnum & Bailey has been an important player in the local legal community. Today, the second-generation partners take pride in the firm's history of careful expansion. According to Biggs, growth for growth's sake is not part of the plans for the future. "We are not looking to become anything other than what we have been for decades now," he explains. "We want to continue to be recognized as one of the finest trial law firms in California."

For 70 years, The Fresno Bee *has been the newspaper of record for Fresno County and the Central San Joaquin Valley. Even as it has strived to enrich the lives of local residents through a commitment to news and public service, it has been much more: an instrument of change, a responsible corporate citizen, and a leader in social consciousness. As the* community has evolved and prospered, so has *The Fresno Bee.* Yet its mission has remained constant: to be the region's primary source of news, information, and entertainment, while demonstrating the strictest standards of journalism and editorial integrity.

MODERN FACILITIES AND EQUIPMENT

Today, *The Bee* is a successful, dynamic institution fueled by a work force of over 850 people. *The Bee* occupies a 19-acre site in downtown Fresno, where it recently completed a 131,000-square-foot expansion and installed state-of-the-art flexographic printing presses and new packaging equipment. The flexo press uses water-based ink and employs an environmentally clean process that generates no waste.

"The industry and our society are evolving, and we must meet the challenge," says Publisher Gary Pruitt. "The Fresno Bee will continue to change, but it will remain the primary source of information for this valley, in one form or another, as it has been for the past 70 years."

promoting awareness of and solutions to the illiteracy problem. It has also taken the initiative to implement a model companywide recycling program, among the most extensive in the newspaper industry.

SEVEN DECADES OF GROWTH IN FRESNO

Established in 1922 by Carlos McClatchy, *The Fresno Bee* was the second in the McClatchy newspaper group. Today, fourth-generation family member James McClatchy, a native of Fresno, is chairman of the board of the company, which currently owns and publishes 20 newspapers in California, Washington, Alaska, and South Carolina.

Formerly a privately held family corporation, McClatchy Newspapers went public in 1988, and its stock is traded on the New York Stock Exchange.

The Fresno Bee's circulation, 150,000 daily and 185,000 on Sunday, is concentrated in Fresno County. Daily readership in the county exceeds 276,000, or 73 percent of the population. Readership in the four-county circulation area (Fresno, Kings, Tulare, and Madera) totals more than 348,000 daily and 442,000 on Sunday, making *The Bee* a highly effective advertising medium.

As the market it serves grows and diversifies, *The Bee* will continue to find new and better ways to distribute its primary commodity: information.

"The information provider of tomorrow will have to use a variety of approaches to reach the many audiences it must serve," says Pruitt. "We will need to offer information in formats other than the printed newspaper, including telephones, computers, and fax machines. And we'll have different products designed to meet the needs of small market segments, perhaps even in different languages. In addition to being a mass medium as we have traditionally been, we will be able to target our various audiences."

He adds, "The industry and our society are evolving, and we must meet the challenge. *The Fresno Bee* will continue to change, but it will remain the primary source of information for this valley, in one form or another, as it has been for the past 70 years."

The Fresno Bee occupies a 19-acre site in downtown Fresno, where it recently completed a 131,000-square-foot expansion.

◀ HARVEY ZIMMERMAN

The new technology, representing a $50 million investment, has resulted in more and better use of color, increased page capacity, the use of non-rub ink, and improved overall printing quality. "The investment we have made in our new building enables us to serve our customers, both readers and advertisers, better than ever," says Publisher Gary Pruitt. "And it reflects a commitment to our newspaper, our community, and the market we serve."

That commitment is evidenced not only by the quality of the product, but also by the role *The Bee* plays in the community and, indeed, the industry. A sponsor of programs and activities throughout the Valley, *The Bee* contributes to hundreds of organizations and causes each year. It has been a leader in

*N*ew England Sheet Metal Works, Inc., a family-owned company founded in Fresno, has made significant contributions to the San Joaquin Valley building industry for 73 years. A full-spectrum mechanical construction company, New England Sheet Metal designs, fabricates, and installs heating and air conditioning systems, energy management systems, controls,

plumbing, pipe-fitting, and fire protection equipment. The company is also noted for its fabrication and installation of architectural metals and its heavy industrial in-plant work.

DIVERSE PROJECTS IN THE VALLEY
Since its founding in 1920, the firm has participated in many large-scale, and in some cases rather unusual, construction projects in the area. One of the company's recent undertakings was Fresno City Hall. Completed in 1991, the project made extensive use of stainless steel inside and out. Ara Yazijian, co-owner and president of the company, says, "We installed more than 300,000 pounds of stainless steel on the roof, exterior siding, support columns, doors, and trim. It was a one-of-a-kind project."

In 1982, New England Sheet Metal helped remodel the Kingsburg city water tower on Highway 99 to resemble a giant teapot, reflecting that community's Scandinavian heritage. "That was one of our fun projects," Yazijian says. "Every day thousands of people drive by that tower, which has become a Valley landmark."

Further back in the company's history, New England Sheet Metal was awarded the air conditioning contract in 1970 for the construction of the Fashion Fair Shopping Center. More than 134 large air conditioning units were air-lifted into place in what was then the largest helicopter installation in San Joaquin Valley history. The firm has completed other major projects for Fresno Community Hospital, Clovis Community Hospital, Fresno County Juvenile Hall, Hilton Hotel, Fresno Police Station, Dow Chemical, Fresno City Schools, Sun-Maid Growers of California, Manchester Shopping Center, Kaiser Permanente Medical Center, Fig Garden Financial Center, and the Leon S. Peters School of Business at California State University, Fresno.

Although the company is best known for its industrial and commercial projects, it has also worked extensively in residential construction, primarily as a heating and air conditioning contractor.

COMING TO FRESNO
New England Sheet Metal was founded by Yazijian's father, A.K. Yazijian, who immigrated to the United States from Europe. After landing in Boston, the elder Yazijian decided to make his home in Fresno when he learned that the San Joaquin Valley's climate and geography were similar to those of his native country, Armenia. He soon established his new company and named it after the region that gave him his first experience of life in America.

A.K. Yazijian served as company president until his death in 1956. His son, Gregg, assumed management of the company for 18 years until his death in 1974. That year, Gregg's younger brother, Ara, took the reins of the family business, serving as president and co-owner with his brother Haig. Since 1920, New England Sheet Metal has moved five times to new and larger facilities and is currently located on five acres at 2731 South Cherry Avenue in a 40,000-square-foot building to accommodate its growing operations.

MAJOR COMPANY DIVISIONS
Today employing nearly 150 people, New England Sheet Metal is organized into major divisions that guide the company's activities. The design/

New England Sheet Metal's 40,000-square-foot office/shop is located at 2731 South Cherry Avenue.

The company's state-of-the-art computerized coil line is used to manufacture rectangular ductwork.

engineering department produces working drawings for field personnel, permit acquisition, plan approval, and architectural coordination. Area contractors and other clients also call on the department to conduct cost analysis for various aspects of prospective construction projects so that effective bidding criteria can be developed.

In order to stay abreast of the ever-changing market conditions, New England Sheet Metal's fabrication department has state-of-the-art computerized rectangular duct fabrication equipment and a laser cutting table for all types of fittings.

The company's service department maintains a fleet of 15 radio-dispatched trucks to service everything from small rooftop units to 1,000-ton units for commercial buildings. "Our service representatives are on call 24 hours a day to handle air conditioning or heating problems," says Yazijian.

As might be expected from a trailblazer among sheet metal companies in Fresno and beyond, the firm's president has held a number of leadership positions in the industry and contributed significantly to his profession. During his 17-year tenure at the company's helm, Yazijian has served as president of both local and state sheet metal contractors' associations. He also served for six years on the National Joint Adjustment Board, which settles union and labor disputes.

Perhaps Yazijian's greatest honor came in 1986 when he was named a Fellow of the Sheet Metal and Air Conditioning Contractors' National Association (SMACNA). The purpose of the SMACNA College of Fellows is to recognize and honor individuals in the sheet metal and air conditioning industry who have made significant contributions to the advancement of SMACNA and the industry. Membership in the College of Fellows is reserved for industry leaders of the highest rank.

Within the next several years, Yazijian plans to retire and hand over the management responsibilities of the company to the next generation of the family: his son, Mark Yazijian, and his son-in-law, James Boone. He is confident that New England Sheet Metal will be in good hands. "I don't plan to look over their shoulders," Yazijian says. "I am confident they will maintain the level of quality service and products we have established over the last 73 years."

In 1991, the company completed work on Fresno's new City Hall, a one-of-a-kind project that required over 300,000 pounds of stainless steel and more than 500 tons of cooling.

More than a century ago, the Fresno Chamber of Commerce was formed as a nonprofit membership group of local businesses and professionals. Since its founding in 1885, the Chamber has provided opportunities for networking among all sectors of the community: business, education, agriculture, and government. As an advocate for the economic and social well-being of the 702,000 residents of Fresno County, the Fresno Chamber of Commerce today serves well over 2,000 members throughout a 6,000-square-mile area.

Located in California's heartland, the San Joaquin Valley, Fresno is one of the state's fastest growing communities and among its most culturally diverse. According to 1990 U.S. census figures, the Hispanic community accounts for nearly 40 percent of the total Valley population. Vietnamese and Hmong refugees, Japanese and Chinese immigrants, Africans, Armenians, Portuguese, and other ethnic groups contribute to Fresno's cultural diversity—unmatched by many cities twice its size. Over the years, Fresno has become a haven for yet another wave of immigrants: city dwellers seeking refuge from the countless problems of California's overcrowded metropolitan areas.

Responding to this level of growth and diversity is one of the Chamber's greatest challenges today. "Not unlike our local city government," says 1992 Chamber President Robert Carter, "we establish goals and objectives based on what our diverse membership needs are."

For more than a century, the Fresno Chamber has provided opportunities for networking among all sectors of the community.

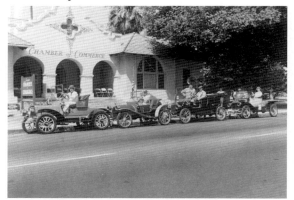

A FOCUS ON AGRICULTURE

With nearly $3 billion in annual crop production, Fresno County is the leading agricultural county in the United States. Agriculture dominates the local economy, with more than 250 crops currently in production. As a result, the Fresno Chamber places a high priority on working with the agriculture industry. In fact, the Chamber presents an annual "Agriculturalist of the Year" award as part of the AgFresno Farm Equipment Show, of which it is a cosponsor.

The Chamber's proactive Agribusiness Development Group keeps members informed on issues through a series of monthly Ag Council Luncheons held at the Fresno Chamber offices.

The Chamber's Ag marketing Committee develops an annual *Fresno County Ag Sourcebook*, a publication designed to promote the agricultural industry. It contains a list of various agriculture resources in Fresno County, as well as articles about leading-edge ag technology developed in the San Joaquin Valley.

▲ DEMI DE SOTO ▶

Another of the Chamber's agriculture advocacy programs is the annual Fresno County Blossom Trail. This 67-mile, self-guided tour highlights Fresno County's 6,000 square miles, which include 1.3 million acres farmed by 7,500 farmers raising 250 different crops worth nearly $3 billion a year. The event is cosponsored by the Fresno Chamber of Commerce, Fresno County Farm Bureau, and the Fresno City and County Convention & Visitors Bureau. The Fresno County Blossom Trail was recently added to the American Bus Association list of the top 100 must-see events in the United States.

The Fresno Chamber of Commerce reaches out to the educational community as well. In 1990, it initiated the first annual Valley Education Conference as a way of bringing business and education together. Major local organizations, including Dow Chemical U.S.A., *The Fresno Bee*, Pacific Bell, and PG&E, help sponsor the annual event. "The Chamber's Employer/Education Committee is responsible for this innovative program aimed at creating a partnership between business and education," states 1993 Chamber President Jim Pardini.

The Fresno County Blossom Trail, a 67-mile, self-guided tour, is cosponsored by the Fresno Chamber of Commerce, Fresno County Farm Bureau, and the Fresno City and County Convention & Visitors Bureau.

SMALL BUSINESS ADVOCACY

Seminars on timely business topics are another important part of the Chamber's program of work. "Being proactive means that we must play an

Thanks in part to the Chamber's efforts, a new optimism has emerged regarding the future of downtown Fresno as a regional business center.

aggressive leadership role in the business community," says Pardini. "But we also have to be reactive, especially to proposed anti-business legislation. We must be an effective lobbying group in order to ensure that the local business community is well represented in the governmental process."

The Fresno Chamber of Commerce works closely with organizations, such as the Central California Small Business Development Center (SBDC) and the Service Corp of Retired Executives (SCORE), in providing services to small businesses. Monthly seminars, counseling services, and business networking opportunities are also an important part of the Chamber's mission to enhance and support the private sector in Fresno County.

DOWNTOWN REVITALIZATION

As is the case in many other metropolitan areas, Fresno has experienced a flight to the suburbs over the past decades, leaving behind an area in need of new private sector investment. An enthusiastic advocate of downtown revitalization efforts, the Fresno Chamber recently spearheaded a coalition of local businesses to promote the privatization of the Fresno Redevelopment Agency. Thanks in part to the Chamber's efforts, a new optimism has emerged regarding the future of downtown Fresno as a regional business center.

"Our downtown has great potential, and an economic and political stalemate had stopped the revitalization process," says Carter. "We assessed the history of redevelopment in Fresno and decided our priority should be to place the process in the hands of the private sector."

AWARD-WINNING COMMUNICATIONS

One of the Fresno Chamber's most visible contributions to the community is *Fresno Business*. The award-winning publication offers the Chamber a forum to highlight its contributions to the evolving Fresno County business community. *Fresno Business* is one of only 13 newspapers in the United States and Canada to receive an Award of Excellence from the American Chamber of Commerce Executives. Communications Concepts of Washington, D.C. also honored the paper with its APEX National Press Award of Excellence. "Our newspaper has been very instrumental in keeping the membership and the community informed about Fresno Chamber of Commerce activities," states Executive Director Stebbins Dean.

Other vital Fresno Chamber communication tools include the award-winning Membership Directory & Business Pages, published by Towery Publishing, and data base marketing resources including mailing lists, labels, and brochures.

A CONTINUED COMMITMENT TO FRESNO COUNTY

During more than a century of small business advocacy, the Fresno Chamber of Commerce has expanded its focus to virtually every aspect of the community. With an eye on tomorrow, Jim Pardini defines the Chamber's challenges in simple terms. "Our responsibilities have evolved into several primary areas: community and business advocacy, agricultural enhancement, governmental and civic affairs, and membership development," he says. "We do not envision a drastic departure from these fundamental roles in the near future."

California Shoe Shine

UNITED CIGAR STORES

SECURITY-FIRST NATIONAL BANK OF LOS ANGELES

FED RAL

NAT NAL BANK

33688

FRESNO
California's Heartland

I 9 2 6 - I 9 5 5

The traffic stopped on Fulton Street in 1931 when the service clubs held their hand car races, this one between the Advertising club and the Lions.

1929	SAINT AGNES MEDICAL CENTER
1932	PRODUCERS DAIRY FOODS, INC.
1934	EDUCATIONAL EMPLOYEES CREDIT UNION
1934	FLOWAY PUMPS
1937	FIRST AMERICAN TITLE INSURANCE COMPANY
1938	COMMERCIAL MANUFACTURING AND SUPPLY COMPANY
1938	THOMAS, SNELL, JAMISON, RUSSELL AND ASPERGER
1939	TOWER THEATRE FOR THE PERFORMING ARTS
1942	LONGS DRUG STORES
1944	DeMERA DeMERA CAMERON
1944	FRESNO PACIFIC COLLEGE
1946	DUNCAN ENTERPRISES
1948	VALLEY ENGINEERS, INC.
1950	RYAN, CHRISTIE, QUINN, PROVOST & HORN
1950	VETERANS AFFAIRS MEDICAL CENTER FRESNO
1952	FRESNO WIRE ROPE & RIGGING CO.
1952	VALLEY CHILDREN'S HOSPITAL
1953	BENEFIT ADMINISTRATION CORPORATION

The Sisters of the Holy Cross, who came to Fresno in 1894 to open a boarding and day school that eventually became Saint Augustine's Academy, established Saint Agnes Hospital in 1929. An article in the May 19, 1929, edition of The Fresno Bee noted that because the site was on one of the highest spots in Fresno, patients would enjoy the benefit of the prevailing cool northwest breeze. It takes a stretch of the imagination to envision a "high spot" in Fresno today, but most residents will acknowledge the benefits of the cool evening breeze during the dry, hot months of summer.

As if it were destined to be, the Sisters at Saint Agnes affirmed their mission and spirit of care by opening the hospital one day early for a young boy who needed emergency surgery. Rather than stand on ceremony, the hospital's first official act, on August 4, 1929, was one of care. Saint Agnes opened officially on the following day.

The original hospital cost $350,000 and opened with a staff of 32. In the first year of operation, 1,334 patients were admitted, and 257 babies were born. Over the years, that facility was enlarged several times. In 1974, in response to population growth and the need for modern facilities, Saint Agnes began construction at its present location on Herndon Avenue. Saint Agnes Medical Center opened in March 1975 and is currently licensed for 323 beds. In 1991, more than 2,000 employees served at Saint Agnes, more than 18,500 patients received care, and 3,559 babies were born.

Saint Agnes Medical Center was also the first hospital in the Valley to be accredited by the American College of Surgeons, a tradition of excellence that is echoed in the 1990 assessment by the Joint Commission on Accreditation of Healthcare Organizations (JCAHO). Among all JCAHO-accredited hospitals, Saint Agnes Medical Center placed among the top 10 percent in "quality of care."

BUILDING FOR THE FUTURE

On May 3, 1991, the medical center hosted a sesquicentennial tribute to the Sisters of the Holy Cross. Sister Ruth Marie Nickerson, C.S.C., medical center president and chief executive officer, acknowledged the occasion with these words: "In celebrating the 150-year anniversary of the Sisters of the Holy Cross, we are not celebrating an organization that's 150 years old. Not at all.

"We are celebrating our beliefs and the sources from which they come—love, hope, and faith. We are celebrating nothing less than our mission and our confidence that the future holds no obstacles, no challenges, no conditions that cannot be overcome by the grace that has sustained us so far."

This confidence is evident in two major medical center building programs currently under way, the Saint Agnes Outpatient Center and The Cancer Center at Saint Agnes.

The Outpatient Center, scheduled for completion in January 1993, is a 65,625-square-foot, four-story addition to the main hospital. With a primary emphasis on outpatient care, it will provide expanded services to outpatients, as well as facilities for magnetic resonance imaging, outpatient laboratory services, and a 19-bed critical care unit.

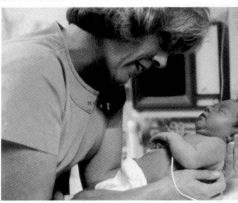

In 1991, 3,559 babies were born at Saint Agnes Medical Center.

The Cancer Center at Saint Agnes, a 32,900-square-foot facility, will realize a vision that began when Saint Agnes Medical Center moved to its present location. The facility is the result of years of planning to meet the needs of the hospital's patients, their families, and physicians and will bring together the experience of outstanding physicians and the latest medical technology for the treatment of cancer. Completion is slated for spring of 1993.

HELPING TO CONTAIN HEALTH CARE COSTS

Saint Agnes works to contain the spiraling cost of health care by helping people learn how to stay healthy and by entering into partnerships with other

Since its founding in 1929, Saint Agnes has grown with Fresno. In 1975, the hospital moved from its original location at Fruit and Floradora streets to a modern medical complex on Herndon Avenue.

providers in order to reduce duplication, improve services, and minimize capital expenditures.

To help people stay healthy, the medical center produces television spots and newspaper articles called "Health Updates from Saint Agnes." Among the topics addressed in 1991 were melanoma, arteriosclerosis, organ donations, immunization, chest pain, breast cancer, testicular cancer, and the durable power of attorney for health care. More than 2,000 concerned residents called for more information.

In conjunction with its public information programs, the medical center also offers free health screenings to the Fresno/Clovis community. Among services provided in 1991 were cholesterol screenings for 5,462 people at a cost of only $5 per person, free prostate cancer screenings for 572 men, and free vision screenings for 1,995 clients by The California Eye Institute at Saint Agnes.

Another example of the medical center's resolve to contain health care costs and meet community needs can be seen in its partnerships with other providers. Among these are ValuCare, the largest health maintenance organization of its type in the Valley; The California Eye Institute at Saint Agnes; San Joaquin Valley Rehabilitation Hospital for inpatient and outpatient care of disabling injuries or illnesses; The Fresno Imaging Center for outpatient diagnostic services; Valley Children's Hospital for neonatal infant care; and The Windham at Saint Agnes, a retirement community for independent living.

COMMITTED TO THE VALLEY COMMUNITY

Saint Agnes also attends to the needs of mature adults by utilizing their talents and skills as volunteers and by providing services to bolster their quality of life. The Saint Agnes Service Guild, the medical center's first volunteer organization, provided more than 100,000 hours of service in 1991. Members of Club 55 Plus, an association of people over age 55 who share interests, hobbies, and travel, also serve the medical center and community

in countless ways as volunteers. In 1985, Saint Agnes broadened its services to mature adults by establishing The Windham at Saint Agnes, a retirement community for 200 residents from age 55 to 85. Life at The Windham is secure, gracious, and active.

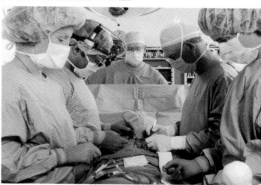

Another aspect of the medical center's community service can be seen at the Holy Cross Clinic at Poverello House and at the Holy Cross Center for Women. Saint Agnes staffs and supplies both of these facilities for needy people. In 1991, the Holy Cross Clinic cared for 7,485 patients. As volunteers in the truest meaning of the word, 68 physicians, dentists, nurses, dental assistants, hygienists, and clerks provided this care without compensation.

In 1990, Saint Agnes was ranked among the top 10 percent in "quality of care" by the Joint Commission on Accreditation of Healthcare Organizations.

The Holy Cross Center for Women served 11,920 clients in 1991: 9,085 women and 2,835 children. These figures represent a 34.4 percent increase since the center opened in 1988. Additionally, Fresno's Commission on the Status of Women awarded the center its 1991 Business of the Year Award.

Everyone at Saint Agnes understands that providing modern medical care is significantly more complicated than it was only a few years ago. Science, technology, costs, and the range of services available occasionally obscure the fact that health care is for people and that each patient is a unique human being with dignity and worth who merits the utmost respect.

The 3,559 births that occurred at Saint Agnes in 1991 offer a joyful illustration of the hospital's stature throughout the Valley. The men and women of Saint Agnes Medical Center are privileged to share the hopes and dreams of their community.

PRODUCERS DAIRY FOODS, INC.

*W*hether it's a cold glass of milk, a dollop of sour cream on a baked potato, or a frosty ice cream bar, Producers Dairy prides itself on having the freshest possible dairy products available in the Central Valley. A family-owned business for over 60 years, the dairy is today run by the father-and-son team of Larry and Richard Shehadey, who agree it is the

freshness of their products that has made Producers succeed.

"Our product can go from a loading box into a refrigerated truck and never be exposed to uncooled air," says Larry Shehadey, president. "It's absolutely guaranteed fresh on arrival to customers."

In addition to its reputation for freshness, Producers Dairy is well known for the advertising campaigns that have made its products familiar to Central Valley residents over the years. Many remember Producers as "Hoppy's favorite." Actor William Boyd, better known as cowboy star Hopalong Cassidy, promoted Producers products from 1952 until his death in the late 1970s. His likeness still adorns the company's milk cartons today. Valley residents young and old identify the dairy with its current advertising jingle: "P-R-O-D-U-C-E-R-S spells Producers. When you know quality, you'll say yes to Producers."

A VALLEY INSTITUTION

Producers Dairy was incorporated in 1932 by a group of ambitious men who wanted to produce quality milk products for the Fresno area. Sixty years later, with a work force of 300 employees, the company produces some 150,000 gallons of milk

and juice daily and a full line of dairy products that it delivers throughout the region. "Producers Dairy is as indigenous to the Valley as grapes," says Richard Shehadey, vice president.

The Shehadey family has been involved in the company since 1949 when Larry Shehadey purchased a major interest in Producers. Just one year later, he became general manager and embarked on a crusade to offer the highest quality dairy products in the Valley.

In 1949, Producers opened its present plant at 144 East Belmont and installed the Central Valley's first half-gallon and quart-size single service packaging machines, which produced the most modern and popular containers of that time. This forward-looking move contributed to Producers' growth in the early 1950s. By 1951, Producers was the first Central Valley dairy to have a 100-percent refrigerated delivery fleet, thus assuring that products would arrive fresh and cold for grocers' shelves.

With his eye still on the goal of product quality, Larry Shehadey in 1959 built an ultra-modern milking parlor for the Producers dairy herd at 4260 W. Madison. As a service to the community, Shehadey included within the new facility an air-conditioned viewing room for school children to

On the production line, quality control is vital, and it's not unusual to see the Shehadeys checking the flow personally.

Producers Dairy maintains a fleet of refrigerated trucks that assure the quality and freshness of its products at all times en route to the retailer.

watch the cow-milking process. Today, more than 20,000 people visit the facility annually.

In 1972, Producers Dairy opened a larger modern milking operation on Whitesbridge Road west of Fresno. Called the Bar 20 Dairy Farms, the operation has the capacity to milk 2,500 cows twice daily. Producers' total herd is approximately 7,000 cows. While the company does not obtain all of its milk from its own animals, its farms were developed as a means of maintaining better control over quality and freshness.

Over the years, Producers' processing plant on East Belmont has been continuously updated with the latest, most modern equipment available for processing and sanitizing. The addition in 1980 of a plastic bottle blow-mold machine to manufacture the company's "space saving" bottle has further increased the quality and efficiency of the processing operation. In addition, an expanded refrigerated cold storage box was added in 1988 to accommodate future business expansion of the dairy. Current expansion plans include computerized processing controls and additional refrigerated storage tanks.

With a continuing rise in sales and the 1991 purchase of an ice cream facility on Hazel Avenue to increase its line of frozen dairy products, Producers has experienced significant growth in the past several years. After six decades of service to the Valley community, Producers is well on its way to becoming the largest independent dairy not only in the Valley, but also across the western United States.

"It is testimony to the quality of our products," says Richard Shehadey. "You don't see brand loyalty much anymore, but Producers has it. In this highly competitive business, the strong survive, and the key to our success has been satisfying the customer."

A COMPLETE PRODUCT LINE
Ensuring customer satisfaction has meant offering a complete line of dairy products in addition to guaranteeing freshness and quality. The Fresno dairy produces an array of milk products, including Jersey Extra Rich, homogenized milk, low-fat milk, Extra Light one-percent milk, non-fat milk, chocolate milk, buttermilk, strawberry milk, acidophilus low-fat milk, and half and half. Other dairy products include sour cream, cottage cheese, yogurt, ice cream products, and novelties. The company also produces fruit punches and orange juice, which originates from a family-owned orange grove in Florida. The juice is transported to Fresno semi-frozen and then pasteurized at the Producers plant.

As has always been the case with its new products, customer satisfaction was the primary goal when Producers introduced strawberry milk in 1990. The product went through 15 formulations until company officials were satisfied they had found the right blend, which uses real natural strawberries.

Producers Dairy serves customers in a distribution area that extends from Bakersfield to north of Stockton and from Santa Maria north through the Monterey Peninsula area and up to San Francisco. "We are close enough to all of our customers to deliver guaranteed fresh products," says Larry Shehadey. "Most chain stores buy milk from outside the Valley. Compare our products and you'll see that they're tastier."

With strict quality controls from "Moo to You" (another familiar Producers advertising line), the company produces, processes, and distributes dairy products for the Central Valley that meet the highest standards. Not resting on its laurels, the company continues to look for new and better ways to serve its customers and energetically looks forward to the future.

"There's going to be significant growth in the Valley, and we want to be part of it," says Larry Shehadey. "My son Richard would agree that Producers Dairy will succeed because quality remains our overriding goal."

Established in Fresno in 1934, Educational Employees Credit Union offers a full line of financial services to school system employees and their families in Fresno, Kings, Madera, Mariposa, Merced, and Tulare counties. With an original investment of $200, the credit union today has assets of over $370 million, making it the largest locally owned credit union in Fresno County

and the sixth largest in the state.

Today more than 60,000 members, the majority of them residents of Fresno County, consider the credit union their primary financial institution. After more than 50 years of serving primarily Fresno County, the credit union began expanding its services to school system employees in nearby counties in 1988.

Recognized as a leader in providing competitively priced financial services, Educational Employees Credit Union offers a diverse line of services including financial planning. Bruce Barnett, president and CEO of the credit union, says, "Our purpose is to understand members' financial needs and to provide quality financial products and services to meet those needs."

From left: Dr. Peter G. Mehas, superintendent of the Fresno County Office of Education, joins the credit union's chairman of the board, Gordon Scott, and its president and CEO, Bruce Barnett.

BUILDING A PARTNERSHIP BETWEEN EDUCATION AND BUSINESS

The credit union also enthusiastically supports the educational programs and efforts of the school systems that employ its members. In Fresno County, the credit union works closely with the Fresno County Office of Education, which represents 39 school districts serving 165,000 students. In all, the county school system employs 6,818 teachers, 640 administrators, and 6,651 classified personnel. Says Barnett, "The traditional philosophy of credit unions is 'People helping people.' We feel our support of the Fresno County school system is one of the best ways we have of demonstrating this to the public."

The Fresno County Office of Education is committed to serving the needs of its diverse student population. Member school districts receive curriculum, migrant, vocational, court, community schools, and special education services, all of which are administered by the County Office. In addition, the organization trains teachers to teach more effectively, fosters leadership skills through the innovative Leadership Academy Program, promotes the use of technology in educating students, and offers educational, staff development, and fiscal expertise to districts and schools.

Dr. Mehas, surrounded by eager Fresno County students, recognizes the importance of building a partnership between education and business.

The Educational Employees Credit Union sponsors a number of educational programs and awards to support the schools in their mission. Three annual awards it presents are the Fresno County Teacher and Employee of the Year and the Management/Leadership Award, which recognize outstanding school personnel for their leadership and contributions to education. A popular program sponsored by the credit union is "Principal for a Day," which offers business leaders the unique opportunity to actually serve as a school principal. This experience gives them firsthand knowledge of a local school and encourages partnerships between business leaders and the schools.

FRESNO 2000

A cooperative effort among the Fresno County Office of Education and the local business community, as well as government officials, civic and community organizations, teachers, and parents, has resulted in the adoption of the Fresno 2000 plan, perhaps the most ambitious and far-reaching endeavor the community has undertaken in decades to raise local educational standards. Educational Employees Credit Union is fully supportive of the America 2000 program, a set of six goals to be reached by the turn of the century. The enthusiasm and dedication of the individuals who worked on the Fresno 2000 plan are reflected in the fact that Fresno was the first West Coast community to adopt the goals of America 2000.

Those six goals state, in essence, that by the year 2000: all children will start school ready to learn; the high school graduation rate will increase to 90 percent; American students will demonstrate competence in challenging subject matter, and every school will ensure that all students learn to use their minds well; U.S. students will be ranked first in the world in science and mathematics achievement; every adult American will be literate, possess the knowledge necessary to compete in a global economy, and exercise the rights and responsibilities of citizenship; and every school in America will be free of drugs and violence and will offer a disciplined environment conducive to learning.

More than 60,000 members consider the Educational Employees Credit Union their primary financial institution.

In addition, the credit union assists the County Office of Education with the advancement of forward-looking technology in the classroom by underwriting costs for Lab Quest computer software. Other credit union-sponsored programs include Computer Competitions, Odyssey of the Mind, and Fresno's Finest Musical Program. Through these efforts, the credit union is reaching students, providing unique support for teachers and administrators, and helping to shape the future of the community.

Commenting on the contributions of Fresno businesses toward the improvement of educational opportunities in the community, Dr. Peter G. Mehas, superintendent of the Fresno County Office of Education, says, "Preparing students of Fresno County for life in the 21st century is a tremendous challenge. Collaboration with our business community will ensure that together we produce graduates who will become contributing and productive members of society."

Gordon Scott, chairman of the board of the Educational Employees Credit Union, believes that the organization's commitment to and active participation in improving the quality of education in Fresno is an investment in the future of the San Joaquin Valley, as well as an obligation the community must fulfill to today's students. He also feels strongly that the credit union's role in bringing about positive change is not only a corporate responsibility but also a privilege. Says Scott, "Educational Employees Credit Union is proud to be a part of this community. We want the community to be equally proud of us."

F irst American Title Insurance Company, one of the oldest and largest real estate title insurance companies in America, has offered peace of mind to generations of Fresnans by providing protection to buyers in property transfer matters. The Fresno office of the company, whose home office is headquartered in Santa Ana, California, writes title insurance for more than

3,000 Fresno County home buyers and property purchasers each year.

Company officials proudly trace the historical roots of the Fresno office to Home Title, which opened in 1937 on Mariposa Street downtown. The homegrown company had served the city admirably for 28 years when, in 1964, First American Title agreed to underwrite Home Title's insurance policies. In 1969, Home Title opened negotiations with First American for a merger of the two companies. The merger was agreed upon, and in 1973 Home Title's name was changed to First American Title Insurance Company of Fresno.

Today the Fresno branch employs 30 people in its main office on Fresno Street, 11 people at an escrow office at Palm and Sierra avenues in north Fresno, and two people at a branch office in nearby

The Fresno office of First American Title Insurance Company writes title insurance for more than 3,000 Fresno County home buyers and property purchasers each year.

Kingsburg. The company's primary activity is preparing and processing title insurance policies, which take the risk out of acquiring property by insuring against defective deeds, forged signatures, unpaid property taxes by former owners, disputed ownership, and other problems that can surface unexpectedly during the transfer of property. Another main focus at First American is the preparation of escrow instructions on the sale of land.

FIRST AMERICAN CORPORATE BEGINNINGS
The history of the parent company, family owned and operated for generations, dates back to 1889 when Orange County was created from the larger Los Angeles County. At that time, there were two

title companies in the newly formed county, Santa Ana Abstract Company and Orange County Abstract Company, both founded by local citizens.

The companies were hired to transcribe by hand all the Los Angeles County records for property that had become a part of the new county. It was a daunting task—some of the land ownership records were in Spanish and dated back to the Mexican colonial period of the early 1830s. With a total of six employees, it took the companies two years, working six days a week.

In 1892, C.E. Parker, a Santa Ana businessman, bought stock in the Santa Ana Abstract Company and in 1894 played a key role in consolidating that firm and Orange County Abstract Company into a new organization known as Orange County Title Company. Parker served as president of the firm for 37 years until his death in 1930. He was succeeded by H.A. Garner, who served until 1943 when Parker's son, George A. Parker, became president. In 1963, George Parker became chairman of the board, and D.P. Parker, grandson of the founder, was elected president.

In 1968, corporate reorganization of the company occurred with the creation of a holding company, First American Financial Corporation. The principal subsidiaries formed were First American Title Insurance Company and First American Trust Company. Two additional subsidiaries, First American Home Buyers Protection Corporation and First American Real Estate Tax Service, Inc., were added in 1986 and 1987, respectively. D.P. Parker became chairman of the board of the holding company in 1989, and his son, Parker S. Kennedy, was named president.

Today, the subsidiaries of First American Financial provide title insurance through more than 300 offices and over 4,000 independent title agents throughout the country, as well as offices in the Bahamas, Canada, Guam, Mexico, Puerto Rico, the Virgin Islands, and the United Kingdom. With total assets of nearly $600 million, the holding company is listed on the NASDAQ market system.

The Fresno office of First American Title Insurance Company benefits not only from the financial strength of its parent organization, but also from over a century of experience in the title insurance field. After decades of business in the Fresno community, First American Title Insurance Company is committed to maintaining its reputation for professionalism and outstanding service for years to come.

loway Pumps is a company with over a half century of experience in the manufacture of vertical pumps for commercial, industrial, municipal, and agricultural applications. Since Floway's establishment in 1934 as Fiese & Firstenberger Manufacturing, Inc., the firm has continually combined theory with practice to produce a quality line of engineered products.

Like Fresno, Floway has continued to grow and flourish. After World War II, the company underwent a number of corporate changes which allowed it to concentrate on the development and production of the vertical turbine pump. In 1957, the trademark, Floway, came into existence. Through progressive engineering, design, and manufacturing techniques, the vertical turbine became a highly versatile pump with many applications in various fields.

By 1965, continued growth had brought about the name Floway Pumps, Inc., adding a sense of identity and unity of purpose to the company. A merger with Peabody International in 1975 met the existing needs and concerns of both firms. An interest in the environment, pollution, and safety issues helped Floway achieve worldwide recognition as a quality producer.

In 1992, the company was purchased by the Weir Group PLC of Glasgow, Scotland. The Weir Group is committed to the continued growth and development of Floway Pumps.

FRESNO OPERATIONS

The company's main manufacturing plant, located in south Fresno on more than 20 acres, contains approximately 200,000 square feet of production and storage space. Floway's 180 management, engineering, sales, production, and administrative support personnel work together to produce thousands of reliable pumping units every year. Branch offices and warehouses in Fresno and Houston, as well as an extensive network of over 300 experienced representatives and distributors, have been established to distribute the company's products domestically and internationally.

Locally, the Valley's farmers are an essential element in the future prosperity of Fresno and the nation. Their needs continue to be served by Floway Pumps, while the company has successfully expanded into other fields. Among these are the

areas of fire pumps, radioactive waste, municipal, and industrial applications. Floway pumps can be found in numerous locations around the world, from Latin America and the Middle East to sites including Chicago's O'Hare International Airport, where the majority of the jet fuel pumps were manufactured by Floway. In Iceland, the company's geothermal units allow hot underground water to be brought to the earth's surface, heating homes and buildings in the cities of Reykjavik and Akureyrar.

Floway is also concerned with the larger community. The company takes pride in the fact that employees are involved in many charitable and civic activities, and the company itself supports Valley Children's Hospital, the Bulldog Foundation, March of Dimes, and the Business Associate program at California State University, Fresno.

With a motivated work force, a quality product that is sold internationally, and new ownership that is committed to the growth of the company and the betterment of the community, Floway Pumps is poised for a future that promises continued success.

Left and above: Floway manufactures pumps for a variety of uses, including municipal and agricultural applications.

The company's main manufacturing plant, located in south Fresno on more than 20 acres, contains approximately 200,000 square feet of production and storage space.

or 55 years, the Longs Drug Stores chain has provided customers with outstanding service and competitive prices. Employees work hard to uphold the company's commitment to be "the best drug store in town." "Our first responsibility is to our customers," says Richard A. Collins, vice president and district manager for the Central Valley. "Everything we do and

sell must be of high quality. Employee training is a priority for us so that we can maintain a high standard of service."

That philosophy has been the foundation of growth and prosperity for the company, whose headquarters is in Walnut Creek, California. Since its founding in 1938, the chain has grown to nearly 300 stores in the '90s. Seven of the 230 California locations are in Fresno. Other states with Longs stores include Colorado, Nevada, Alaska, and Hawaii. In 1992, Longs recorded an impressive annual sales average of $8.8 million per store.

ROOTS IN NORTHERN CALIFORNIA

The company traces its beginnings to the late 1800s and Godwin Scudamore, the great grandfather of the chain's founders, Thomas J. Long and Joseph M. Long. Scudamore was the co-owner of three drug stores in Lake County, comprising what may have been the first drug store chain in northern California.

In 1902, Scudamore's son, Thomas E. Long, opened the family's first general merchandise store in Covelo, California. Long died in 1903 and left the store to his son, Edward. Tragically, the store soon burned to the ground. Edward and a partner reopened the store in 1911, and it survived until 1928, when the country was heading into the Depression. Edward's sons, Tom and Joe Long, were born into the business and learned first-hand from toddler to college age about running a store.

The brothers graduated from college in 1932 and started their careers, Tom in accounting and Joe in city management. Then in 1938, they chose a new path following in the entrepreneurial spirit of their ancestors. M.B. Skaggs, then president of Safeway grocery stores, loaned them the necessary capital to open their first store, which Skaggs suggested should be a self-service drug store. That year, the brothers founded Longs Self-Service Drugs on Piedmont Avenue in Oakland, California. That first store has been in operation through the years and will soon relocate behind the original site and nearly double in size.

By 1940, the brothers opened two more stores in northern California. The first Fresno location opened on May 25, 1942 at a downtown site and

Today, Longs pharmacists fill the expanded role of "consultant," enhancing the value of the pharmacy and furthering the company's commitment to customer service.

Longs opened its first Fresno location on May 25, 1942. The popular downtown store has moved twice since then, each time increasing in size.

has moved twice since then, each time increasing in size. Over the years, many top managers have apprenticed at the downtown Fresno store. By 1948, after a decade of hard work, the Longs chain operated six stores in California.

AN ERA OF RAPID GROWTH

The years between the late 1950s and the late 1960s heralded an era of rapid growth for Longs, with the opening of 31 additional stores in California. In 1971, the company's listing on the New York Stock Exchange signified its growth and success.

Longs reached a milestone in 1976 with the opening of its 100th store in Kailua, Hawaii. The chain celebrated another milestone in 1981: $1 billion in annual sales. Expansion has continued throughout the '80s and early '90s, bringing the chain to nearly 300 stores in five western states.

The company has never sacrificed quality for quantity. Longs continuously makes improvements in store operations to satisfy and serve customers better by applying new technology and keeping abreast of industry advancements. For example, in 1988 Longs introduced "Super Pharmacies," which can dispense more than 500 prescriptions a day with the help of computers, conveyors, and other automatic equipment. In addition, Longs pharmacists fill the expanded role of "consultant," enhancing the value of the pharmacy and furthering the company's commitment to customer service.

"Longs Drug Stores anticipates continued growth in the '90s," says Richard Collins. "We will remain committed to excellent service, competitive prices, and being the best group of drug stores anywhere!"

or more than half a century, the historic Tower Theatre for the Performing Arts has served as the architectural centerpiece of a lively entertainment, shopping, dining, and residential district north of downtown Fresno. Closed for major restoration in the late 1980s, the Tower Theatre reopened in 1990, transformed from an aging movie house into an elegant cultural center

for the performing arts.

Before its development, the Tower Theatre property served as a temporary playground in a neighborhood where attractive Norman and Spanish revival-style homes were built beginning in 1919. A. Emery Wishon, an executive with Pacific Gas & Electric Co., owned the two-plus acres of land. In the late 1930s, he leased the property to Fox West Coast Theaters, marking the beginning of the Tower's long history in Fresno.

A DAZZLING ART DECO COMPLEX

The theater chain hired famed Art Deco architect S. Charles Lee to design the Tower Theatre building as a mixed-use complex: a cinema flanked by two wings of retail shops. When the dazzling $100,000 theatre opened to the public on December 15, 1939 with a double feature, *Dancing Coed* and *Henry Goes Arizona*, it was the talk of the town. The walls of the 900-seat auditorium were adorned with fluorescent murals painted by the Dutch-born artist Anthony Heinsbergen and illuminated by black lights. Architect Lee, who in his career designed over 400 theatres worldwide, had tried the startling new lighting effect in only one other location in the United States. An 80-foot fluted concrete tower, which today remains ablaze with multi-colored neon lights, was patterned after the 130-foot monument *Star Pylon*, the symbol of electricity at the 1939 World's Fair in New York City.

▶ RUSSELL ABRAHAM PHOTOGRAPHY

THEATRE RESTORATION

Around 1960, the theatre was acquired by the late Ralph Coelho and two partners. In 1987, Coelho's daughter, Aileen C. "Dotty" Abbate, and her mother, Aileen L. Coelho, began a $1.6 million restoration project designed by Kennedy Lutz Seng & Boudreau Architecture, Inc. and executed by Cumming Construction Company to transform the

movie theatre into an elegant performing arts center.

Architectural historian John Edward Powell guided the theatre's historic restoration along with interior designer Gary Steinert. John Lind and Ron Eichman of VenueTech Management Group in Napa, California played critical roles in the project's development. Today, VenueTech continues to manage the highly successful theatre.

The foyer carpets, etched-glass doors, gold-leaf casework, hard-wood paneling, and ceiling murals were all meticulously restored. The auditorium wall murals were brought back to life by the original artist's son, A.T. Heinsbergen. A stage and dressing rooms were built, and lighting and sound systems were installed. New handicapped accessible restrooms were added downstairs, and the elegant, tiled restrooms upstairs were preserved.

The Tower Theatre today seats 761 patrons and features an eclectic mix of stage plays and entertainers. Broadway shows such as *Ain't Misbehavin'* have graced the Tower stage, along with internationally acclaimed artists including Ben Vereen, The Smothers Brothers, Ray Charles, Harry Connick Jr., Joan Rivers, Bobby McFerrin, and the Vienna Choir Boys. The theatre is also available for special events, weddings, and private gatherings. The Tower Building wings, as well as the surrounding streets, are filled with interesting shops. The Daily Planet restaurant, a building tenant since 1981, is a popular night spot, as are the neighborhood Java Cafe coffee house and Butterfield's microbrewery and restaurant.

Following the restoration, the Tower Theatre was placed on the National Register of Historic Places. The graceful structure also won the 1992 National Historic Preservation Award from the League of Historic American Theatres.

...cently restored to its ...iginal 1939 grandeur. ...Tower's interior lobby ...tures exotic paneled ...ods, gold-leaf ...ents, and striking ...ling murals.

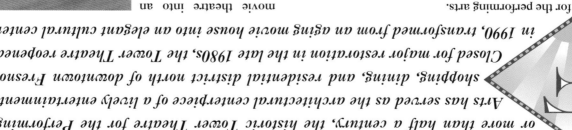

Featuring more than 40 nationally and internationally acclaimed artists each year, the Tower Theatre today is Central California's most elegant and vibrant performing arts center. (Point Anderson photo)

Commercial's processing systems are designed to handle a multitude of products and capacities.

COMMERCIAL MANUFACTURING AND SUPPLY COMPANY

Located since 1938 in the heart of one of the world's richest agricultural regions, Commercial Manufacturing and Supply Company is dedicated to providing the food processors of the world with equipment to meet their varied needs. ◆ Established originally as a machine and welding shop by three Fresno brothers, Commercial Manufacturing and Supply entered the food processing arena by designing and constructing machines to clean and process raisins for processors in the San Joaquin Valley. Soon, other dried fruits and nuts as well as canned, fresh, and frozen vegetables and fruits were added to the company's processing equipment capabilities.

SOLVING FOOD PROCESSING PROBLEMS

Owned by the son of one of its founders, Commercial Manufacturing and Supply today plays an integral part in putting food on dinner tables around the world. Whether it's processing bean sprouts in Japan, walnuts in China or Kashmir, vegetables in New Zealand or Bulgaria, or raisins in Central Asia or America, Commercial Manufacturing's equipment serves the needs of the food processor. Over the years the company has developed equipment to clean, weigh, grade, blend, size, can, freeze, and dehydrate a variety of foods. An "A to Z" listing of products available from Commercial Manufacturing and Supply runs to over 100 items, ranging from air cleaners, air knives, and aligners to many kinds of washers (reel, shaker, flood, tank, and riffle).

Housed at the same location in south Fresno for more than half a century, Commercial Manufacturing and Supply and its employees have been responsible for the design, development, engineering, and manufacturing of innovative, one-of-a-kind

machinery. The in-house engineers, design specialists, and draftsmen are complemented by highly qualified welders and machinists in addition to office and management personnel. A long-term commitment to creative problem solving led the company to design the first stainless steel raisin processing plant for greater productivity and improved sanitation. Commercial Manufacturing and Supply continued that spirit of innovation by developing a more efficient stem removal system for raisins and other fruits.

Since its founding in 1938, Commercial Manufacturing and Supply has designed innovative equipment to meet the needs of food processors worldwide.

As the food industry has evolved, so have the company's designs and applications. Some of the more recent additions to Commercial Manufacturing and Supply's product line have the capability to blend soup ingredients, measure out and mix 10 tons of snack food per hour, combine frozen vegetables, or de-stem 12 tons of raisins per hour.

SERVING FOOD PROCESSORS WORLDWIDE

Food processors worldwide are turning to Commercial Manufacturing and Supply for its quality, service, and flexibility in supplying the industry with either customized single pieces of equipment or complete processing plants. For example, in 1989 the firm designed, engineered, and built an entire raisin processing complex for the Soviet Republic of Uzbekistan. Soviet workers were subsequently trained on location by Commercial Manufacturing and Supply's personnel experienced in the installation and operation of processing plants.

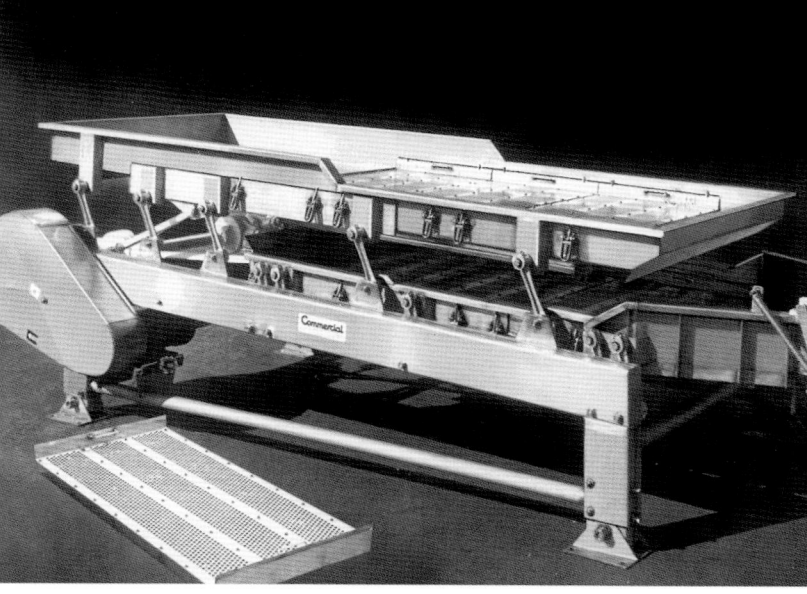

Dozens of America's food processing companies, including Gerber, Pillsbury, Stokely, Sun-Maid Growers of California, General Foods, Del Monte, Campbell, Quaker Oats, and Nestle, have also called on Commercial Manufacturing and Supply to provide answers to their problems.

The company takes pride in identifying the needs of its clients and then providing specific solutions in an efficient manner. Dedication to innovation, flexibility, and quality will continue to be the key to growth for Commercial Manufacturing and Supply as it enters the 21st century. From its home base in Fresno, the company looks forward to meeting the needs of its customers for years to come.

THOMAS, SNELL, JAMISON, RUSSELL AND ASPERGER

homas, Snell, Jamison, Russell and Asperger is one of the oldest legal firms in Fresno and one of the city's leading full-service business law firms, particularly in its historical field of specialization, tax law. ◆ The firm was founded in 1938 by Joseph Kimble (now deceased) and Howard Thomas, and within four years William Snell, Oliver Jamison, and

T. Newton Russell had joined. Paul Asperger became a partner in 1951. The original partners practiced together for decades, and their outstanding legal careers and contributions to community life set the standards for other attorneys who have made their careers with the firm. In the past several years, the five named partners have discontinued full-time legal practice. Sixteen partners and nine associates remain, who continue the outstanding work of their predecessors.

"The strong foundation established by the original partners is one of our strengths," says Janet L. Wright, who joined the firm in 1986. "The original partners were a unique group of individuals with diverse legal and community interests who stayed together over a long period of time and committed themselves to building a successful practice. Those of us who compose the firm today hope to continue their commitment to the profession and our community."

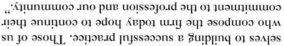

From left: Partners Janet L. Wright, John C. Mengshol, and David M. Gilmore gather in one of the firm's conference rooms.

BRINGING TAX SPECIALIZATION TO THE VALLEY

When Thomas, Snell, Jamison, Russell and Asperger was founded in the days preceding World War II, legal specialization was an emerging trend; it was tax law that caught the attention of the firm's attorneys. "Our firm was responsible for bringing tax specialization to the San Joaquin Valley," says retired partner T. Newton Russell, who today serves as an advisor to the firm. "Our practice grew in large part through referrals from accountants up and down the Valley."

To service these clients, the firm established conference offices in Merced, Modesto, Visalia, and Delano. The firm developed expertise in all aspects of tax law, including income, corporate, estate, property, sales, and excise taxes, and at all levels—local, state, and federal. "Everyone pays taxes, so we found ourselves working not only with many individuals but with virtually every industry in the area," Russell says.

Over the years, the firm's reputation in tax law has prompted demand from clients for legal services in other areas. In response, the firm has branched out, developing expertise in business litigation and

planning, including all aspects of business formation and operation. According to Wright, the firm has worked with two and three generations of management at several area companies and has developed an expertise in supervising transitions in management and property to the next generation.

To meet client needs over the years, the firm has also developed expertise in environmental law, water law, commercial law, and bankruptcy. Consequently, the firm has an active litigation practice in state, federal, and administrative courts.

TOP LEGAL PROFESSIONALS

"The firm can rightfully claim longevity as a strength, but more importantly its reputation has been established through the efforts of some of the best legal professionals in the state," says Wright, adding that the firm's attorneys have graduated from outstanding law schools such as Harvard, Boalt Hall (UC Berkeley), Stanford, USC, and UCLA. "Many attorneys who started with the firm have gone on to establish their own practices, enter government service, or join other organizations and have had distinguished careers," says Wright. "Many of the top practicing attorneys in Fresno have been affiliated with our firm. We have an eye for talent."

From left: Partners James O. Demsey, Charles E. Small, Gerald Vinnard, and Howard B. Thomas.

Wright adds that she and the other senior attorneys with the firm have, like the original partners, committed themselves to both legal and community service. The broad range of current community service activities includes participation in the Chamber of Commerce Leadership Fresno program (Donald P. Asperger and Hilary A. Chittick), chair positions in local, state, and national bar associations (Samuel C. Palmer III and Janet L. Wright), and Rotary Club and Boy Scouts of America volunteer work (David M. Gilmore).

Says Wright, "The primary goal of the firm's next generation of attorneys will be to maintain the quality of service, stability, and integrity our clients have enjoyed for 50 years."

From *its 13,000-square-foot headquarters in the Shaw-Fruit Plaza, the accountancy corporation of DeMera DeMera Cameron assists more than 1,500 clients in the western United States, Japan, and Mexico. ◆ The firm attributes its success to the consistently applied professional efforts of its qualified and dedicated owners and staff. "Despite our volume of business,*

each client receives our personal attention. Individually and collectively, our clients are our most important asset," says Managing Director Mark Cameron. "Satisfying their individual accounting needs through caring and personalized service is our top priority."

The professional services provided to these clients include auditing, accounting, estate planning, business valuation, computer system design, litigation support, management consulting, and income tax planning and preparation. With a full-time staff of highly educated and experienced professionals, DeMera DeMera Cameron serves a diverse client base, including auto and truck dealerships, transportation firms, construction companies, agricultural operations, financial and real estate firms, manufacturing concerns, health care providers, regional and national fast food franchises, and retail organizations.

"I think it's fair to say that we have one of the most varied and comprehensive client lists in the Valley," says Cameron. "Our firm and our clients have a great deal of name recognition in the communities we serve."

DECADES OF ACCOUNTING EXCELLENCE

James DeMera Sr. established the firm in 1944 in the historic Brix Building in downtown Fresno. He was joined by his sons, James DeMera Jr. in 1951 and Howard J. DeMera in 1955. Together, they built one of the Valley's largest and most diverse accounting practices.

In the 1970s, after nearly three decades of primarily family involvement, DeMera DeMera Cameron incorporated and further expanded its practice. The firm currently has eight shareholders: Howard DeMera, who serves as president; Mark D. Cameron; John B. Houlihan; Karen M. Bradley; John A. Renna; R.M. "Tripp" Pound III; James Hering II; and Craig M. Horn. All are members of the American Institute of Certified Public Accountants and the California Society of Certified Public Accountants. "We feel our caliber of professionalism is unmatched by any other accounting firm in the area," Cameron says, "and equaled only by our commitment to the community."

Indeed, civic involvement plays a major role in the firm's philosophy. "We have always considered it important to give back to the community," Cameron says, "and we welcome opportunities to be of service. For instance, the firm was a major donor in the procurement of a bloodmobile for the Central California Blood Bank."

In addition, Howard DeMera chairs the Finance Committee for St. Agnes Hospital, Jim Herring serves on the Board of Directors of Fresno Community Hospital, and Mark Cameron is treasurer of the Fresno Athletic Hall of Fame and past president of the West Fresno Boys Club Board of Directors. The other owners and employees also donate a great deal of their time and talents to local civic and service organizations, including Valley Children's Hospital, Fresno Philharmonic, Fresno County Historical Society, Fresno Chamber of Commerce, San Joaquin Memorial High School, and Rotary, Lions, and Elk clubs. "A community is as strong as the involvement and support it receives from its citizens," Cameron says. "Through our active participation in these various organizations, we feel we can truly help our community flourish."

From its headquarters in the Shaw-Fruit Plaza, DeMera DeMera Cameron provides diverse services for more than 1,500 clients.

HIGH STANDARDS FOR THE FUTURE

In December 1990, DeMera DeMera Cameron completed its first intensive evaluation under the American Institute of Certified Public Accountants Quality Review Program. The California Quality Review Committee for Accounting and Auditing accepted the unqualified opinion issued by the reviewer. "This was the most comprehensive review a firm like ours can experience," Cameron explains. "Passing quality review is essential if a firm is to continue membership in the American Institute of Certified Public Accountants, the most prestigious organization in our profession."

During the past 50 years, DeMera DeMera Cameron has been a part of Fresno's enormous growth. Today, Fresno is California's sixth largest community and its fastest growing city. Throughout this period of expansion, DeMera DeMera Cameron has remained an important force in the San Joaquin Valley. "Our staff is second to none," Cameron says. "I think the forecast for Fresno and the Valley is very bright, and I feel confident DeMera DeMera Cameron will play a vital role in helping to meet the challenges that lie ahead."

or nearly 50 years, Fresno Pacific College has enjoyed a rising reputation as the only accredited liberal arts college in California's Central Valley. ♦ In addition, Fresno Pacific has gained national attention in a survey published by U.S. News & World Report, which named the school one of the "Best of the West." Using guidelines established by the Carnegie

Foundation for the Advancement of Teaching, such as academic reputation and student satisfaction, the report ranked Fresno Pacific in the top 10 among regional liberal arts colleges in the 15 western states.

A COLLEGE OF DISTINCTION
Founded in 1944, Fresno Pacific provides a personalized education in a setting conducive to academic creativity, an innovative faculty, and a distinctively Christian orientation in every program. With a total enrollment of approximately 1,450 students, the college offers the bachelor of arts degree in a variety of majors within five academic divisions, and the master of arts in education.

The impact of the college's programs is unusually broad. An estimated 15,000 teachers in California and around the world take classes each year through the Professional Development Division to stay abreast of educational innovation or simply to broaden their academic background. In turn, these professionals serve their respective communities by preparing thousands of children for adulthood.

A COLLEGE OF DIVERSITY
Whether preparing teachers, managers, musicians, or social workers, the Fresno Pacific experience is based on dedication to excellence. "Excellence in academics is one goal we constantly strive to attain," says President Richard Kriegbaum. "The college is here to meet the real needs of the community by providing opportunities for individuals to develop spiritually, culturally, and professionally. Pacific literally changes people for the better."

Fresno Pacific College approaches this responsibility through a variety of methods, with diverse programs for a diverse student body.

The Center for Conflict Studies and Peacemaking offers training in conflict mediation for school personnel, community and business organizations, and churches.

Through the Center for Degree Completion, working adults with 60 units of college credit may complete a bachelor's degree in as few as 13 months of night classes while maintaining their regular employment.

The OASIS program offers in-home assistance to the elderly, enhancing and extending their ability to remain independent in their own homes. Day care is also available for older adults who need more

The 30,000-square-foot faculty and administration office building is the latest addition to Fresno Pacific's 43-acre campus

assistance, and OASIS was the first agency in the Central Valley licensed to provide overnight respite care for individuals with Alzheimer's disease.

Music and drama presentations on campus and throughout California provide valuable points of artistic contact between college performers and the wider community.

Fresno Pacific's athletic program combines serious academics with serious competition. Since 1984, nine Sunbirds teams have competed in NAIA national playoffs, including three in men's soccer, three in women's basketball, and three in women's volleyball. In 1989, the volleyball Sunbirds captured the women's national championship. In addition, several Sunbirds athletes have brought home national championships in individual track and field events.

A VALUABLE ASSET
Through a fulfilling combination of academic, cultural, and public service programs, Fresno Pacific College makes a unique contribution to the community. Over the past 50 years, it has become a truly valuable asset to the quality of life throughout the San Joaquin Valley and far beyond.

Duncan Enterprises, the world's largest ceramics manufacturer, is concerned with the avocation of one group and the vocation of another. From its headquarters in Fresno, the company is committed both to producing quality products for millions of crafters and hobbyists around the globe and to creating a positive work environment for its 400 employees. ◆ "Every day I think about what we need to do to satisfy our customers," says Larry Duncan, president. "And when I say customers, I mean my 'internal' as well as 'external' customers."

BUILDING A HOBBY INTO A BUSINESS

The Duncan Enterprises complex, which today covers 35 acres in east Fresno, had its beginnings in the garage of Erma Duncan, Larry Duncan's grandmother, in the late 1930s. What started as a ceramics hobby quickly evolved into a family business involving her husband, Lee Duncan, and sons, Bob and Dick Duncan.

In the early years, the flourishing family enterprise was engaged in the retail selling of ceramics paints and supplies, as well as teaching ceramics classes. The business moved in 1946 from the garage to its first commercial studio on Blackstone Avenue. By the early 1950s, the Duncans had reduced retail operations and shifted their focus to the manufacture and distribution of ceramics supplies. In 1955, the business was incorporated with Bob Duncan as president, Dick Duncan as vice president, and Erma Duncan as secretary-treasurer. The company moved to its present site on East Shields Avenue in 1961. Mrs. Duncan retired from active participation in the company in 1965. Larry Duncan became president of the company in 1983 when his father, Bob, went into semi-retirement.

...oday, Larry Duncan ...ads the company that ...gan as a ceramics hobby ...his grandmother's ...rage in the late 1930s. ...arry Krauter photo)

CORPORATE FOCUS:
CUSTOMER SATISFACTION

Today, Duncan Enterprises, which has annual sales exceeding $50 million, boasts a diversified and growing product line. In addition to ceramic glazes and craft and fabric paints, its leading products, the company manufactures brushes, tools, molds, kilns, craft items, and kits for ceramics and other craft hobbies.

The company's "external" customers are located in over 40 countries throughout the world and include more than 200 ceramic distributors, 30,000 ceramic retailers, many other crafts distributors and retailers, and major school and institution catalog houses. Many American mass merchandisers also sell Duncan Enterprises' products.

THE DUNCAN TEAM

As much as Larry Duncan enjoys talking about the history of the business and its product line, he becomes even more animated when describing the company's relationship with its employees, who are referred to as "team members" to emphasize their importance to the success of Duncan Enterprises. "The most important thing that makes one business different from another is the quality of its employees, and our team members are outstanding," he says. "We put a lot of effort into trying to keep them satisfied because happy people do better work than unhappy people."

The company's 400 employees are an important part of the team atmosphere at Duncan Enterprises. (Larry Krauter photo)

Duncan Enterprises shows its concern and respect for its team members by following a team approach to management, which gives employees at all levels a role in the decision-making process and offers ways for individuals to make meaningful contributions. Team member involvement includes a stock-sharing program, and Duncan awards bonuses up to $10,000 to workers who develop new ideas or products. The company recently gave every team member a $500 savings bond in recognition of outstanding work performance.

The Duncan Enterprises compound is a further reflection of the management's interest in creating an enjoyable workplace. The buildings of the complex are colorfully painted and decorated with ceramics, and there is a team member recreational park with a sports field and picnic tables. The company also has a gym that is open 24 hours a day, a drive-through recycling center, and a library with audio and video tapes and book selections ranging from parenting tips to self-improvement programs.

By demonstrating this sort of respect for team members, Duncan Enterprises provides a pleasant, rewarding work environment that draws continual creativity from its people. This creativity has contributed enormously to the company's success in the form of new products and new approaches to doing business. "We have tried to create a win-win situation at Duncan Enterprises so that everyone benefits," says Duncan. "We want both our customers and our team members to have a positive experience."

hen a French contractor defaulted on a hydroelectric power project in 1989, Valley Engineers, Inc., a general engineering construction firm headquartered in Fresno, was called in to complete the job. Located in a rugged and remote area of the High Sierra, the worksite was accessible by hiking trail only. Nevertheless, Valley Engineers, Inc. mobilized its crews within two days and worked throughout the winter coping with rain, mud, snow, and ice.

Construction crews installed 8,000 feet of 32-inch diameter welded steel penstock pipe snaking along steep mountain slopes. Completion of partially constructed stream diversion structures and a power house added to the challenge. Pipe sections, concrete, steel, lumber, supplies, and equipment were airlifted into place with helicopters.

Valley Engineers, Inc. is the oldest locally founded engineering firm in Fresno. The company was established in 1948 by three Price brothers as Valley Trenching Company. Thomas R. Flynn, current president, joined the firm in 1953, and the company was reorganized with Pete Price and Flynn as partners. At that time, the company's name was changed to Valley Engineers, Inc. Price retired in 1974, and Flynn entered into a new partnership with Bob Sondag, who died unexpectedly just five years later. In 1982, Bruno Dietl joined the company and remains a partner today. With a staff of 40 permanent employees, many of whom have been with the company for more than 20 years, Valley Engineers, Inc. employs up to 500 skilled craft workers and continues to meet new challenges.

TACKLING DIVERSE ENGINEERING
CHALLENGES
Throughout its 45-year history, Valley Engineers, Inc. has undertaken more than 1,000 challenging projects up and down the West Coast and in Arizona, Nevada, New Mexico, Oregon, and Nicaragua. Its major public and private construction projects include pipeline systems for natural gas, oil, refined products, wastewater, and water; oil, water, and wastewater pumping and treatment plants; hydroelectric power plants; irrigation transmission systems; ocean outfalls; tunnels; and many other civil engineering and heavy mechanical projects.

The firm won a national award in 1992 from the Associated General Contractors of America for innovative construction and design of a tunnel only eight feet below the Pacific Coast Highway near Newport Beach in Southern California. For this challenging project, Valley Engineers, Inc. employed a construction method never before used.

Perhaps the most unique area of expertise for Valley Engineers, Inc. is geothermal construction for the energy industry. The firm completed its first geothermal project in 1971 for UNOCAL. Valley Engineers, Inc. has since constructed over 100

miles of gathering systems that move steam from well heads to geothermal power plants located 100 miles northeast of San Francisco near the geysers, the largest geothermal power generating area in the world.

Valley Engineers, Inc. has also been involved in many Fresno area projects. In 1992, the firm installed a 44-inch, one-mile-long welded steel pipeline for the Orange Cove Irrigation District to produce hydroelectric power and to transport water from Friant Dam to the state fish hatchery.

Valley Engineers, Inc. has recently completed the installation of 400 new fire hydrants throughout Fresno as part of the city's fire protection upgrading plan. A new domestic water system for Fresno County's Beran area southwest of the city, and a 1.5-mile trunk sewer extension project to accommodate rapid growth in nearby Clovis have added to the area's infrastructure improvement.

Whether it's atop the High Sierra or in the Central Valley's oil fields, industrial areas, farmlands, cities, and counties, Valley Engineers, Inc. has put its decades of experience to work for diverse clients. Says Flynn, "Over the years, we have contributed to the livelihood of the Valley—over 15 million man-hours of employment."

Clockwise from top left: Valley Engineers, Inc. has completed diverse projects involving the domestic water supply, a gas condensate facility, an irrigation turnout structure, geothermal wellsites, city gas mains, and the state fish hatchery water supply.

I n 1865, President Abraham Lincoln made a promise to American men and women serving in the armed forces. For their sacrifices to preserve freedom, he pledged the country "to care for him who shall have borne the battle and for his widow and his orphan." This promise has become the mission of the U.S. Department of Veterans Affairs. ◆ For more than four

decades, veterans in the San Joaquin Valley have been provided quality medical care pledged to those who honorably serve in the U.S. armed forces. Since 1950, Veterans Affairs Medical Center Fresno has attended to the health care needs of thousands of Valley residents who are veterans. Many, due to their economic status or severity of illness, have turned to the Medical Center seeking treatment for their medical and psychological problems.

The 265-bed facility currently employs more than 1,000 Fresnans and treats over 5,000 inpatients and 110,000 outpatients each year at an annual operating expense of $51 million. Among the hospital's programs are Medicine, Surgery, Psychiatry, Dental, Radiology, Neurology, Ambulatory Care, Alcohol and Drug Dependency Treatment, Rehabilitative Medicine, Nuclear Medicine, Speech Pathology, Respiratory Care, Oncology, and Hospital Based Home Care. The Medical Center complex also includes a 60-bed Nursing Home Care Unit.

The complex includes a 60-bed Nursing Home Care Unit with an ambulation course.

Currently, the Medical Center serves a geographic area nearly the size of West Virginia. Patients living in communities from Merced to Bakersfield and from the High Sierra to San Luis Obispo on the coast take advantage of its many programs. The facility is accredited through the Joint Commission of Accreditation of Healthcare Organizations, College of the American Pathologist, American College of Surgeons, and American College of Graduate Medical Educations.

Since 1974, the Department of Veterans Affairs (VA), through its affiliation with the University of California, San Francisco (UCSF) and several other community medical centers, has provided support and training for some 170 medical residents each year. Approximately 50 percent of residents trained in these programs have elected to continue their practice of medicine in Central California.

VA administrators believe the partnership has not only provided local educational opportunities in the field of medicine but also improved health care to Central Valley veterans. "Our affiliation with UCSF has contributed greatly to our educational mission and the quality of care provided to veterans in our service area," says Malcolm Anderson, M.D., the Medical Center's chief of staff. "It has also enhanced our ability to recruit recognized leaders in the health care profession."

The Medical Center's 265-bed facility currently employs more than 1,000 Fresnans and treats over 5,000 inpatients and 110,000 outpatients each year.

INTERACTING WITH THE COMMUNITY

The Fresno community has honored its veterans through local civic, veteran, and fraternal organizations offering both monetary and volunteer support for the VA Medical Center. Each year, an estimated 40 groups provide more than 100,000 hours of volunteer work at the Medical Center. In 1991 alone, donations totaling $250,000 were collected.

Medical Center administrators admit the enormous contribution is essential to the facility's success. "Our volunteers make a significant contribution to our patients' morale and recovery," says Director Wayne C. Tippets. "I'm not sure what we would do without their compassion and concern for our nation's veterans."

He adds, "We are very proud to provide quality care to our veterans. It is this local recognition of our efforts that helps maintain the VA Medical Center's high standing in the Fresno community. Our mission is to continue this level of health care for our veterans in the face of increasing challenges to America's health care delivery system."

*V*alley Children's Hospital is the one and only regional medical center devoted exclusively to providing the highest quality health care services available to children living in the San Joaquin Valley. It remains the only freestanding children's hospital in rural America, serving 10 counties, 60,000 square miles, and more than 800,000 children. ♦ Caring for the Valley's

children for 40 years, Valley Children's Hospital is currently licensed for 182 beds. Increasing demand for hospital services to serve the fastest growing population area in the state has created the need to build a larger facility. Plans are under way for a new 210-bed facility to be opened in early 1997.

More than 50 acres near the scenic San Joaquin River have been generously donated by a local family for the new campus and medical office buildings. The location and size of the new site will allow Valley Children's Hospital to continue its mission, offering the one-of-a-kind care that the region's children have depended upon for more than four decades.

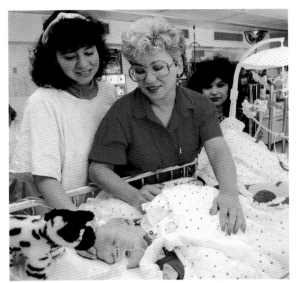

The hospital's Neonatal Intensive Care Unit is the only Level III NICU in the San Joaquin Valley.

A nonprofit, private hospital, Valley Children's is governed by a 20-member Board of Trustees made up of leaders from throughout the Central Valley who believe in the importance of ensuring a bright future for children. The Valley Children's Hospital Foundation is the beneficiary of numerous fund-raising efforts by organizations and individuals including the Padrinos, a group of men dedicated to granting wishes of chronically, critically, and terminally ill children. The foundation also hosts Children's Miracle Network Telethon, the American Dream Home Giveaway, and the Kids Gig.

Valley Children's Hospital offers specialized care to more than 800,000 children from 10 San Joaquin Valley counties.

The hospital receives additional support from its 16 guilds, whose chapters spread across the entire San Joaquin Valley. More than 1,400 dedicated women host special events, including home tours, black tie dinner dances, nut sales, fashion shows, and much more to raise money that directly benefits hospitalized children. Two guilds individually own and operate a thrift shop and gift boutique whose proceeds benefit the hospital, as do the profits from the Valley Children's Gift Shop.

A SPECTRUM OF HEALTH CARE SERVICES
Valley Children's Hospital provides a spectrum of children's health care services unequaled in the 10-county area it serves. Nowhere between Los Angeles and San Francisco is there another health care facility offering a full spectrum of pediatric services and facilities: a Level III Neonatal Intensive Care Unit, a 10-bed Pediatric Intensive Care Unit, the only pediatric Rehabilitation Center in the Central Valley, cardiology and cardiothoracic surgery, developmental and behavioral pediatrics,

diabetes/endocrinology, emergency medicine, gastroenterology, genetics/prenatal detection (including amniocentesis and ultrasound), genetics/metabolism, hematology/oncology, home infusion, infectious diseases, neurology, occupational/physical therapy, orthopaedic surgery, physiatry/physical medicine, pulmonology, radiology, speech-language pathology and audiology, and a trauma receiving center. In each of these disciplines, a team of skilled professionals evaluates every child's care and shares recommendations with family members and referring physicians.

Among other on-site, state-of-the-art technology and support services are magnetic resonance imaging (MRI), CT scan, complete pharmacy and laboratory, child life services, and comprehensive social services support including interpreters.

Valley Children's Hospital also offers a variety of one-of-a-kind services to the community. The Physician Referral Service, for example, helps new and established families find the right physicians for their children.

Pediatrics Plus, an urgent care center in north Fresno, is staffed by Valley Children's board-certified pediatricians and health care professionals. This facility offers a full range of medical services, including X-ray and lab, to children whose regular physicians may not be available.

The Rotary House for Respite Care is the first center of its kind in California offering daytime and overnight respite care for medically fragile children. Staffed by nurses, Rotary House provides a place for parents and caregivers of children with special needs to leave their children for a few hours each

The hospital's volunteer program offers community members the chance to participate in the healing process through patient care and behind-the-scenes work.

day, secure in the knowledge that their physical and emotional needs will be met by highly skilled, caring pediatric professionals.

Valley Children's Hospital is also closely affiliated with the Ronald McDonald House, which provides a warm, homelike place where families from all over the San Joaquin Valley can stay while their children are cared for at Valley Children's.

A STANDARD OF EXCELLENCE

Excellence in the provision of quality care is the standard at Valley Children's Hospital. Its 150 active medical staff members and 1,500-plus employees work diligently to keep quality of care at a superior level. In 1991, the Joint Commission for Accreditation of Health Care Organizations and the California Medical Association granted Valley Children's a three-year accreditation based on its quality of care delivery. This accreditation is a reflection of the dedication to children's health exhibited by Valley Children's physicians, nurses, and staff.

In addition, a survey by an independent research firm rated quality of care at Valley Children's superior to all other hospitals in the Valley providing care to children. More than two-thirds of Fresno County parents surveyed said Valley Children's nurses and physicians are the best providers of health care for children, and eight of 10 rated the hospital's facilities the best for treating children.

Valley Children's is affiliated with the University of California San Francisco Medical Education Program, training 18 pediatric residents and subspecialists each year. These young doctors have the chance to learn from some of the nation's finest physicians, which in turn ensures that future generations of area children will continue to receive the best possible care.

Providing first-rate medical services is only part of Valley Children's commitment to children and families. The hospital also believes that educating children and parents is the best way to prevent illness and injury. Valley Children's interacts with the school system, local media, and community agencies, sponsoring and supporting quality programs that serve to strengthen the family and meet the needs of children. Community education programs sponsored by the hospital include the annual Safe Kids Fair, which teaches youngsters the importance of good health and safety, and Super Sitter classes, which help adolescents learn how to be responsible baby sitters, and in turn, responsible adults. Valley Children's also offers CPR classes, and in the name of fitness and fun, a series of fun runs and duathlons for children.

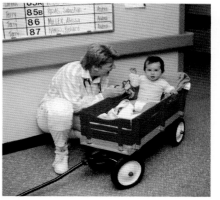

From the Emergency Department to the Rehabilitation Unit, everything at Valley Children's Hospital is designed with children in mind. Members of the hospital staff realize that children aren't tiny adults. They don't fit in big wheelchairs; adult blood pressure cuffs don't fit arms the size of a grown-up's finger. Likewise, children react differently than adults—both physically and emotionally. Valley Children's Hospital is equipped to handle these differences through the latest technology and, perhaps most importantly, through a staff that chooses to work with children.

Little red wagons are a Valley Children's trademark and the preferred method of transportation for many patients.

Valley Children's Hospital, the regional medical center just for children, is here for all families. Every child is welcome, no matter what the family's ability to pay. The hospital and its staff believe in children, and they believe that each child deserves the best in health care and in life.

n business for over four decades, Ryan, Christie, Quinn, Provost & Horn is a full-service accounting firm with a reputation for quality work and the credentials to affirm its good name. ◆ Founded in 1950, the firm originally offered general accounting, financial planning, and estate planning services. Currently employing 10 certified public accountants and a

support staff of 10, the firm has over the years added some two dozen services including mergers and acquisitions, criminal and civil tax fraud defense, expert witness testimony, and business and tax seminars. Although the firm offers comprehensive accounting services, it considers business consulting its primary area of expertise.

Ryan, Christie, Quinn, Provost & Horn is headquartered in the Santa Maria Building.

In 1990, the firm's outstanding work was officially recognized when it became a member of the "PCPS" Division for Certified Public Accounting Firms, whose accreditation is conducted by the American Institute of Certified Public Accountants for the purpose of establishing a superior standard of quality in the accounting profession. "Of the nearly 200 accounting firms in Fresno," says partner Paul Quinn, "only a handful are members of this group. It's one of the most comprehensive quality control measures our profession has to offer."

QUALITY WORK SPURS GROWTH
The superior work consistently delivered by the team of professionals at Ryan, Christie, Quinn, Provost & Horn has resulted in remarkable growth for the firm. Experiencing nearly a three-fold increase in its client base in the past five years, the firm today has more than 475 year-round business clients and about 1,300 seasonal tax preparation customers.

The firm's broad business client base includes physicians, contractors, agricultural concerns, real estate companies, and developers, among many others. Through its affiliation with the "PCPS" Division for Certified Public Accounting Firms, the firm is working more frequently with area banks. "Because of the current savings and loan crisis, most banks require that the accounting firms they employ meet the stringent requirements of that group's accreditation process," explains partner Joey Christie. "Banks continually call on us for business audits as well as other services."

Ryan, Christie, Quinn, Provost & Horn is also one of the most sought after accounting firms in Fresno for litigation matters. "Local law firms that are involved with IRS audits, divorces, or bankruptcies frequently ask us to provide professional assistance in resolving those cases," Christie says.

COMPUTER CONSULTING EXPERTISE
Topping the firm's extensive list of services is a specialty in computer consulting. Michael Salles, whose computer expertise complements his broad accounting background, leads a team of professionals who can set up computerized accounting procedures for virtually any type of business. The firm's consultants determine the hardware and software combination that best suits the client's needs, procure and install the appropriate equipment, and train clients in its proper use. Ryan, Christie, Quinn, Provost & Horn's staff members then act as a computer and accounting support network after installation and training. "We are among the few accounting firms in the Fresno area to provide this level of computer expertise," says Christie.

This field of specialization also enhances the firm's tax preparation capabilities. "Most other Fresno accounting firms utilize outside computer services for processing, which can often take up to a week," says Christie. "With our computer capabilities, we are able to process in-house, frequently cutting turnaround time by more than half."

The firm expects its remarkable growth pattern to continue. Looking ahead to the next five years, the partners anticipate a 10 to 15 percent annual growth rate. Christie considers this a realistic expectation in light of the firm's history and the talent and commitment of its staff.

"Ryan, Christie, Quinn, Provost & Horn will continue to offer a full array of accounting services," says Quinn, "but our specialization in business consulting will be our focus and the way in which we can best serve the Fresno business community."

*I*n 1952, Richard and Billie Becker had dinner with a friend who made a suggestion that would change their lives. The friend, who was a traveling rope and wire cable salesman, suggested the Beckers open a "rigging loft" in Fresno, a business that would sell all types of rope, cable, and related products. He noted that, at the time, there was no rigging loft between Bakersfield and Stockton. Richard Becker, who was then working as a salesman, was somewhat reluctant, but his wife prodded him on. So with one coil of cable, Becker started his new business, Fresno Wire Rope and Rigging Co. His wife, Billie, continued to work as a nurse and raise their twin daughters, sometimes helping with the books at night.

Fresno Wire Rope and Rigging Co. had some lean times in the beginning, Mrs. Becker remembers, but by the late 1950s the company was growing and she was able to quit her nursing job to join the business full time. In 1960, the company purchased property for its current facility at 2360 East Avenue in downtown Fresno's industrial district. In the early 1960s, Fresno Wire Rope and Rigging enjoyed a brisk business selling supplies to the state government for the construction of the San Luis Reservoir and the California Aqueduct in the western San Joaquin Valley.

> "I have always told my employees that customers are our lifeblood," says Billie Becker, co-founder and president. "I believe such an attitude is what has made this company prosper for four decades."

family business on her own. "If you let fear stop you, you'll never get anywhere."

THE RIGGING LOFT TODAY

Fresno Wire Rope and Rigging today has seven employees and sells an extensive line of wire rope, winches, straps, and related products for equipment and tools such as logging chains, augers, cable hoists, hand trolleys, chain hoists, land levelers, trucking equipment, and tractor scrapers. The company even sells the huge replacement teeth for the big jaws of the scoop buckets on heavy earth-moving equipment.

Pacific Gas & Electric Co. is the firm's biggest customer, followed by companies in the agriculture, trucking, and timber industries, and the general public. While most of the firm's sales are to businesses or residents in the San Joaquin Valley, Mrs. Becker says she occasionally fills out-of-state and even out-of-country orders.

Indeed, wire rope is a different product from when the Beckers reluctantly entered the business 40 years ago. Today's virtually indestructible rope is coated and impregnated with a plastic polymer material that penetrates the strands of metal wire to the core. The polymer cushions the wires and strands of the cable as they move and slide, keeps the wire clean and rust-free, and protects it from sunlight and cold weather.

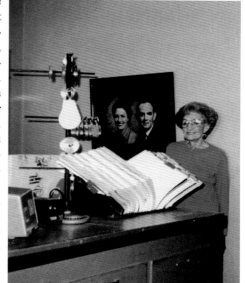

Billie Becker, who helped her husband found the "rigging loft" in 1952, still runs the business today.

The company sells an extensive line of wire rope, winches, straps, and related products for a range of equipment and tools.

Since her husband's death in 1975, Mrs. Becker has continued to operate the company, despite offers to buy it made by several customers who claimed it was too much for her to handle. "Nearly 18 years later I'm still running the business, so I must be doing something right," jokes Mrs. Becker, who says she never doubted she could manage the

As she reflects on the past, Mrs. Becker believes the company's reputation, outstanding service, good will, and word-of-mouth referrals have accounted for much of the new and repeat business the firm enjoys. "I have always told my employees that customers are our lifeblood," she says. "I believe such an attitude is what has made this company prosper for four decades."

oasting nearly four decades of history in California's Central Valley, Benefit Administration Corporation (BAC) has always been a forward-looking organization. ◆ Today, BAC employs state-of-the-art equipment in administering health programs, pension funds, vacation and miscellaneous trust funds, and benefit plans for corporations, government entities, health

care agencies, and labor unions throughout the San Joaquin Valley. The firm designs and manages benefit programs tailored to individual needs, including record keeping, claim payment, preparation of government reports, bookkeeping, financial statement preparation, and specialized auditing.

The backbone of BAC's business is labor-management jointly administered trust funds for the construction and service industries, as well as government and school district trust funds, including those for the City of Fresno. In recent years, the firm has added corporate self-funded plans to its expanding list of clients.

BAC is managed by the experienced team of Bob Cardinal, president, and Mirth Lundal, executive vice president.

CUSTOMER SERVICE AND PROFESSIONALISM

BAC provides only professional services and has never sold any products or taken commissions. "We have no conflicts of interest in serving our clients and can work with any broker or consultant the client desires," says owner, president, and CEO Robert J. Cardinal.

Over the past three years, BAC has installed an estimated 50 personal computers in a Local Area Network (LAN) and has reorganized its management staff in pursuit of improved client service. "We take pride in the work we do for the people we represent," Cardinal says. "We're very service-oriented, and we believe our company offers a high degree of professionalism." Both Cardinal and Executive Vice President Mirth Lundal hold the coveted Certified Employee Benefit Specialist (CEBS) designation. This certification, issued through the International Foundation of Employee Benefit Plans and the Wharton School of the University of Pennsylvania, requires 10 exams and years of study.

After establishing the company in 1953, Sheldon P. Lewis built a personal and professional reputation of high regard throughout the community and the industry. A former president of the Chamber of Commerce, he once served as a Foreman of the Fresno County Grand Jury. Since BAC changed hands in 1989, Lewis has remained involved on a part-time basis.

During that transition, Cardinal brought his own impressive list of management and administrative

credentials to BAC. Before moving to Fresno, he was president and CEO of the third-largest benefit administrator in the United States. He is chairman of the Administrators Committee of the International Foundation of Employee Benefit Plans, a past director of the Society of Professional Benefit Administrators, and a frequent speaker and author on health care cost containment and benefit administration.

"Sheldon and I first met years ago while working together on national industry committees. He was a national leader for 40 years, and I am continuing the tradition," Cardinal says. "It's rather unique for Fresno to have an organization of this kind with the national visibility we have."

MEETING THE CHALLENGES OF A GROWING INDUSTRY

As insurance and health care costs continue to skyrocket, corporations are moving toward self-funded employee health and benefit packages. According to Cardinal, BAC is well-prepared to serve those growing needs far into the future. "Almost all of our clients are instituting managed care health plans," he explains. "We work with all of the local medical and dental care providers and most of the care organizations in California."

Adds Cardinal, "We deal with corporations that are trying to obtain the best quality care at the lowest possible price. As demand for our services increases, we expect to see a 10 to 15 percent yearly growth in our business."

A driving force behind the increasing demand is the intervention of the federal government in regulating employee benefits. According to Mirth Lundal, who monitors client compliance with governmental regulations, the Employee Retirement Income Security Act passed in 1974 was a landmark piece of legislation designed to protect workers' rights. However, the act and the subsequent benefit legislation which she has seen in her 21 years at BAC have also had a dramatic impact on the complexity of the industry. "The regulations are extremely complicated," says Lundal. "It's an absolute explosion of paperwork."

Despite the challenges presented by the changing atmosphere of benefit administration, company officials believe the firm is up to the task. "BAC is one of the oldest companies in this business," Cardinal says. "That longevity should provide us with the experience to keep pace with the industry."

The experts said it was a hazard to attorneys and other nobility and that an earthquake would make it come tumbling down. In 1965, however, it took days for the best demolition people to tear down the old Fresno County Court-house to make way for a less stately though safer replacement.

It was high time that the clock tower went up, signaling the completion of the Fulton Mall in down-town Fresno in 1964, an experiment in urban planning that was hailed as the wave of the future.

Preceding page:
Mountain texture
Photo by Rick Preston

FRESNO
California's Heartland

stablished in 1970, the Fresno office of Boyle Engineering Corporation provides engineering design services in California's heartland. The firm helps find solutions for the water needs of the San Joaquin Valley agriculture industry and works with area communities to develop water treatment and distribution systems. Fresno engineers also design roads and bridges and

provide general civil engineering in the Central Valley. Says Lonnie Schardt, P.E., who manages the Fresno office, "As engineers, we welcome the opportunity to design projects that contribute to the quality of life here in the Valley."

Fresno is just one of the firm's 23 offices in nine states. Company headquarters are in Newport Beach, California. Since its founding in 1945, Boyle Engineering Corporation has been involved in a variety of projects nationwide, but today focuses on the design and construction of water and wastewater treatment systems, irrigation and drainage systems, and traffic and transportation projects. A privately held, employee-owned corporation, Boyle is consistently ranked by *Engineering News Record* in the "Top 100" among the 500 leading design firms in the country.

Boyle's Fresno office is headed by Schardt, who has over 30 years of experience in a wide variety of projects. These include overseeing the infrastructure design of the world's largest women's prison and guiding research into high-tech irrigation technologies. The workplace philosophy of Schardt and his 24-member team of engineers, scientists, and support personnel is that problems are really challenges, and solutions are the inevitable result of careful planning and preparation.

In Madera County, Boyle's Fresno engineers were instrumental in the construction of the Central California Women's Facility, the world's largest women's prison.

PROJECTS IN THE VALLEY

Boyle's Fresno office has completed significant projects throughout the Valley. In western Fresno County, for example, Boyle Engineering has responded to farmers' irrigation and drainage problems by demonstrating the feasibility of new water-conserving irrigation technologies. At a 160-acre test field at Harris Farms, Boyle specialists experiment with subsurface drip systems, sprinkler systems, surge flow, and other techniques to help farmers reduce water use and produce less drainage

water. In the Tulare County community of Visalia, a growing city of 80,000 people, Boyle engineers designed a complete, computer-aided management system for the city's sewer system and storm drains.

In Fresno, Boyle Engineering is helping overcome local water quality problems and well contamination caused by the banned pesticide DBCP. The firm's engineers have developed plans for modifications to the Fresno water department's pumping, chlorination, monitoring, and testing equipment at three well sites. Boyle conducted similar studies and developed plans for a wellhead treatment system at the California Air National Guard base at the Fresno Air Terminal.

In Madera County near Chowchilla, Boyle's Fresno engineers were instrumental in the construction of the Central California Women's Facility, the world's largest women's prison, which houses 3,800 inmates and employs nearly 800 people. Under contract with the California Department of Corrections, Boyle did much of the predesign work, geotechnical site surveys, and the environmental impact report for the $135 million facility that was completed in 1990. The firm also designed offsite and onsite roads, water systems, and a wastewater system for the prison.

The Department of Corrections has retained Boyle to provide the site engineering services for a second women's correctional facility, a 55-building complex located across the street from the existing prison. The Boyle-designed sanitary sewer system, which will serve the new prison as well, recycles treated wastewater to irrigate prison farmlands.

Boyle also designed a wastewater system for the women's prison, which houses 3,800 inmates and employs 800 people.

Boyle's Fresno staff has designed and developed specifications for numerous bridges throughout Fresno County. At the Elkhorn Slough in the southwestern portion of the county, engineers designed a new bridge that meets current highway standards, but left the original, historic Teilman Bridge structure intact. The firm has also designed several Fresno area road rebuilding projects, including widening Bullard Avenue at California State University, Fresno.

In addition, Lonnie Schardt's expertise in water rights has helped settle disputes between American

In southwestern Fresno County, Boyle designed a new bridge that meets current highway standards, but left the original, historic Teilman Bridge structure intact. (Fred Emmert photo)

Indians and state governments around the West. Among a number of advisory roles, Schardt was a consultant to the Idaho Attorney General's office in a water rights dispute between the Shoshone and Bannock tribes and the state of Idaho. Four years of negotiation came to a successful close in 1989 when an agreement was reached that allocated 500,000 acre-feet of water to the Indians from the Snake River and its tributaries.

CORPORATE ROOTS IN ORANGE COUNTY

The founder of Boyle Engineering Corporation, J.R. "Lester" Boyle, began his engineering career in 1942 in Orange County, California. In 1945, he formed a partnership in Santa Ana with Harold Patterson; their goal was to help private industry and governmental bodies—such as cities, states, water districts, and agencies—solve water problems. Boyle took over the business as sole proprietor in 1948 and renamed it J.R. Lester Boyle, Consulting Engineer.

The business grew quickly, and Boyle incorporated the firm in 1952 as Boyle Engineering. The corporation's first years were devoted to helping solve problems caused by the phenomenal growth of Orange County. The firm created the original master plans for the sewer systems for two Orange County sanitation districts. In the 1980s, Lester Boyle also helped form an alliance between the massive Metropolitan Water District of Southern California, the Municipal Water District of Orange County, and 20 other water districts to build several major water pipelines to serve Orange County's rapidly growing communities.

The company soon began expanding its client base, including work for the U.S. Department of Defense. That federal agency has continued to rely on Boyle Engineering's expertise in site/civil and infrastructure design for military installations. By the early 1970s, offices had been added in Bakersfield, Lancaster, Fresno, San Diego, and Ventura, and out-of-state in Las Vegas and Phoenix.

Lester Boyle continued as president of the firm until 1971 and as chairman until his retirement in 1973. Thomas S. Maddock succeeded Boyle as president of the firm from 1971 until 1991, when he became chairman of the board. Hank Haeseker today serves as the company's president.

During Maddock's 20-year term as president, Boyle Engineering added California offices in Los Angeles, San Bernardino, Sacramento, and San Luis Obispo; out-of-state offices were established in Denver, Colorado; Albuquerque, New Mexico; El Paso and Dallas, Texas; Washington, D.C.; Charlotte, North Carolina; and four cities in Florida. Under Haeseker's leadership, a Santa Rosa, California office was opened in 1992.

With 1991 revenues of nearly $60 million, the firm, which started out with just two men in 1945, today has 650 employees in offices from coast to coast. Although staffed by engineers highly skilled in several fields, the company maintains its focus on water management, distribution, conservation, and treatment.

Among other services, the firm helps find solutions for the water needs of the San Joaquin Valley agriculture industry.

Says Lonnie Schardt of the Fresno office, "Boyle's engineers have long recognized that water is America's most precious natural resource and that conserving and recycling it makes good environmental and economic sense. The company hopes to continue making significant contributions in this area for years to come."

People-oriented is the term that best describes the Fresno accounting firm of Moore, Grider & Company. Its 12 partners strive to promote a family-like working atmosphere—a commitment which has been the cornerstone of the organization for nearly four decades. ♦ The partners feel that maintaining a staff of talented and happy workers has been crucial to the

firm's success over the years. "We are a reasonably informal type of organization," says Ken Aldag, general partner. "We try to make sure the atmosphere in the office makes people *want* to come to work."

From left: The firm's retired founding partners are Bob Grider, Bob Cowan, Jerry Moore, and Stan Griggs.

A satisfied work force has translated into the kind of stability that clients look for in an accounting firm. In fact, over 3,000 individuals, businesses, agricultural entities, not-for-profit organizations, and professionals in the Fresno area regularly take advantage of the services available from Moore, Grider & Company. "We are one of the three or four largest accounting firms in Fresno," Aldag says. "Last year, we prepared approximately 2,700 individual, corporation, partnership, and fiduciary income tax returns."

ACTIVE OUTSIDE THE WORK ENVIRONMENT

Each year, April 15 marks the end of another successful season for the family of partners and employees at Moore, Grider & Company. "We're usually pretty worn out in April," Aldag says. "We do about half of our business during the first three to four months of the year. When its over, we like to unwind by throwing ourselves an after-tax-season party."

The firm sponsors other social events for its employees throughout the year, including an annual Christmas party and a dinner party for all employees and spouses. The firm has also hosted an employee softball team and Monday night golf outings. Management believes this kind of socialization outside the office has enhanced the attitudes of the employees and strengthened the firm in general. "It helps us build a strong team mentality," Aldag explains, "and it has contributed to our stability. I think one thing that sets us apart from many other firms is that our employees and partners, with very few exceptions, tend to stay with the firm for most, if not all, of their professional careers."

This philosophy of companywide socialization has spilled over into the area of community service. "Many of our firm members are very committed to the community," Aldag says. "Many of us have

been either officers or board members of the Chamber of Commerce, YMCA, Ronald McDonald House, Friendship Center for the Blind, Youth for Christ, United Way, Boys' Club, Fresno Art Museum, and Valley Children's Hospital. The list goes on and on."

The firm is also active in professional accounting organizations. "Three current and past partners have served as president of the Fresno Chapter of Certified Public Accountants," Aldag says. "One partner is now the vice president of that organization, and another is the chair of the Professional Conduct Committee of the California Society of CPAs. We are very proud of our professional and civic participation."

AREAS OF ACCOUNTING EXPERTISE

In an effort to deliver the best, most comprehensive services with the greatest possible efficiency, Moore, Grider & Company has departmentalized its service areas.

The tax department, headed by partners Mike Bowers and Rick Holland, offers tax planning and preparation for corporations, partnerships, trusts, estates, and individuals. The firm also works in cooperation with area attorneys and other professionals to provide financial, estate, and retirement planning. George Belyea heads the tax litigation service area.

The accounting and management services department, led by Deryl Jordan, Gary Sabbatini, Tom Bell, and Doug Gentry, provides an array of

From left: Partners Cheryl Storer, Rick Holland, and Mike Bowers meet in the firm's office on Divisadero Street.

services. Business planning and consultation are emphasized in this area, along with general accounting, financial reporting, and preparation of payroll tax, sales tax, and other government reports.

Cheryl Storer, who concentrates in health, welfare, and retirement benefit accounting and reporting for local companies, spearheads the employee benefits division.

The firm's computer counseling division, which assists clients in establishing their own in-house computerized accounting systems, is led by Doug Gentry. Clients rely on his skills in the areas of computer hardware and software, employee training, and systems development to guide them through today's rapid technological advances in computerized accounting.

Audit and review services are the special focus of Ken Aldag and Denise Hurst. They put their collective experience to work in providing clients with reports that offer assurance on the fairness and accuracy of their financial statements.

Insolvency planning, bankruptcy consulting, and litigation support are perhaps the newest areas of concentration at Moore, Grider & Company. George Belyea, who guides these activities, brings to the firm three decades of experience in these fields.

The firm has also structured a division specifically targeting Fresno's progressive medical industry. The medical services department, which brings together the diverse resources of all other company divisions, has experienced steady growth since it was established early in the firm's existence. Necia Collins-Wollenman devotes her time exclusively to this area of the firm's practice, coordinating the accounting, income tax, and management services offered to many clients in the medical field.

Bob Fowler, who serves as managing partner for the firm, offers the administrative expertise that

helps keep the various departments working toward the ultimate goal: client satisfaction.

Partner Doug Gentry and Rena Avedikian, a firm associate, disucss a computer application.

DECADES OF GROWTH

Moore, Grider & Company traces its current level of prosperity to 1956, when Jerry Moore established the firm's first office on San Joaquin Street in downtown Fresno. Bob Grider, who served clients primarily in tax planning and return preparation, joined the firm in 1962. Stan Griggs and Bob Cowan, both now deceased, followed as partners over the next several years. The firm spread its influence throughout the Fresno area initially through the efforts of these partners and a growing staff. With Moore now retired, Bob Grider is the last active name partner. Although officially retired, he continues to serve clients.

In 1966, the firm and its 10 employees moved to the current location on Divisadero Street at the northern end of downtown Fresno. By 1974, the employee roster had grown to 25, prompting the company to expand. A further expansion in 1980 boosted the firm's office space to 10,000 square feet to accommodate its 35 employees.

Still today, growth continues at Moore, Grider & Company. Its 40-plus employees keep pace with an expanding client list, and company officials envision more of the same for the future.

"The growth of the San Joaquin Valley, and particularly Fresno, has brought us much of the success we currently enjoy," Aldag says. "We don't presently feel the need to expand to other communities, which could tend to blur our local perspective and people-oriented philosophy. The Fresno area continues to provide many opportunities that will undoubtedly increase demand for our services."

Partners Gary Sabbatini and Denise Hurst (standing) and Tom Bell and Necia Collins-Wollenman (seated) gather in the firm library.

ig Garden Village, built in 1956 as Fresno's first suburban shopping center, has retained its original, unique ambiance while continuously working to enhance its retail mix and make improvements to maintain its place as the premier shopping center in the San Joaquin Valley. ♦ Located in the attractive, upscale Fig Garden district of northwest Fresno, the shopping center combines the charm of rustic, natural wood architecture with the beauty of a garden-like setting. Its eight restaurants and more than 50 fashion, gift, and specialty shops, most of which are locally owned or regionally based, are housed in a dozen freestanding buildings arranged in a horseshoe configuration with a central parking lot. Shoppers frequently remark to shopping center personnel on the convenience of pulling up to the front door of the establishment they choose to patronize.

"We're very service-oriented," says Annette Newman, general manager, "and our unique personality encourages more than just shopping. We are also known as a community gathering place where friends can meet and enjoy the pleasure of an open-air environment, and where community organizations can draw crowds for fund-raising events."

The 30-acre Fig Garden Village has a wide variety of shops and stores, including a department store, specialty fashion and food operations, and branches of national and regional chains.

For dining, entertainment, and nightlife, The Village offers a cinema with four screens, as well as some of Fresno's most popular restaurants. Among The Village's service establishments are two banks and a United States Post Office contract station, one of the most active post offices in the city.

Left and opposite: Throughout the seasons, shoppers enjoy The Village's unique, colorful banners.

GROWING SINCE 1956

The only locally owned and managed shopping center or mall of its size in Fresno, Fig Garden Village is part of a 12,000-acre residential and farming development project named Fig Gardens, which originated in the 1920s. Although the surrounding countryside produced figs during the 1950s, the land occupied by the shopping center was used for grain farming and peach production. Allen Funch Jr., who as a child played and hunted on the property where his family home was located, today serves as proprietor of the development.

Beginning in 1956, Fig Garden Village was built in phases, growing year by year until the crowning structure was completed in 1969. Designed to complement the existing retail section, an additional office complex, housing 23 commercial suites on three floors, was added in 1978 on Shaw Avenue, just to the east of the center.

In order to maintain The Village's original rural personality and style, few changes were made to the shopping center until 1982, when the property underwent an ambitious landscaping program. The renovation was so successful that Fresno honored The Village with the city's first "Envy Award of Excellence" in 1986.

The Village made further improvements when, in the mid-1980s, it resurfaced and landscaped the

Fig Garden Village is home to some of Fresno's most popular restaurants.

Newman says the broad array of tenants and the helpful, friendly attitudes of merchants and store personnel have made Fig Garden Village one of the most successful shopping complexes in Central California. "The cooperative relationship between the shopping center management, our advertising agency, and the Fig Garden Village Merchants Association is a key to our success. We work very closely together, and everyone, including our customers, benefits."

rear parking lot and added a new lighting system. The latter effort won an award from the Illuminating Engineers Society for excellence in design and functionality in the western United States.

A GATHERING PLACE FOR THE COMMUNITY

Over the years, Fig Garden Village has established itself as an outstanding corporate citizen, not only for its efforts to maintain and develop an attractive, first-class facility, but also for its active participation in community affairs. The Village's calendar is filled with charitable and civic events hosted on the property, and the Village Merchants Association is known for its energetic participation in and contributions to community endeavors.

Among the many annual events sponsored by The Village is the North Fresno Rotary Pancake Breakfast. On the first Saturday after the Fourth of July, approximately 1,500 people converge on the shopping center for their first meal of the day and then shop at sidewalk sales. "This is a real team effort," Newman explains. "The Rotary Club collects all proceeds from the breakfast for its community programs, and local residents take home some great bargains."

Another annual gathering sponsored by The Village is the "Kids Gig," a spring festival featuring rides, music, a petting zoo, face painting, food,

The 30-acre shopping center includes eight restaurants and more than 50 fashion, gift, and specialty shops.

games, and prizes. In 1992, the event raised more than $6,000 to benefit Valley Children's Hospital.

One of Fig Garden Village's most ambitious community endeavors is "Daffodil Days," the annual local kick-off event for the American Cancer Society's fund-raising campaign. Held in March, the event displays more than 15,000 daffodils which have been planted and nurtured by The Village's maintenance personnel.

Some of the many other organizations that benefit from The Village's commitment to the community are the Fresno Women's Network, Girl Scouts, Central California Blood Bank, Salvation Army, Association for Retarded Citizens, and the YWCA. "Our shopping center is more than a commercial enterprise," says Newman. "We also see it as an important part of community life in Fresno."

In keeping with its involvement in community life, Fig Garden Village publishes a monthly newspaper, *The Villager.* Launched in the 1970s, this general-circulation, tabloid-size publication profiles merchants, promotes Village events, and informs residents of other area activities. Reaching more than 50,000 readers in north Fresno and adjacent areas, the newspaper has one of the largest circulations among San Joaquin Valley periodicals.

Because the shopping center has reached its potential in terms of size, explains Newman, the focus for the future will be on maintaining the heritage of Fig Garden Village through community involvement and customer service, while constantly seeking ways to improve the retail mix for contemporary consumer tastes.

"We've been very successful at keeping pace with the needs of the community," says Newman. "Our challenge now is to maintain our high standards."

The Village has become a gathering place for the community, hosting numerous charitable and civic events year-round.

I n business for almost four decades, *California Industrial Rubber Co.* is a family-owned firm that distributes rubber products throughout the Central Valley to businesses involved in the state's agriculture industry. The Fresno-based firm sells hundreds of rubber products and parts such as hydraulic hoses, adhesives, gaskets, and sheet rubber used in irrigation, harvesting, and planting equipment.

Owners of the company are husband-and-wife team Larry and Carol Ann Cain. Larry serves as president of the company, overseeing sales, warehousing, and a new manufacturing division; Carol is chief financial officer and credit manager. "Our objective is to provide quality service and on-time delivery to clients in the agriculture industry," says Larry. "Keeping our clients' equipment operational is essential to our success as well as theirs."

The company's administrative offices, manufacturing facility, and main warehouse are located on South Cherry Avenue in Fresno's Enterprise Zone.

The company's administrative offices, manufacturing facility, and main warehouse are located on South Cherry Avenue in Fresno's Enterprise Zone. Satellite locations in Tulare, Bakersfield, Merced, and Yuba City and an outlet in Fresno serve as distribution facilities and retail sales outlets. All branch locations are locally managed for enhanced customer service. Says Larry Cain, "I'm very much in favor of empowering people on the front line to make decisions. I think local accountability is important to our customers."

CAIN INVOLVEMENT SINCE 1987

The Cains acquired California Industrial Rubber Co. in 1987 from Robert and Edith Edmunds, who founded the firm in 1958. Before the purchase, Larry himself had served as manager of the company's branch location in his hometown of Yuba City. Impressed with the organization and operation of the company, the Cains decided to buy the business when the Edmunds announced they would retire.

As new owners, the Cains immediately embarked on an expansion program that has nearly doubled the company's volume to its present $15 million in annual gross sales. California Industrial Rubber added the Bakersfield outlet in 1987 and the Merced facility in 1990. In 1992, a new retail location was built in Fresno within blocks of the company's corporate offices. The additions have boosted total warehousing capability to 130,000 square feet and the company's employee roster to more than 80.

The Cains believe the company's significant growth is due primarily to the expertise and experience of its employees. "This company has been in business for close to 40 years, and our employees have acquired a thorough understanding of the needs of the agriculture industry," Larry says. "In addition to an outstanding staff, we have policies and services our customers appreciate, such as no minimum purchase and free delivery at all times. We even offer free after-hours emergency deliveries."

Also contributing to company growth is the belt fabrication operation the Cains initiated in 1987. The company's primary product is conveyor belting for an advanced European-style conveyor system used in many agriculture packing houses and for field operations such as harvesting, sorting, and loading. The belting is a light-weight monofilament product that requires less energy and less heavy machinery to drive than standard conveyor belting materials. The Cains hope this innovative product will open doors for them in new markets, such as bakeries and confectioners.

In addition, the company fabricates cleated conveyor belting for nut hulling and processing operations for products such as walnuts, almonds, and pistachios. The sales and service division also offers while-you-wait assembly of all types of hoses.

On the heels of their expansion program and the company's subsequent growth, the Cains view the future of California Industrial Rubber Co. in very positive terms. They visualize as many as five additional branch outlets throughout the Central Valley by the end of the decade, as well as expansion into surrounding states in the more distant future.

"Our vision is to be a dominant force in the Valley," says Larry Cain. "And it is conceivable that we will some day be a viable business concern throughout the western United States."

The firm sells hundreds of rubber products and parts such as hydraulic hoses, adhesives, gaskets, and sheet rubber used in irrigation, harvesting, and planting equipment.

McGlasson & Associates
Consulting Engineers

m. H. McGlasson launched a one-man civil engineering and land surveying business in Fresno in 1960. More than three decades later, McGlasson & Associates Consulting Engineers, with 25 employees on staff, does a variety of engineering projects throughout the San Joaquin Valley and is recognized for its expertise and creativity in using computer technology to solve

engineering as well as other business problems. The firm is today run by David McGlasson, who became president in 1991 when his father entered semi-retirement.

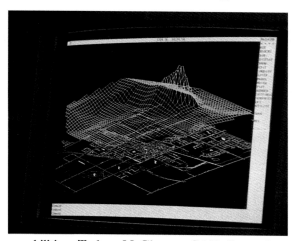

Since 1988, McGlasson CAD Group has specialized in developing the company's computer-aided design capabilities.

SAN JOAQUIN VALLEY PROJECTS

Over the years, McGlasson engineers have worked with many governmental bodies and special districts as well as private companies on major projects throughout the Valley. Among its numerous projects in Fresno, the firm was hired to do design and preconstruction work for the concourse apron at Fresno Air Terminal. The company has also been involved in street reconstruction and the design of new sidewalks, curbs, and gutters in downtown Fresno.

McGlasson & Associates, with 25 employees on staff, does a variety of engineering projects throughout the San Joaquin Valley.

McGlasson & Associates has long served as city engineer for the nearby community of Lemoore. Some of the firm's largest projects there have included the design of the water and sewer system and the police and fire stations. McGlasson & Associates also played an important role in the completion of an industrial park that was a joint project of the City of Coalinga and a private developer. The firm conducted aerial surveys, developed designs for two miles of gas and water mains and widening of a state highway, and did other engineering work during the construction phase of the park. Likewise, McGlasson & Associates provided engineering expertise for the design of industrial parks in Lemoore and Paso Robles.

At Bass Lake in the Central Sierra, the firm is currently completing one of its most challenging projects to date: surveying, determining boundary lines, and calculating assessments for 651 properties in a $20 million assessment district in the Pines Village area. McGlasson engineers also have been involved in designing new and revising existing irrigation and canal systems for several irrigation districts in the San Joaquin Valley.

A GROWING COMPUTER DIVISION

When Bill McGlasson started the company 30 years ago, computers had little, if any, role in the engineering business. But in recent years computer know-how has placed McGlasson & Associates on the cutting edge of engineering firms. In 1988, the company established a computer division with the goal of developing its computer-aided design (CAD)

capabilities. Today, McGlasson CAD Group is a significant and growing aspect of the McGlasson operation and plays a major role in civil engineering and surveying industrywide.

The company clearly relishes its role in staying on top of the latest technological changes. "We're primarily a bunch of computer enthusiasts," laughs Vice President Fred Lusk. "Some of our engineers write their own software programs. It's unusual for an engineering firm to have that kind of computer expertise."

McGlasson & Associates has recently begun sharing its knowledge with area engineering firms and other businesses. McGlasson CAD Group's Group Training and Support program conducts workshops and seminars on the use of software programs such as AutoCAD, Image Systems, Softdesk, Microsoft Windows, and Novell. "These seminars provide a forum for learning and the testing of new ideas in an atmosphere of encouragement," says Lusk. "We also guide participants so that they apply their knowledge in a focused, practical way."

Adds Lusk, "Our GTS program uses teaching methods that work. People and organizations have a difficult time embracing change and altering the way they work even when they know they should. We believe that our workshops and training staff encourage and enable productive change."

From a one-man shop to a full-service engineering firm and beyond, McGlasson & Associates has served the San Joaquin Valley for over three decades by offering outstanding professional services. In the process of developing its own potential, the firm has also contributed to the advancement of fellow firms and area businesses.

*A*t Patrick James, Purveyor to Gentlemen, outstanding service is a tradition not taken lightly. Custom fitting is often done in a client's office, and employees routinely deliver tailoring to the airport to customers who are traveling business executives. ◆ Patrick J. Mon Pere, owner and founder of the chain of 13 better men's stores located in California and Washington, likes to

tell the story of one of his managers who drove three hours to deliver tailoring to a customer who was leaving on a trip the next day. Another Patrick James manager made a "house call" to an attorney who was dressing for the symphony and needed help with his tuxedo. It didn't matter that he had bought the tux at another men's store. "Obviously, now he's a very good customer," says Mon Pere.

Attention to clients' needs has been a integral part of the Patrick James philosophy since the first store was opened in Fresno in 1962. "Everybody talks service, yet they suffocate the word with overuse," says Mon Pere. "We offer a high level of service— one that is almost non-existent today. It is an endangered species. We operate almost like an Old World tailor."

Attention to clients' needs has been an integral part of the Patrick James philosophy since the first store was opened in Fresno in 1962.

QUALITY: A GUIDING PHILOSOPHY

The standards for quality at Patrick James are just as high and exacting as they are for customer service. Each store's handsome decor and fine furnishings offer the first indication of the clothing quality a customer will encounter. All Patrick James stores are decorated with antiques the owner has collected over the years, and the ambience created throughout recalls the various rooms of an elegant old home.

Just as the quality materials and style of a fine home last for years, so does the fine clothing at Patrick James. "The essence of the store's guiding philosophy is quality," says Mon Pere. "We want a

client to have a wardrobe with no planned obsolescence. We want him to have the finest fabrics, as well as the styling that will enjoy a long life."

The fact that clothing offered at Patrick James is made to last was demonstrated recently when a customer brought in two suits to be altered that he had purchased at the Fresno store some 25 years ago. At Patrick James, a customer can find the same tweeds that were, for an earlier generation, the unofficial daily uniform at Yale and Princeton, as well as beautifully tailored suits that define good taste today. "We provide clothing that, rather than being worse for wear, actually gets better with age," says Mon Pere.

The stores carry fine clothing from manufacturers such as Southwick, Burberry, H. Freeman, Major, and Corbin. A Patrick James line of clothing is also featured, and a custom shirt department was added two years ago to better serve customers. Mon Pere participates in the buying for all the stores.

FROM FIG GARDEN VILLAGE TO WASHINGTON

Prior to opening the first Patrick James store in Fresno in 1962, Mon Pere worked for other local clothing stores as a buyer and manager. During that time he developed his own concept of what a small, better men's specialty shop should be. Customers, he believed, should be treated with care and courtesy, and attention to detail ought to be foremost. He selected the upscale Fig Garden Village shopping center as the location to test his ideas.

That first store met with unqualified success, and four years later was moved to a larger location in Fig Garden Village on the corner of Palm and Shaw avenues. Since then, Patrick James has expanded into an adjacent space, and the entire store was remodeled in 1991 to position it for the '90s and beyond.

The company began opening additional locations in the late 1960s, and today operates stores in the California communities of Aptos, Carmel, Campbell, Danville, Mill Valley, Palo Alto, Sacramento, San Francisco, San Luis Obispo, Santa Rosa, and Stockton. There is also a shop in Bellevue, Washington.

The Patrick James stores cater to professionals who understand the value of better clothing and dressing well. "Our customers know the difference between a hastily made sweater that resembles a

Patrick James stores are decorated with antiques the owner has collected over the years, and the ambience created throughout recalls the rooms of an elegant old home.

Shetland and the genuine article, made in Scotland by hand," says Mon Pere. "They can spot the difference between an authentic Harris tweed and an Asian look-alike in a minute. And they wear the difference with pride."

HIGHLY TRAINED SALES STAFF

Sales personnel at Patrick James are professional, career clothiers who offer customers superior knowledge regarding the clothes they purchase. "Customers will have the undivided attention of their salesperson. That's critical to how we do business," says Mon Pere. "Our salespeople are far better trained than most in retail. Our customers ask very intelligent questions, and they are not disappointed with the answers."

Employees of Patrick James undergo extensive sales training in the form of seminars and store meetings. They also travel frequently to cities in the Northeast to meet directly with manufacturers, ensuring that they fully understand the clothing they are offering their customers. "There is not a point they miss," says Mon Pere. "Successfully selling fine clothing requires a lot of education. We work hard to provide an entirely different shopping experience."

Each salesperson keeps profile cards on his or her customers, and a client is called when a new piece of clothing arrives that the employee feels would be a good addition to his wardrobe. Thank-you cards are sent to customers whenever they make a purchase, and salespeople with longstanding customer relationships often send cards and notes on birthdays, anniversaries, and other special occasions.

Not surprisingly, customers are very loyal, and they become an important part of the Patrick James family. "It's not uncommon for our employees and customers to develop strong friendships," says Mon

Pere. "A lot of clients regard us as critical to their careers and social lives. We clothe many of California's top professionals. We give them the time and concentration required to do the job right."

Despite troubled economic times in the retail sector, Patrick James remains a Fresno firm characterized by growth. With annual sales of approximately $13 million, the company plans to add two to three new stores each year in the Northwest. And though Patrick James continues to open shops far from home, the company's headquarters will remain in Fresno. "We take a great deal of pride in every aspect of our operations," says Mon Pere, "and we are equally proud that we are Fresno-based."

People throughout Fresno County readily associate the name Paul Evert with quality recreational vehicles. And rightfully so, since Paul Evert's RV Country is today one of the largest dealers of its kind in the San Joaquin Valley. But what the company really sells is dreams. ♦ "People who buy RVs are buying into a brotherhood," says Paul Evert, founder and owner of the company. "In an instant, they have a million friends they never had before. There are no strangers in an RV park."

Evert's dreams come in all colors, shapes, and sizes, from van conversions, to mid-size travel trailers and fifth wheels, to full 36-foot homes on wheels. Likewise, the range of available amenities would impress even a home builder. In addition to the essentials like a galley, restroom and shower, and living and sleeping quarters, many of Evert's vehicles offer little luxuries such as color TVs, VCRs, full air conditioning, closed circuit video monitors, microwaves, dishwashers, and stereos. And the job of driving these land cruisers has not been overlooked. The driver gets amenities like cruise control, power windows, power steering, and tilt wheel control, just to name a few. Virtually every conceivable owner need has been included either as standard equipment or as part of an options package. "Our customers come to us to buy fun and adventure," Evert muses, "but they need not sacrifice comfort in the process."

The diversity of available accessories is matched only by the variety of vehicles. The company maintains an inventory of about 300 units on a 14-acre site located adjacent to Highway 99 just south of Fresno. The stock includes recognizable RV names such as Pinnacle, Flair, Fourwinds, Monaco, Southwind, Silver Eagle, Dolphin, Seabreeze, Alfa, Road Ranger, Dutchmen, and Lance. In 1990 alone, Evert sold more than 900 units, and in the recessionary year of 1991, the dealership managed to roll 764 "dreams" off the lot.

"RVing is one of the most wholesome and family-oriented activities I can think of," says Paul Evert, owner and founder.

MAKING DREAMS COME TRUE

Paul Evert's personal story, so important to his business success, is also about dreams, and about a boy who made his dreams come true. Evert attended California State University, Fresno and majored in business administration. After college, he worked at Schenley Industries/Roma Wine. Soon, he was promoted to the position of head scheduler for 11 west coast states.

In 1955, he took an additional part-time job selling new cars for a local automobile broker, a career move that changed his life forever. "Even as a teenager, I always knew I would head my own business," Evert recalls. "Back then, I thought I would be in ranching. I always wanted to own land."

But Evert became hooked on vehicle sales from his earliest days with the auto dealers. Realizing he had found his calling, he committed the next 10 years to learning the trade by selling new and used cars. By the time Evert was ready to go into business for himself at age 32, he had formulated his own theory on establishing a successful dealership. As Evert puts it, "I realized that most dealers try to build their business primarily around sales, adding parts and service later. I had always thought that if it were me, I would start the other way around."

Opening his own used car lot in 1963 on Abbey Street in downtown Fresno, Evert and his first five employees began selling Corvettes and Porsches to other dreamers. Holding true to his ideas of a successful auto business, Evert's service department and auto detail services preceded his focus on sales. "I was committed to selling a quality product, taking care of my customers and their vehicles, and making a fair living," says Evert.

After a successful first two years, Evert seized an opportunity to grow. When the two-story building next door burned down, he purchased the land, cleaned off the debris, and expanded his original lot. Within just 10 years, he had purchased another two nearby lots, bringing his total holdings to half a city block in the heart of Fresno's commercial district. "I guess I never got over my dream to own land," Evert says.

The new property was finally occupied in 1975 after Evert leased the original used car lot to a

Proof of its longtime dedication to service, Paul Evert's RV Country supports a 22-bay service area.

business acquaintance who needed a location for his RV dealership. In 1977, the tenant decided to move to San Diego and offered to sell his inventory to Evert rather than move it 350 miles south. "I looked the books over and went into a few of the vehicles," Evert recalls. "I decided that no one who went into a Midland RV could pass up buying it, so I took the Midland and County Campers vehicles off his hands. Within a year, I was hooked. RVs were for me."

Evert proceeded to sell off his automobile inventory and fill four different lots with an impressive stock of RVs. He also leased the Frontier Chevrolet Truck Service Center and converted it into an RV service shop with eight bays.

Today, the operation runs on service, as evidenced by the 22-bay service center at his current location. Evert believes a happy customer is his best advertisement. "We will call every customer who comes here for service to ask if he or she is satisfied," he says. "Quality control and customer satisfaction are top on our list of services. We work very hard at that."

CONSOLIDATING THE BUSINESS

Recognizing the many drawbacks of being spread over several locations, Evert began searching for a single site that could house his growing inventory, sales offices, administrative offices, and parts and service facility, and still have room for further expansion. In 1979, Evert made the move to his present location on Highway 99 at Central Avenue. As Evert's dream continued to grow, he saw the need for additional management assistance: "I wanted to find managers who shared my ideas and one or two who would carry on the business once I retired."

In 1991, Evert welcomed two partners to help relieve the stresses of overseeing a major dealership alone. Curt Curtis, general sales manager, took over the areas of sales, financing and insurance, detailing, and marketing. Lorna Milligan serves as controller, overseeing the parts and service division, accounting, and legal matters. "For the sake of efficiency," Evert says, "we have all agreed on an overall division of duties."

Evert concedes his career may be nearing its maturity, but his drive to follow his dreams has not. In 1992, he completed an RV park capable of handling 10 vehicles for customers who need to stay overnight while their units are being serviced.

Evert offers a comprehensive selection of parts and accessories for RV owners.

The Paul Evert RV Club, established in 1987, provides information on service specials and group trips of interest to members. Through the years, an estimated 10,000 owners, including friends, relatives, and customers, have purchased RVs from Evert.

The company maintains an inventory of about 300 units on a 14-acre site located adjacent to Highway 99 just south of Fresno.

Looking to the future, Evert plans to further expand the company's parts, service, and administrative facilities. Currently, the sales office is being temporarily housed in a separate building, but in the new facility, all offices will be under one roof. When completed, the expanded office and service complex is expected to total over 22,000 square feet.

In the meantime, Evert, with the help of his new partners, plans to continue his successful ways. Indeed, the future seems unlimited for the Fresnan who has for over 30 years shared his dreams with his customers. "RVing is one of the most wholesome and family-oriented activities I can think of," Evert says, "and it has been my pleasure to be involved in this rewarding business in Fresno."

The Fresno County Economic Opportunities Commission has spent nearly three decades making investment in people its business. When Congress passed the Economic Opportunity Act of 1964, EOC committed itself to advocate for and serve Fresno County's poor. ◆ Today, EOC stands at the forefront as one of 955 community action agencies in the nation. Its mission is to provide services which will enhance the quality of health, education, and economic well-being of the disadvantaged—services which focus on developing self-sufficiency skills in the low-income and disenfranchised population.

SEIZING THE OPPORTUNITY

Beginning with a budget of $500,000, EOC reached 1,900 clients during its first year of service. Today, the nonprofit agency offers 36 programs to over 150,000 clients with an annual budget of over $33 million.

EOC's programs are further distinguished by their diversity. *The Fresno Bee* noted in a 1990 editorial, "To run a finger down EOC's directory of services is to remind yourself of almost everybody who needs help in Fresno County: the hungry, the homeless, the unemployed, senior citizens, teenagers at risk of being juvenile delinquents, pregnant teenagers, and preschoolers."

Surviving drastic cutbacks in the 1970s, EOC focused services on providing nutritious hot lunches to the elderly and shut-ins through its Hot Meals/Meals on Wheels program. In 1973, EOC aggressively studied the effects of the energy crisis on low-income residents of Fresno County. The results set the stage for EOC's front-seat position in assisting the elderly and low-income families in energy conservation.

EOC's job training services benefit both program clients and local employers.

STRENGTHENING THROUGH DIVERSITY

Facing more financial uncertainties in the '80s, EOC explored and implemented new directions for economic development. San Joaquin Business Investment Group, Inc., authorized by the Small Business Administration in 1987, was designed to boost community economic development by offering financing to small businesses owned by socially or economically disadvantaged persons. Executive Plaza on Mariposa Mall, purchased in 1988 as EOC's home office, marked an investment for the future in downtown Fresno and a sound development project for the agency.

Not losing sight of its mission, EOC continued to address emerging community needs by launching several programs: Project Pride for serious youth offenders; Palm Village homeless shelter for families; Head Start for low-income preschoolers; WIC

Each month, nearly 200 senior volunteers help EOC distribute surplus food.

nutrition services for women, infants, and children; and Employment and Training for youth and adults.

Since 1970, Joe Williams has served as executive director of EOC, which is administered by a 24-member volunteer board. "Our strength," Williams notes, "lies in our board representation from both the private and public sectors."

BUILDING COMMUNITY PARTNERSHIPS

Over the years EOC has grown to meet the changing needs of the community. The agency has aggressively planned and implemented programs that link agencies in providing the most comprehensive and cost-effective services, especially in areas addressing youth issues. EOC's employment and training services, including such programs as construction trades and summer jobs for youth, have built close alliances with local businesses.

EOC's School Age Child Care Program offers a safe environment, tutoring, and recreational activities to latchkey children.

Building community partnerships can best be demonstrated by the Sanctuary, a runaway youth shelter that offers comprehensive services through its Youth Opportunities Unlimited Center. The collective efforts of public agencies, community-based organizations, and private citizens will determine the continued success of this and many other EOC programs.

In a quiet tree-lined section of downtown Fresno, surrounded by stately old homes, Hope Manor has for more than 30 years provided quality health care and a safe, clean environment to the senior citizens who call the facility home. In addition to a pleasant, community-like atmosphere, Hope Manor offers expert medical attention, nutritious and tasty meals, and a variety of interesting activities for its 225 residents.

Whether it's a favorite sofa, a cherished desk, or a collection of family pictures, residents can bring treasured personal items to help maintain a home-like atmosphere and to express their individual tastes. In addition, the brightly lit, carpeted hallways at Hope Manor are lined with colorful paintings and jigsaw puzzles completed by residents. Beautiful flowering plants also frame many windows in the facility's spacious private and semiprivate rooms.

"There's a very friendly atmosphere here at Hope Manor. You can sense that people get along," says Genie Einhart, administrator. "It's a home, not an institution."

RESPONDING TO A VARIETY OF NEEDS

With a reputation for excellence in serving "yesterday's youth," Hope Manor is one of Fresno's largest nursing home facilities. The caring staff of 155 prides itself on being responsive to both residents and their families.

For instance, family members have 24-hour access to an administrator and a member of the nursing staff. Individual and family counseling services are available, as well as a support group for employees. Likewise, a licensed social service supervisor monitors residents' activities and communicates with family members.

Residents of Hope Manor often bring treasured personal items with them to help maintain a home-like atmosphere and to express their individual tastes.

TIM FLEMING

Residents can choose from three levels of care which cover a broad range of requirements: residential care, intermediate care, and skilled nursing care. For those who require minimal assistance, the residential care option includes a 24-hour attendant, meals, housekeeping, and an emergency call button for added peace of mind. Both the intermediate care and skilled nursing care levels provide licensed nursing service 24 hours a day, as well as a number of certified nursing assistants to respond to residents' needs. In all of its programs, Hope Manor caters to the individual with sensitivity and skill.

A variety of activities and entertainment options are also available. Residents play bingo, listen to classical music, do arts and crafts projects, and attend parties at Hope Manor. There are also current events and world affairs discussion groups, trivia games, and regularly scheduled outings.

OVER THREE DECADES OF CARING

Over the years, many generations of families have called Hope Manor home. The facility was originally purchased in 1960 to serve as a 24-bed home. Mrs. Einhart and her husband, John, expanded the facility in 1965 to 59 beds. A decade later, construction began on a high-rise addition, which was licensed in 1977. Since her husband's death on September 30, 1980, Mrs. Einhart has continued as Hope Manor's administrator, perpetuating the tradition of excellence begun over 30 years ago.

Today, the five-story complex has 99 nursing beds, 56 intermediate care beds, and 70 residential beds. All rooms, which measure approximately 15' x 20', include a large bay window with a view of the Hope Manor grounds. They are designed for single, double, or triple occupancy to meet residents' individual needs.

Serving more than 200 residents, the five-story complex has 99 nursing beds, 56 intermediate care beds, and 70 residential beds. (Tim Fleming photo)

The ground floor of the facility houses administrative offices, a main dining area, a large activity room, a beauty shop, and a physical therapy room. Also on the main floor are the kitchen area and a popular television room with skylights and exposed ceiling beams. Hope Manor offers regular in-house podiatry and dental care as well. A 24-hour surveillance camera and security patrol round out the amenities, making the facility a safe place for its 200-plus residents.

After more than three decades of quality care for the elderly, Hope Manor and its administrator still strive for improvement. Mrs. Einhart, who enjoys the close interaction she has with the people of Hope Manor, believes in maintaining a good mix of staff and residents to ensure a homelike atmosphere: "We just keep getting better as we go along."

PROVOST & PRITCHARD, INC., ENGINEERING GROUP

ater is arguably the most coveted natural resource of the San Joaquin Valley, and its effective short- and long-term management is of critical importance to the economic livelihood of the area. For almost 25 years, Provost & Pritchard, Inc., Engineering Group of Fresno has focused the majority of its resources on the supply, management, and conservation of water

and its interaction with land development.

"Municipal and agricultural development in the Valley have always depended on the availability and management of water," says James Provost, managing principal, "and our firm has built a reputation based on our expertise in this area."

Founded in Fresno in 1968 by Paul Pritchard, principal in charge of municipal and private development, the firm currently employs 13 engineers and 26 support personnel. In addition to water management, Provost & Pritchard provides engineering services for numerous urban planning projects, municipal improvement plans, commercial ventures, and large residential developments. Specific services consist of project planning and management, as well as design of on-site and off-site improvements including streets, bridges, flood control facilities, grading plans, and water and waste water systems. In 1990, the firm opened a branch office in Napa, California, in the heart of the state's wine country, to better serve clients in Northern California.

A LEADING ENGINEERING FIRM
IN THE VALLEY

As the largest civil engineering firm based in Fresno, Provost & Pritchard is unique in that it has the depth of expertise and experience generally found only outside the Valley. "Our strength lies in the professionalism of our staff and their dedication to providing quality services on a timely basis," says Provost of the firm's reputation in the Fresno market. "Our personnel are fundamentally and technically prepared with the experience to solve problems, work with affected public agencies, and provide prompt, meaningful communication with our clients."

Provost & Pritchard has completed more than 1,000 major projects in its 25 years of service to the Valley. Current public agency clients include 15 San Joaquin Valley water districts, the Fresno Metropolitan Flood Control District, the City and County of Fresno, the City of Clovis, and other nearby communities such as Malaga, Armona, Caruthers, and Huron. Commercial and residential development clients are represented by Spencer Enterprises, Valley Children's Hospital, Community Hospitals of Central California, Kesterson Development Company, Chestnut-Central Industrial Park, and Zacky Farms.

One of Provost & Pritchard's most exciting and challenging community planning projects is the Brighton Crest residential development located near Millerton Lake, about 20 miles northeast of Fresno. Started in 1989, this community, planned around a championship signature golf

Founded in 1968, Provost & Pritchard provides engineering services from site selection through construction management.

course, is being developed in phases and is the hallmark land development project of the Fresno area. "Brighton Crest is the first freestanding planned community to utilize a treated surface water supply," says Pritchard. "We also designed a STEP (Septic Tank Effluent Pump) wastewater collection and treatment system for the project. We were the first to import this advanced technology, developed in Oregon, to the San Joaquin Valley."

Provost notes that most of the firm's municipal and private clients are attracted to the firm because of the diversity of expertise it offers. Provost & Pritchard has extensive project experience ranging in scope from land surveys and parcel maps to design and construction management of water and wastewater treatment plants.

"Our staff has a successful track record of providing engineering and management services for projects from the conceptual phase through the permitting process, and from design through completion of construction," Provost adds. "We also understand the financial requirements necessary to implement a project. We are knowledgeable of the funding programs of various governmental agencies and have developed good working relationships with their staffs. Furthermore, the firm has been instrumental in the formation and implementation of more than a dozen assessment districts in the local area."

Water resources and land development engineering will remain the focus for the Provost & Pritchard, Inc., Engineering Group as it moves toward the 21st century. "The San Joaquin Valley is growing rapidly," Provost acknowledges, "and there is a critical need for water management and land development expertise. Provost & Pritchard has the experience, ability, and commitment to meet this need."

ounded in Fresno in 1966, BSK & Associates, an employee-owned corporation and nationally recognized firm listed in the Engineering News Record (ENR) Top 500 Design Firms in the Country, provides a diversified range of services in Geotechnical Engineering and Environmental Sciences, Geology and Hydrogeology, Analytical Laboratory Testing, and

Construction Materials Testing and Inspection. "BSK is the only Fresno-headquartered company on the ENR list," says Hugo Kevorkian, founder, chief executive officer, and president. "We can take a project from beginning to end, from consulting to design, inspection, and remediation. We are among the few companies of our kind that can do it all, and that's part of what sets us apart. In fact, some of our competitors occasionally use our laboratory facilities."

SK & Associates provides a diversified range of geotechnical engineering and testing services.

As an example of the company's full-service capabilities, Kevorkian says the firm can survey a property for contamination, which includes taking soil and water samples, and then analyze the samples for pesticide, lead, or petroleum products. If contaminants are found, BSK can recommend remediation procedures, supervise clean-up, and consult with the client on proper documentation for environmental regulatory agencies.

The geotechnical engineering services offered by the firm include determining soil strength and characterizing soil conditions necessary to meet design criteria on projects from complex buildings and warehouses to roadways, bridges, and major public works facilities. Among the firm's engineering geology services are hydrologic and groundwater resource studies, slope stability analyses, and seismic risk evaluations. A full spectrum of construction consulting services includes materials testing and laboratory and field testing for projects during construction.

One of BSK's most active organizations in Fresno is its state-certified analytical laboratory located on Stanislaus Avenue two blocks from the main office on E Street downtown. Clients include Fresno-area private individuals, water districts, engineering firms, environmental contractors, industrial and manufacturing companies, agriculturalists, builders, developers, and state and local municipalities. Among the services offered by the laboratory are organic analysis, chemical analysis, trace metal analysis, microbiological analysis, hazardous materials analysis, and professional consultation.

City, county, and state agencies, architects, school districts, developers, and industrial concerns are a sampling of the corporations and public agencies that have taken advantage of the firm's expertise and services since its founding 27 years ago.

KEEPING PACE WITH CITY AND STATE GROWTH

BSK was organized on the perception that the Fresno design and construction communities needed a professional company with a strong orientation in geotechnical engineering and testing services. "We recognized the need in Fresno for our kind of expertise in what was, even then, a fast-growing community," Kevorkian says. "Company business philosophy was, therefore, strongly influenced by the objective of providing quality professional services and of developing the strongest expertise in our field of practice."

Outgrowing its original facility, BSK & Associates moved its operations in 1970 to the building on Stanislaus Avenue which today houses its main Fresno laboratory. The following year, the firm opened an office in Visalia, and in 1972 added a Bakersfield facility. The Pleasanton/San Francisco Bay Area regional office was established in 1984, and the Sacramento office opened in 1990.

▲ TIM FLEMING

Since its founding in 1966, BSK & Associates has grown from a one-office operation into a network of offices and laboratories employing some 150 people. The firm is today recognized throughout the state for its high standards and outstanding capability in Engineering and Geosciences.

Recently, the firm was chosen to work on the Kaiser Permanente Medical Center project in Fresno.

"We started when Fresno was little more than a farming community, and we have kept pace as it has grown into one of California's most productive cities," Kevorkian says. "But just as Fresno has not yet reached its potential, neither has BSK & Associates. There is reason to believe Fresno will dominate the entire Central Valley in the coming years, and we hope to be a part of that growth."

I t is not widely known that Fresno is home to one of the premier law schools in the state of California, but outstanding statistics and word-of-mouth praise are working to enhance the reputation of San Joaquin College of Law. ◆ Graduates of the college consistently rank among the best when tackling their last hurdle to become practicing attorneys. From 1987 through 1991, graduates logged an average 76.1 percent first-time bar examination passage rate. In the category of law schools in the United States that are not accredited by the American Bar Association (ABA accreditation is granted exclusively to major research institutions), San Joaquin College of Law has no rival. The second-place law school holds a mere 58.2 percent first-time pass rate.

"What do you call a school whose students have an average Law School Admission Test score at the 50th percentile and a 75 percent bar exam passage rate for first-time takers?" asks Janice Pearson, dean of the college. "Well, I think you call us remarkable when you consider the fact that the graduates of the country's top ABA schools who pass that same bar examination at a first-time rate of 85 to 90 percent also have average LSAT scores at the 95th percentile level."

A LASTING MISSION

San Joaquin College of Law was founded in 1969 by a group of Valley judges and attorneys who believed local students with a great deal of talent were being denied the opportunity to enter the law profession due to financial constraints and logistics problems. Previously, Fresno residents who wanted to attend law school had to leave town to do so. When the school began its night classes in 1970, the focus was on providing working adults an opportunity to obtain a quality law degree locally so that they could continue in established jobs and careers and not disrupt family life or obligations.

"The founders believed these graduates could greatly benefit the San Joaquin Valley in the years to come, and they were right," says Pearson. "Many of our graduates have remained in the area to assume roles in the legal community and have contributed to the quality of life here in many ways."

Moreover, graduates of the college are among the most sought after legal professionals in the state. In the school's 22-year history, 91 percent of its graduates, an estimated total of 376, have passed the bar exam and gone on to careers in law.

Over the years the success rate has added to the school's prestige and broadened interest in its program. The annual number of graduates has steadily grown in recent years, from a couple of dozen in the late 1980s to 75 forecast for 1993. Although the average student age today is 32, students from 21 to 75 years of age are enrolled at the school. Consequently, San Joaquin College of

Law has made changes to meet increasing needs.

The original curriculum for pursuing a Juris Doctor degree was a four-year, semester-system evening program. The school then expanded by adding an accelerated three-year program and began offering daytime courses. Taxation and paralegal programs have also been added in recent years. "Our mission is much the same as it was when the school was founded," Pearson says, "but we are serving a larger audience."

College officials credit the faculty—70 adjunct and five full-time instructors—for the overwhelming success of the program. Most professors at San Joaquin College of Law are prominent local practicing attorneys and judges. Although they are paid for their services, the stipend is very modest and not regarded as a primary incentive for teaching. "The attorneys who teach here are essentially volunteers," Pearson says. "Our law professors have a sincere desire to promote the quality of our legal community, and it is astonishing how hard they work to accomplish that."

The success of the San Joaquin College of Law is no secret in Fresno. Its graduates make important contributions to every aspect of community life, and aspirants of any age to the legal profession need look no further.

Graduates of the San Joaquin College of Law are among the most sought after legal professionals in the state.

Over the course of three generations, the DeFrancesco family has become the heartland's "first family of dehydrated garlic and onions," shipping millions of pounds of these and other products annually to food manufacturing customers across America and around the world. ♦ The company's headquarters, farming operation, and processing plant in Firebaugh

in west Fresno County are the legacy of Mario DeFrancesco Sr., who founded the company in 1968 in Gilroy, California, the state's garlic capital. Before establishing his own company, Mr. DeFrancesco helped found (in 1959) and managed Gilroy Foods, now a division of McCormick & Co., Inc., the world's leading manufacturer of seasonings and flavoring products. Mr. DeFrancesco was joined in his new venture, which processed and packaged dried garlic and onion products, by his sons, Mario Jr. and Al, who had gone into farming after graduation from college. Mr. DeFrancesco's wife, Pauline, also assisted in the business.

In 1973, the family moved the headquarters and processing plant to Firebaugh, where two years before the company had purchased farmland and begun growing some of its own garlic, which now is supplied primarily by contract growers. Mario Jr.'s sons, Mario III and Frank, have since grown up to join the family operation.

Today, the huge enterprise, which employs 120 people year-round and up to 250 during the harvest season, has a product line that includes dehydrated garlic and onions in powdered, granulated, and chopped forms (its principal products), as well as parsley, beets, and asparagus in powdered and other dehydrated products. Since his father's death in 1990, Mario Jr. has served as president. His son, Mario III, is in charge of the farming operation. Al also operates a trucking firm (Westside Transportation, Inc.) in Gilroy, which is another family-owned enterprise. According to Mario Jr., his mother Pauline "is 78 and still makes it her business to find out how the companies are doing."

EXPANSIVE FIREBAUGH OPERATIONS
Although most of the fresh vegetables processed for the company's products are grown by contract growers throughout the West from Oregon to the Mexican border, DeFrancesco & Sons grows some of its own vegetables—including garlic, onions, parsley, and asparagus—on 1,700 acres of farmland. Another business owned by the family markets fresh asparagus under the name Almar.

The impressive Firebaugh plant features state-of-the-art processing equipment and acres upon acres of warehouse space. Harvesting time for DeFrancesco & Sons begins in mid-April in the Imperial Valley and, moving north with the season, contin-

ues into the middle of October in Oregon. In the company's research and development department, scientists propagate their own secret varieties of garlic and onions to ensure outstanding flavor. Contract growers who supply these crops to the company plant only DeFrancesco's seed.

DeFrancesco's customers include spice packers, canners, and meat packers, as well as processors of dehydrated soups, salad dressings, and other foods. "We do business in western Europe, eastern Europe, South America, Canada, the Pacific Rim, and all across the United States," says Mario Jr. "A substantial percentage of our business is foreign, and it's growing all the time."

DeFrancesco adds that one of his greatest pleasures is taking "wide-eyed" foreign customers and visitors on tours of the processing plant and the surrounding lush, green fields, both of which visually boast the virtues of American agricultural technology and ingenuity.

Where do the DeFrancescos see the company as it moves into the 21st century? According to Mario Jr., the family is satisfied in its role as a worldwide supplier. He sums up their vision for the future by saying: "I see DeFrancesco & Sons becoming bigger and better than it is today, and I see it remaining family-owned."

The company's impressive Firebaugh plant features state-of-the-art processing equipment and acres upon acres of warehouse space.

*B**y tuning in to KFTV Channel 21, Central California Hispanics can dance to "El Show du Xuxa," laugh with "Paul Rodriguez," play along with "Sabado Gigante," and be informed by "Arriba Valle Central."* ♦ *Since 1972, the local Hispanic population has enjoyed countless hours of entertainment and news through the Spanish-language station, owned and*

operated by Univision, that today reaches close to 700,000 people from Bakersfield to Modesto. KFTV, which celebrated its 20th anniversary in 1992, has the largest broadcasting area of any television station in Central California. Its 30-minute evening newscast, "Noticias 21," was the most popular weeknight newscast among Hispanics and non-Hispanics in Central California in 1992, according to Arbitron ratings.

"We play a dominant role and gladly accept the responsibility of being a leading broadcaster," says Mario M. Carrera, vice president/general manager. "Overall, our ratings are very high, and we have made continuous improvements in our local and network programming. In addition, it's important to us to be involved in community activities on behalf of our Spanish-speaking viewers in the Valley and in Fresno where we are based."

RUBEN FLORES

HANFORD BEGINNINGS

Present-day KFTV Channel 21 came on the air in September 1972 as an affiliate of the Spanish International Network (SIN), renamed Univision in 1987. Broadcasting from the small community of Hanford, 35 miles southwest of Fresno, KFTV Channel 21 began as a repeater station airing programming from KMEX Channel 34, an SIN affiliate in Los Angeles.

RUBEN FLORES

In May 1984, KFTV Channel 21 moved into a new $3 million facility in northwest Fresno.

Locally produced programming began slowly, but within months the station was broadcasting five minutes of community-oriented news daily, several additional news reports weekly, and a weekly 15-minute public affairs program. In spring 1973, local programming began in earnest with "El Noticiero 21," a weeknight 15-minute newscast and the predecessor of "Noticias 21," which was an ambitious undertaking for the small staff and limited equipment at the Hanford facility. Early on, the station also was restricted by its location more than half an hour from Fresno, the largest city in

the area. As a result, KFTV Channel 21 had to battle skepticism that it could reach large numbers of viewers who would patronize advertisers.

Despite these difficulties, KFTV Channel 21 became more important to Central California Hispanics, who in ever increasing numbers were tuning in to view local programming, as well as the national and international news, soap operas, musical variety shows, and other quality programming supplied by SIN from Mexico, Spain, and several Latin American countries. Thanks to an agreement in 1981 between SIN and Televisa, Mexico's top television network, SIN affiliates, including KFTV Channel 21, began airing a live national newscast from Mexico on weeknights. This addition opened the way for more live programming from different parts of the world.

Other developments also strengthened KFTV Channel 21. From the beginning there had been discussion regarding a relocation of the station to Fresno, and in May 1984 this goal was realized when KFTV Channel 21 moved into a new $3 million facility in the northwest part of the city. A year later the large metropolitan area of Bakersfield, approximately 100 miles south of Fresno, began receiving KFTV Channel 21's signal, which replaced KMEX TV Channel 34's signal from Los Angeles. With the addition of the Bakersfield market, KFTV Channel 21 became the station with the largest broadcasting area in Central California.

In 1990, the station began producing and broadcasting a live, one-hour, weekday morning show called "Arriba Valle Central."

*KFTV's success through-
out the Central Valley
stems, in part, from a
belief in reinvesting in its
people and state-of-the-
art broadcast equipment.*

A COMMUNITY PARTICIPANT

With growth and improvements, KFTV has become an important player in Fresno and the surrounding San Joaquin Valley communities. "At first people viewed us as the station from the other side of town. However, with proven results and a quality of work that is second to none, we have earned respect," says Jess Gonzalez, programming/creative director. "Our primary mission is to serve our viewers in every way we can, and the station's philosophy is hands-on involvement with the community."

The station broadcasts community-oriented programming and telethons, one of which generated significant revenues for the National Hispanic Scholarship Fund in 1991. Likewise, "Navidad En El Valle" (Christmas in the Valley) raised more than $30,000 for needy children throughout the Valley in the same year. The station also promotes

events for the New United Way, Arte.Americas: The Mexican Arts Center, Radio Bilingue, and other worthy community organizations.

"We've never been afraid of tackling major projects," says Daniel Rodriguez, news director/host, adding that in 1990 the station began producing and broadcasting a live, one-hour, weekday morning show called "Arriba Valle Central." "We decided there was a real need for it, but we knew it was going to be a challenge. Our ratings for this program are very high, I'm happy to say." So high, in fact, that the show recently beat out "Good Morning America" and "The Today Show" among all of Central California's viewers.

KFTV Channel 21's most popular show, however, is the network telecast of "Sabado Gigante," a three-and-a-half-hour variety, game, and public affairs show that is broadcast Saturday nights. "Our viewers are overwhelmingly Hispanic, but people who don't speak Spanish tell us they enjoy the show anyway," says Gonzalez. "Our other music and variety shows also draw non-Spanish-speaking viewers."

A GROWING HISPANIC MARKET

The Nielsen and Arbitron ratings companies did not begin rating Hispanic stations until recently, although the Spanish-language market has been significant for some time, says Bram J. Watkins, general sales manager. "Spanish-language broadcasting is a viable means to promote a product or business. The Hispanic market is growing by leaps and bounds and will continue to do so. The average Hispanic household is comprised of four people, whereas the general market household has 2.8 people. Hispanic income is comparable to that of the general market, and more than 50 percent of Hispanic families own homes," he says.

Statistics do tell an important story. From 1980 to 1991, the Hispanic population in Central California grew 82 percent. Currently, the San Joaquin Valley is 38 percent Hispanic and is projected to be 50 percent Hispanic by the year 2000. KFTV Channel 21's coverage area, including Bakersfield and Fresno, is the eighth largest Hispanic market in the United States and the third in California. The annual buying power

of Central California Hispanics is more than $5 billion. All of this means that KFTV Channel 21 is likely to play an increasingly important role in San Joaquin Valley broadcasting.

"As a station, we work very hard to meet the needs of the Hispanic community," says Carrera. "Furthermore, we take a great deal of pride in knowing we represent an emerging majority population and the future of our Valley and state."

*The station strives to enhance the lives and economic well-being of Valley Hispanics through mass media education, information, and entertainment.
(Ruben Flores photo)*

ounded by four Fresno tool and die makers with a goal of being self-employed businessmen, United Western Industries, Inc. was formed to specialize in tool and die fabrication of steel, aluminum, and plastic parts for manufacturers. Today, employees at the company's modern, 15,000-square-foot facility produce hundreds of thousands of quality precision parts.

United Western Industries was established in 1971 by Clifford Gartin, president; L.G. Simmons, corporate secretary; Zenon Dominguez, treasurer; and Douglas Denham, now deceased. During their years of employment with other Fresno companies, the partners had developed a mutual respect for each other's talents. Combining decades of experience and expertise, they joined forces and opened a shop in northwest Fresno.

Employees at the company's modern, 15,000-square-foot facility produce hundreds of thousands of quality precision parts.

At its founding, the new firm was one of only a handful of tool and die fabricators in Fresno. Today, with a staff of 15 shop employees and three of the four partners still active, the company reports more than $1.3 million in annual sales. Gartin is in charge of marketing efforts, Dominguez heads outside tooling, and Simmons manages the shop and directs tool engineering and design.

PRECISION PARTS OF ALL DESCRIPTIONS

United Western Industries serves approximately 100 manufacturers in the San Joaquin and Silicon valleys and from as far away as Canada and Mexico. These customers, who produce everything from trucks and water pumps to wheelchairs and conveyors, rely heavily on United Western Industries' proven ability to manufacture parts to meet customer requirements. The shop has a department that fabricates parts in large quantities and a tool and die department that custom builds and repairs dies and specialized parts.

United Western Industries, which has occupied its present location since 1974, has a wide range of specialty equipment such as drills, presses, milling machines, grinders, welders, saws, and heat treating ovens that enable the company to accommodate the demand for tooling, metal fabrication, prototypes, and special machinery. This diversification provides the customer with the convenience of economic one-order service purchases. The company can produce almost any kind of precision part in any quantity through processes such as blanking, piercing, forming, and welding.

"We don't actually sell a product; we are tool and die makers," explains Clifford Gartin, general partner. "Our customers come to us for custom-designed finished parts or the specialized equipment necessary to produce those parts."

OUTSTANDING SERVICE, CUSTOMER LOYALTY

The partners believe their broad experience and good working relationships with one another, as well as the quality materials produced by the shop, have played an important role in the company's success. Another equally important ingredient in United Western Industries' success is outstanding customer service. "We take the tough jobs that other companies prefer not to do, or do not have the expertise to do," says Gartin. "We also specialize in panic jobs. If a manufacturer needs some parts right away, they usually call us because we have established a reputation for service."

For over 20 years, United Western Industries' attentive staff and willingness to place customer needs first have helped build a roster of loyal and faithful clients. "Most of our customers have been with us for years," says Gartin.

According to company officials, United Western Industries' path to continued success will include the same focus on quality and customer service that has brought the company to where it is today. "We believe in keeping pace with changing technology," says Gartin. "Maintaining stable, satisfied customer relationships is our primary goal for the future."

United Western Industries offers production machining tailored to each customer's individual specifications. (Dana Pearce photo)

CALIFORNIA SCHOOL OF PROFESSIONAL PSYCHOLOGY

ollowing World War II, Americans saw a widespread need for psychological services as veterans returning home struggled for assimilation into peacetime society. Early attempts at meeting those needs meant providing money to research universities that restricted psychological training to a select few. Therefore, during the 1950s and '60s, psychological

services were limited and mental health needs went unfulfilled. The major universities produced few practice-oriented psychologists, and even they had been taught to value research over practice.

The California School of Professional Psychology (CSPP) stepped in to fill the treatment void by creating a new approach to graduate education in the field of psychology. CSPP's goal was to educate professionals primarily for psychological practice and applied research. Training was focused on the assessment and treatment of an array of problems, such as substance abuse, family dysfunctions, and other mental health disorders. CSPP was in the right place with the right idea and has been riding the crest of the movement ever since.

▲ TIM FLEMING

Campus quality of life is enhanced through community interaction in CSPP's open courtyard.

small and large group process, consultation skills, and applied research. The Organizational Development Center provides consulting and training to local businesses and industries.

A LEADER IN PSYCHOLOGY TRAINING

Since the establishment of its San Francisco campus in 1969 as the nation's first independent graduate school of professional psychology, CSPP has become the largest graduate training program of its kind in the United States. Today, CSPP has campuses in Berkeley, Los Angeles, Fresno (since 1973), and San Diego. Nationwide, nearly one in five clinical psychologists graduated from the CSPP system, and the school accounts for an impressive 65 percent of all clinical psychologists in California trained in an accredited graduate program.

CSPP has also been a leader in the important area of minority programs, awarding more degrees in clinical psychology to ethnic minorities than any other school in the nation. Located in one of California's most culturally diverse cities, CSPP-Fresno launched an Ethnocultural Mental Health program in 1990 to address the unique problems faced by individuals from different cultures whose needs are overlooked by traditional services.

CSPP also offers training options in Health Psychology and Neuropsychology. The Echosystemic Child Clinical Psychology program at CSPP-Fresno looks at life from a child's point of view. Students learn to treat children with emotional and behavioral problems and to intervene with the family, school, court, and varied service agencies to provide the best care for the children.

Another, newer application of psychological science to the solution of human problems is the area of organizational psychology. In 1989, CSPP-Fresno launched a masters program in Organizational Behavior. The program, designed for working professionals, stresses applied learning in organizational problem-solving, decision-making,

A BROAD-BASED COMMITMENT TO MENTAL HEALTH

In 1979, CSPP was recognized for its superior academics by the American Psychological Association (APA) with a Presidential Citation for Excellence, and received full APA accreditation in 1984. But it is public service that CSPP administrators speak of with the greatest fondness. Despite the school's primary focus on academic training, students hone their skills through practical application. Every year,

CSPP students generously donate more than 600,000 hours of mental health services systemwide through the school's field training and internship programs.

The Fresno campus contributes a substantial share of those hours through its Psychological Services Center. In keeping with the school's commitment to care for those who otherwise could not afford treatment, the Center offers a wide range of services such as juvenile probation and family court assessments and hospital-based evaluations. Programs also provide help with the treatment of eating and anxiety disorders, domestic violence, and many other mental health problems. All program costs are based on a client's ability to pay.

It is this broad-based commitment to the mental health of all the communities served by the CSPP system that has made the California School of Professional Psychology a leader in professional education and psychological services.

Play therapy is among the many services provided through the Psychological Services Center.
(Tim Fleming photo)

BANK OF FRESNO
A SUBSIDIARY OF VALLICORP HOLDINGS, INC.

*W*indows of opportunity are open wide for Bank of Fresno," says Mike McGowan, president of the 20-year-old local financial institution. ♦ A changing national banking atmosphere—sparked by a savings and loan crisis and subsequent tougher federal regulations—has prompted many large California banks to reorganize their lending portfolios.

Founded in 1973, Bank of Fresno is today capitalizing on windows of opportunity in banking.

Consequently, some segments of society, such as small to medium-size businesses, are finding it more difficult to obtain financial services. Bank of Fresno officials have found this phenomenon has created niches in the financial industry that are being filled by community banks.

"As many of the larger banks continue to cut back in certain areas, numerous marketing opportunities are created for us," says McGowan. "Their constriction of service only enhances the appeal of the service-oriented attitudes we, as Fresno's local bank, embrace."

home improvement loans increased to approximately 12 percent ($37 million) of our total loan portfolio," McGowan says. "That represents an increase of 63 percent over the previous year."

True to its focus on serving the banking needs of the entire community, Bank of Fresno has also established itself as a local leader in the small-business loan arena. As the proud recipient of the 1991 award for "Outstanding Achievement in Economic Development," the bank granted 17 Small Business Administration (SBA) loans totaling $3.9 million—more than any other bank, according to the southern San Joaquin Valley SBA office. In fact, Bank of Fresno is the only independent financial institution based in Fresno County with SBA Certified Lender status. "Lending to companies with annual sales of less than $10 million is one of our most desirable credit segments," McGowan says.

A NICHE-BANKING STRATEGY
In the San Joaquin Valley, Bank of Fresno has set its sights on several customer segments whose unique needs are not being met by larger banking systems.

One example is the agribusiness market. Fresno area farmers who concentrate on high-value specialty crops such as table grapes, fruits, nuts, dairy products, and poultry are taking advantage of the bank's array of targeted services, and many need special lines of credit to cover operational expenses until harvest time. Bank of Fresno responded in 1990 by creating an agribusiness department, which greatly increased the bank's visibility in the market. At the end of 1991, approximately $22 million (7 percent) of the bank's loan portfolio was represented by agribusiness loans.

Another niche-marketing program serves local health care professionals. An estimated 30 percent of Fresno area physicians take advantage of the bank's "lifestyles" services, such as traveling notary, a daily courier service, special terms for practice-related loans, and rapid approvals for auto and recreational vehicle loans.

In 1990, Bank of Fresno penetrated the home improvement loan market by working with local brokers on swimming pool construction contracts. Since then, the bank has developed a significant niche in this area. "During 1991, our portfolio of

FINANCIAL STABILITY FOR
LOCAL CUSTOMERS
Bank of Fresno has successfully taken advantage of these windows of opportunity, thanks in part to its relationship with parent company ValliCorp Holdings, Inc. Sharing headquarters with Bank of Fresno on East Clinton Way, ValliCorp is the largest independent, multi-bank holding company headquartered in the San Joaquin Valley, an eight-county market with more than 2.7 million people and a $43 billion economy.

Tapping the area's potential has yielded a tremendous return on ValliCorp's investment, lifting its assets to almost $500 million in 1992. Through the added resources of its parent company, Bank of Fresno consistently offers local residents financial stability; and, by maintaining its management focus on community banking through services such as on-site loan processing, the bank has established itself as the area's number one community bank. "We are Fresno's bank," McGowan says.

Two decades have passed since Bank of Fresno opened its doors in 1973 with 13 employees. Its

The bank's airport branch also houses its corporate offices.

original 3,000-square-foot office did not even have a vault. But despite its size, the bank quickly developed a reputation for innovation.

Shortly after its inception, Bank of Fresno became one of the first local financial institutions to offer extended banking hours. Customers could access banking services from 10 a.m. to 6 p.m. Monday through Thursday, and until 8 p.m. on Friday. "I feel we were very innovative for our time," says Vicki Giese, one of the original 13 employees. "We were also among the first to enter the ATM market."

During its 20 years of service, the bank's employee roster has grown to include more than 280 people, and nine additional branches have been established to better serve Fresno and nearby communities such as Clovis, Kingsburg, Madera, and Sanger. In January 1991, the Bank of Fresno acquired Madera Valley Bank in the neighboring community of Madera, a move which boosted the bank's total assets and total deposits, as well as increased its market service area.

A COMMUNITY FOCUS

As part of its commitment to being a community bank, Bank of Fresno strives to design each of its branches according to the character of the area it will serve. "We are proud of our efforts to customize our branches so that they complement their neighborhoods architecturally," Giese says. "Our Kingsburg location, for instance, has a Swedish motif in keeping with the architectural heritage of the city's downtown area."

Bank of Fresno also maintains local management, a policy which allows customers easier access to banking officials. Individual managers are encouraged to design their service packages for commercial, industrial, real estate, or consumer loans with the needs of the local community in mind. Likewise, loan decisions are made on-site, allowing officials to consider individual circumstances and expedite approval.

Carrying the community focus one step further, the bank initiated a Mentor Program in 1991 with McLane High School of Fresno. Fifteen bank employees volunteer their time serving as big brothers and sisters to at-risk students. These "mentors" work with the students in a one-on-one counseling atmosphere, offering academic tutoring, guidance, and friendship. "The employees who participate in this program receive a great deal of personal satisfaction," McGowan says, "and we are proud of their efforts to help so many young Fresnans."

The bank has also earmarked a portion of its resources for promoting the city's various ethnic communities. In 1991, Bank of Fresno established a Minority Advisory Board comprised of four minority community representatives. This virtually autonomous group, unique among California banks, uses its $30,000 annual budget to support local minority programs. "This board represents the kind of commitment we've made to supporting the efforts of our minority organizations and events," explains McGowan.

After two decades of service, Bank of Fresno's successful niche-banking approach has made it the area's largest locally managed financial institution. Through employee commitment to the community, tailor-made services, access to huge financial resources, and a management style designed to address local concerns, bank officials believe they have found a formula for long-term success.

"Clearly, growth is very important to us," says McGowan, "but we feel growth is only possible by serving the needs of the community. That focus has made us what we are today, and we will continue seeking ways to improve on and demonstrate our winning philosophy."

DANTEL, INC.

*I*n the summer of 1971, three men joined forces in Fresno to launch a small manufacturing operation that has evolved into a highly successful Information Age company with more than 250 employees. Dantel, Inc. has eight regional sales offices across the nation, as well as sales arms in Canada, Europe, and Asia. ♦ Twenty-two years ago, J. Pierre Sicard and Robert Berg were out-of-work engineers, and Harold Kreisher was an investor willing to commit $20,000 to the engineers' efforts to start an innovative new company. Their idea was to build a business that would offer consulting services and manufacture equipment for microwave communications systems used by telephone and utility companies. At the time, microwaves were commonly used in long-distance communications systems since they can easily pass through rain, smoke, fog, and the ionosphere.

Dantel occupies nearly 70,000 square feet of space in two buildings on North Argyle Avenue near the Fresno Air Terminal.

Within a year Dantel had six employees and was beginning to turn a profit. The company received a big boost in the 1970s when it was chosen to design and install a selective signalling communications system for the construction crews camped along the 800-mile Alaskan pipeline.

Since its inception, Dantel's most important products have been supervisory alarm and control systems, which monitor unmanned facilities at remote sites. Although originally designed for microwave systems, the emphasis today is on monitoring fiber optic communications. A key fea-

Dantel's supervisory alarm and control systems, of which the 46085 Multi-X.25 Interface module (above) is one part, are designed to monitor unmanned facilities at remote sites.

ture of all Dantel alarm systems is the ability to pinpoint the source of a failure or disruption in the customer's system—such as a failed fiber optics terminal—and relay that information quickly and accurately to a control center. From the control center, commands can be issued to Dantel's control modules to activate back-up systems when failures occur.

With the divestiture of AT&T and the introduction of a new line of alarm and control equipment in the mid-1980s, Dantel became a leading provider of monitoring equipment in the telephone industry. Today, 80 percent of its business is with the various Bell companies throughout the country. However, Dantel also serves independent telephone companies, cellular carriers, long distance carriers, other manufacturers of communications equipment, commercial businesses, utilities, and government agencies.

TWO DECADES OF GROWTH

From a small start in Sicard's house, the company has moved three times into successively larger facilities. Today, Dantel occupies nearly 70,000 square feet of space in two buildings on North Argyle Avenue near the Fresno Air Terminal. A branch production facility, Dantel-Lac, which manufactures communications multiplexing equipment, is located in south San Francisco. Digital Prototype Systems, started by a former employee of Dantel, provides software and software-based hardware for Dantel.

Today, J. Pierre Sicard serves as co-chairman of the board with Alan J. Brown, who is principal shareholder. Upon his retirement in 1980, Robert Berg sold his interest to Brown. Harold Kreisher, another of the company's founders, remained involved with Dantel until he passed away. Jim Vogt, who previously served as president of Telesciences Transmission Systems of Chicago, became president of Dantel in 1992.

With a $20,000 investment more than two decades ago, these forward-looking leaders have helped nurture a thriving company whose sales exceeded $20 million in 1991. As it moves into a third decade of service, Dantel is poised to keep pace with the changing needs of a growing client base.

Products are increasingly software-oriented as computers become more dominant in the telecommunications industry. In response, Dantel is expanding its market with new networking systems that collect and transmit not only alarm information but any data required by telecommunications companies to operate their networks. Customers also expect better service, and the company has implemented a Total Quality Management program striving for total customer satisfaction and continuous quality improvement.

*O*ne of the most successful firms of its kind in Fresno, Westcal, Incorporated is a family-owned residential development company that specializes in single-family home building for both entry-level and move-up markets. Since its founding in 1974, Westcal has built more than 4,000 single-family homes, and it is consistently ranked among the top three local residential developers with average annual sales of 275 units. Westcal homes range in price from $90,000 to $190,000 and vary in size from 1,000 square feet to 2,500 square feet.

"I think that knowing what people want is a major ingredient to success in this business," says Jerry De Young, Westcal's president. "Another important ingredient is our ability to build for less."

THE ADVANTAGE OF SIZE

By virtue of its size, Westcal can purchase building materials in large quantities at a reduced cost, giving the company an edge over many smaller firms. Westcal also acts as its own general contractor, which results in lower overhead costs. Stable relationships with business associates translate into further cost savings. "By guaranteeing steady work to our subcontractors," says De Young, "we are able to ensure advantageous price controls."

Another size advantage is that the company has the financial resources to purchase property far in advance of immediate needs. By the time suburban development reaches Westcal's land holdings, adjacent property bought by smaller developers working on a project-to-project basis has increased in price, which adds to the sale price of a house built there. As a result, Westcal's homes are often more attractively priced.

While the firm understands that price is an important selling point, Westcal has not sacrificed quality. For each housing development, the company offers up to eight models, which represent a variety of styles and sizes. The finest in amenities are available for its premier models, including bathroom skylights, private patios for the master suite, see-through fireplaces, built-in entertainment centers, formal dining rooms, tile roofs, covered patios, and natural oak cabinets.

NEARLY TWO DECADES OF GROWTH

Founded in 1974, Westcal, Incorporated built its first homes in Madera County on parcels ranging from one-half to five acres with a beginning sale price of $29,900. In 1977, upon completion of approximately 300 homes in Madera County, Westcal launched Northridge Estates, its first major development and also its first community in Fresno. By the time the firm completed the 300-home development, new sites were already on the drawing board, and the company was on the road to success.

Jerry De Young, who graduated from California State University, Fresno with a degree in construction, was hired in 1974 as vice president of field operations. Today, as president of the company, he directs land procurement and development. Through his brokerage license, De Young Realty, he also oversees all sales and marketing.

John Bonadelle Jr. serves as vice president of the company. A graduate of the University of Southern California with a degree in public administration, he directs sales and construction for the Brentwood projects built by Westcal.

Paula Bonadelle De Young, who completed a degree in public relations from the University of Southern California in 1977, is vice president of marketing and public relations for the company. She and De Young were married in 1978.

Jerry, Paula, and John hold general contractors licenses and are well-versed in all aspects of the business. Paula and John, also licensed real estate agents, are the children of Pauline and John Bonadelle Sr., a successful developer and builder in the Fresno area.

Westcal moved into its current offices on West Bullard Avenue in 1989 and today has an in-house staff of 22 employees. The three company principals thoroughly enjoy their work and are proud of Westcal's success and continued growth. For the future, they are dedicated to upholding the Bonadelle family tradition of excellence. "One of my father's primary purposes has always been to provide quality homes that the average person can afford," John Bonadelle says. "We want to follow in those footsteps, and we hope our children will feel the same way."

Since its founding in 1974, Westcal has built more than 4,000 single-family homes.

Jerry De Young, president, and John Bonadelle Jr., vice president, each hold a general contractors license and are well-versed in all aspects of the construction and land development business.

ith a client base that ranges from small farmers and corporate farming operations to a variety of agribusiness concerns, Doane Western Company prides itself on being the only full-spectrum agricultural service company in the western United States. "We have the unique capability of integrating farm management with financial and real estate services," says President Dean Dennie.

It is only fitting that the headquarters of Doane Western, also one of the fastest growing agricultural service companies in the United States, is located in the Central Valley, the most productive agricultural region in the world. The Fresno company offers agricultural real estate sales, farm and ranch management, and consulting services; makes mortgage and production loans; and conducts appraisals throughout the western United States.

Fresno-based Doane Western Company prides itself on being the only full-spectrum agricultural service company in the western United States.

The company has a strong western tradition, dating back some 50 years. Western Farm Management, as the company was originally known, was founded in 1933 in Phoenix, Arizona. In 1975, the firm moved its corporate headquarters to California, and six years later merged with Doane Agricultural Service, an internationally recognized farm management company based in St. Louis, to create Doane Western Company. The merger was short-lived, however, and the company divided into two entities once again so that each could better utilize its employees' areas of expertise to recognize the diversity between midwestern and western agriculture.

In addition to the Fresno headquarters office, there are full-service branches in Sacramento, California; Phoenix, Arizona; and Bozeman, Montana. Field service offices, which offer farm management, real estate, and appraisal services but do not handle loan servicing, are located in Bakersfield, California and Reno, Nevada. Fifteen employees are based at the Fresno corporate office, while the other offices are staffed by an additional 26 people.

A FULL SPECTRUM OF SERVICES

Doane Western manages close to 350,000 acres of land throughout the region, 100,000 of which are devoted to crops such as citrus, pistachios, almonds, Asian pears, plums, wine and table grapes, wheat, cotton, and sugar beets. Rangeland comprises the balance. The Fresno office itself manages land from the Coachella Valley in the south to Santa Clara County in the north.

As one of the largest farm management companies in the country, Doane Western is in charge of the daily supervision of property for investors, owner-operators, and lenders with troubled properties. Farm managers oversee every facet of a farming or ranching operation, including all cultural practices, the hiring and supervision of labor crews, managing harvests, commodity marketing, and maximizing the cash return to the owner.

Doane Western farm managers are business professionals, as well as farming and ranching specialists who are accredited by the American Society of Farm Managers and Rural Appraisers. "Our farm managers bring a creative, innovative, and progressive approach to farming," says Dennie. "They stay up-to-date on the latest agricultural practices and technological advances, as well as environmental and political issues that affect their area of expertise. They also provide clients with periodic property reports which include monthly financial statements of their agricultural investment, plus develop annual operating plans and budgets for each property."

Doane Western professionals also assist clients in bringing their operations to full potential through the development of business plans, by conducting cash flow analyses, and through consulting services that address specific project evaluations.

A RANGE OF REAL ESTATE OPPORTUNITIES

The company's real estate sales division assists buyers and sellers in taking advantage of the most desirable sale or purchasing opportunities throughout the region. Doane Western's clients are a cross section of ranchers, farmers, investors, corporations, and financial institutions. The company's six offices provide its real estate professionals with the opportunity to present a diverse portfolio of listings and to have knowledge of properties not being actively marketed.

The company also specializes in the complex task of determining agricultural property values. "An accurate appraisal requires specialized knowledge,

monitors loan obligations and covenants, and assists insurance companies when certain types of problems arise. The firm may act on behalf of an insurance company lender by conducting an extensive analysis of farm cash flows and property values for a property being considered for a loan.

The loan servicing department, established more than 35 years ago, assists insurance companies, small mortgage firms, government agencies, and other institutions by collecting interest and principle payments, overseeing property tax payments, evaluating loan modifications and releases, determining substitutions of loan collateral, and conducting periodic on-site reviews of the security. "We also act on behalf of our institutional clients by collecting delinquent loan payments and restructuring problem credits," says Dennie. "In addition, we assist both owners and lenders in analyzing macro trends in the agricultural marketplace."

The company recently added a production loan department to provide further penetration into the agribusiness marketplace. Explains Dennie, "We see a need in agriculture for both long- and short-term financing. Our goal is to become a merchant banker for agriculture, and we believe that goal is attainable within three years."

As a merchant banker, Doane Western will analyze a client's credit needs and negotiate with nationwide investment firms lending to the agricultural community in order to have those needs fulfilled. "We'll be the intermediary between western agriculture and Wall Street," adds Dennie.

With more than 50 years of experience, Doane Western will continue to build on a tradition of helping clients in the agricultural industry maximize their profits through the 1990s and beyond. Says Dennie, "Our scope of services, range of specialists, and dedication to service have allowed us to become one of the fastest growing and most successful agricultural service companies in the United States."

Doane Western manages close to 350,000 acres of land throughout the region, 100,000 of which are devoted to crops such as citrus, pistachios, almonds, Asian pears, plums, wine and table grapes, wheat, cotton, and sugar beets. (Paul Rutigliano photos)

training, skill, and experience—qualities that our appraisers, all certified, have," says Dennie.

As a loan correspondent for major insurance companies and through ongoing relationships with other financial institutions, Doane Western offers mortgage and production financing on open crop land, permanent plantings, ranches, dairies, and agribusiness concerns. "One of the strong points of Doane Western is our longtime association with insurance companies that has enabled us to provide long-term loans to clients," says Dennie.

In its role as correspondent, Doane Western also

*I*n 1975, the Veterans Administration joined hands with the University of California, San Francisco (UCSF) to bring Fresno its own physician training program. After assurance from the State of California that the program would continue to be supported once in place, the Veterans Administration generously contributed $10 million in start-up funds and

another $3.2 million for a Medical Education Building to be constructed on the grounds of the VA Medical Center in Fresno.

Since that time, the UCSF-Fresno Medical Education Program has offered quality medical education and practical training in a variety of medical fields, including emergency medicine, family practice, internal medicine, obstetrics-gynecology, pediatrics, psychiatry, diagnostic radiology, and surgery, with an emphasis on primary care. "This program allows Fresno and the Central Valley the opportunity to tap into the resources of one of the premier medical institutions in the country," says Dr. David Altman, associate dean of the school. "Our doctors receive some of the finest educational experiences available."

The school's three-story building serves as the administrative site for 50 to 60 medical students and about 170 post-doctoral students.

FULFILLING A LONGTIME LOCAL NEED

From the earliest days of the city's history, Fresnans had recognized a shortage of health care professionals in the area. But it was not until 1970 that the Carnegie Commission on Higher Education and National Health formally expressed the need, identifying Fresno as a desirable location for a medical training center.

Prompted by the report, Milo E. Rowell, a Fresno attorney, assembled representatives from several local medical institutions to form the San Joaquin Valley Health Consortium. In 1972, the group applied for and received federal funds to develop a physician training program, one of 11 Area Health Education Centers funded nationally, to be jointly operated with the University of California, Los Angeles and UCSF.

Three years later, the Veterans Administration provided major additional support, and the program was given the opportunity to rise to the level of success it enjoys today. "With a facility of our own," Dr. Altman recalls, "we were able to consolidate our resources into a single location. The move also brought our program broader recognition, and interest on the part of physicians and the public took a tremendous step forward. That in turn gave a significant boost to our recruiting capabilities."

Today, the three-story building serves as the administrative site for 50 to 60 medical students and about 170 post-doctoral students by 125 full-time faculty members. Another 375 clinical practitioners in the community serve as volunteer instructors. School officials view the program as the primary means of marketing Fresno to physicians-in-training who are contemplating where they wish to practice.

"We hope to get new doctors excited about medicine here in the Valley," Dr. Altman says, "and our efforts have shown a measure of success. We believe UCSF-Fresno has been instrumental in elevating the quality of medical care available to Valley residents."

LEARNING FROM THE FINEST IN FRESNO

After nearly 20 years in operation, the UCSF-Fresno Medical Education Program remains true to the consortium concept which guided its founders. As a result, students have access to a vast array of medical training opportunities. In addition to educational services provided by the school itself, students gain unparalleled training experience at some of the San Joaquin Valley's finest medical institutions: Valley Medical Center with 417 beds and over 12,000 admissions annually; the Veterans Affairs Medical Center, which provides service to an estimated 150,000 veterans living in the Valley; and Valley Children's Hospital, the institution devoted to the care of the Valley's children. Several other medical institutions, including the Community Hospitals of Central California, Saint Agnes Medical Center, the Kaiser-Permanente facility in Fresno, Selma District Hospital, the Sequoia Community Health Foundation, and Kaweah Delta District Hospital, play indispensable roles in the educational process.

"In addition to the experience our doctors receive, they are exposed to the level of commitment Fresno-area medical institutions are known for," Dr. Altman says. "This area is rapidly becoming a place to benefit from some of the most up-to-date and advanced medical techniques in California."

What does all this mean to the future of Fresno and the physicians who chose to stay in the Valley? "Our institution has joined hands with the local medical establishment to provide Fresno residents access to the best quality care available," says Dr. Altman, "and I expect the future of health care in the Valley to be quite bright."

*T*he Rich Products plant in downtown Fresno produces thousands of pounds of bakery dough daily for everything from french bread and pizza to hoagie rolls, cookies, donuts, and cinnamon rolls. But a passerby who expects to encounter the warm, sweet aroma of fresh bread baking will have to wait. That's because Rich Products prepares frozen, unbaked dough products

that are shipped throughout the region to food service and bakery customers who, in turn, bake the dough in their own ovens.

The Fresno facility, located on O Street, is one of 12 plants in the Bakery Division of Buffalo, New York-based Rich Products Corporation, the nation's largest family-owned frozen foods manufacturer. Overseeing the Fresno operation is General Manager Howard Briar, who has been at the helm since the facility opened in 1974. The plant's customers, located throughout 11 western states and the Orient, include retail bakeries, convenience stores, delicatessens, restaurant chains, supermarket in-store bakeries, pizza chains, schools, and other food service businesses.

HIGH-TECH FOOD PRODUCTION

A tour of the Rich Products plant is a feast for the eyes and an enlightening education in high-tech food production, state-of-the-art sanitation, and space-age food freezing methods. With more than 125 employees, the facility operates around the clock, seven days a week. Industrial-size mixers blend the ingredients of the various bakery items. Afterwards, the raw dough is machine-chopped, rolled, and shaped into the appropriate product.

The fresh dough items are placed on conveyor belts that move thousands of units per hour to quick-freeze chambers that preserve their freshness. Later, the frozen items are packaged and stored in huge, arctic-like freezers at the downtown plant or at nearby cold-storage facilities to await shipping.

Also housed at the plant is a laboratory bustling with technicians who test dough and develop new products. In addition, the plant operates a food service school where students—employees of school cafeterias, supermarket in-store bakeries, and other food service businesses—learn how to handle frozen dough products and decorate cakes. The company also operates a satellite school on Blackstone Avenue in north Fresno. Together, the two schools enroll approximately 1,000 students annually from throughout the region.

A PROGRESSIVE COMPANY

Built on a foundation of discovery and development of new products and processes which have revolutionized the frozen food industry, Rich Products emerged as a dominant force in the food industry by pioneering developments in the very market segment it helped create—non-dairy foods.

The corporation, as it is known today, began with a startling development by Robert E. Rich Sr., founder and chairman of the board. Rich directed a laboratory team to search for a vegetable-based replacement for whipped cream derived from a new source—the soya bean. During the development stage, Rich discovered that the new soybean substance could be frozen, thawed, and whipped.

The revolutionary product, Rich's® Whip Topping®, was immediately hailed as "the miracle cream from the soya bean." It transformed food processing and opened up a new world of non-dairy products to the growing frozen food industry. Today, Robert Rich presides over an $890 million enterprise which produces more than 2,000 frozen food items.

The Bakery Division of Rich Products has benefited from the same foresight and progressive thinking that the company founder exemplifies and encourages in all his employees. In the early 1970s, company executives were convinced that the frozen dough business was going to take off. They were right. As supermarket chains began establishing their own in-house bakeries, frozen dough sales exploded. Between 1972 and 1979, the company's frozen dough sales jumped 433 percent. The enormous and continuing success of the Fresno plant, established during those early boom years, is proof of their vision.

The Rich Products plant in downtown Fresno produces thousands of pounds of unbaked dough products daily that are shipped to food service and bakery customers throughout the region.

The fastest things on two wheels were the motorcycles that raced on the wooden track in front of the grandstand at the Fresno District Fair in the 1920s.

▲ FRESNO HISTORICAL SOCIETY ARCHIVES

At the Fresno Fairgrounds it was "Gentlemen, start your motorcycles" for the Fresno Mile. In the 1992 race, the top cyclists averaged 100 miles per hour, one of the fastest such runs on the West Coast.

▲ TIM FLEMING / FLASH FOTO

1 9 7 6 - 1 9 8 4

1976 ALL AMERICA TRENCHING, INC.

1976 DMC CONSTRUCTION INCORPORATED

1976 FRANK B. HALL & COMPANY

1978 CALIFORNIA VALLEY BANK

1978 INDUSTRIAL MEDICAL GROUP OF FRESNO

1978 SCHAAL/LECHNER CORPORATION

1980 INTERNATIONAL ENGLISH INSTITUTE

1980 QUICKIE DESIGNS INC.

1980 REGENCY BANK

1980 VALLEY INDUSTRIAL & FAMILY MEDICAL GROUP

1981 DRITSAS, GROOM & GOYA

1981 PARDINI'S, INC.

1982 APPL, INC.

1982 SAN JOAQUIN SURGICAL CENTER AND WOODWARD PARK SURGICENTER

1983 CALIFORNIA ORTHOPEDIC AND MEDICAL CLINIC-FRESNO

1983 CMB INDUSTRIES

1983 FRESNO PRIVATE INDUSTRY COUNCIL

1983 MAULDIN-DORFMEIER CONSTRUCTION, INC.

1984 FRESNO SURGERY AND RECOVERY CARE CENTER

1984 GRISANTI & ASSOCIATES, INC.

Dan McAweeney, founder and president of DMC Construction Incorporated, learned early in his construction career that to be successful in the industry, a company must provide quality work, top-notch personnel, and exemplary services. Consequently, in the 16 years DMC has been in operation, McAweeney and his team have developed markets in construction

management and bonded contracts, and the company has flourished.

CONSTRUCTION MANAGEMENT

Construction management is the composite of all modern project management methodologies having as their objective the control of time, cost, and quality in the design and construction of a new facility.

A relatively new specialty in the industry, construction management is offered primarily and most successfully by experienced construction firms. In this role, a contractor is hired to manage a building

Dan McAweeney, DMC's founder and president, oversees an expansion project for the Fresno Art Museum.

project from start to finish, creating a professional service relationship rather than a traditional "builder" contract. According to McAweeney, a construction manager must be well versed in every aspect of the construction industry, including planning, design, contracts, regulations, inspections, and local market conditions.

"Sometimes we act as managers and sometimes as facilitators," he explains. "Builders from out of town have hired us to assist them with getting projects approved by city and county agencies, and to advise them on the Valley subcontractor market. The 3M Corporation recently consulted DMC for an expansion of its facility in Stockton, California. On this project, we assembled the complete construction team—the architect, engineers, outside consultants, subcontractors, and interior designers—to develop a beautiful new facility that met all of 3M's current operating needs. Few general contractors have the expertise to be successful as

construction managers, but it is something DMC does very well."

A BONDED CONSTRUCTION FIRM

As a bonded contractor, DMC is able to offer clients financially backed assurances that each project will be completed according to contractual agreement.

"Only reliable and financially stable construction companies are qualified to obtain bonding. This distinction has helped to establish DMC in an industry plagued by non-performance and uncompleted contracts. Most public construction and other major commercial clients require that a reputable surety stand behind the contract," says McAweeney. Currently, about 95 percent of DMC's work is in bonded construction.

EXPERIENCE

Over the years, the company has developed expertise in various building specialties. In the 1980s, DMC was involved in constructing public projects throughout Central California. In 1987, 75 percent of the company's total work program involved some sort of publicly funded educational or medical construction.

Much of DMC's background is in public construction, and the experience has been of continuing benefit to the company. The myriad of rules and regulations in public work has helped DMC develop exceptional methods of controlling safety, payrolls, schedules, and contracts. The necessity to be the "low bid" has taught the company innovative ways to control costs and streamline operations. DMC has also

developed long-term relationships with the Valley's most competitive subcontractors. *The firm recently completed the new California Citrus Pulp Producers plant in Lindsay.*

The firm has been duly recognized for its talents in public construction. In 1990, DMC was named "Contractor of the Year" by the American Association of Public Works Officials.

DMC has also done extensive hospital work and is proud of its record in this highly specialized field. For example, the firm has completed numerous radiology and magnetic resonance imaging projects throughout the Central Valley, as well as entire new hospitals and many remodeling projects for existing facilities.

McAweeney considers medical contracting the

DMC is managing the construction for the five-story State Compensation Insurance Fund building in Fresno.

epitome of complex construction. "After you've built a hospital, anything else is like baking a cake," he says. "The amount of technical information that must be disseminated between the contractor, the client, and members of the construction team at all levels is simply staggering."

Although DMC is proud of its medical expertise, the company continues to actively manage all types of industrial, commercial, and church construction. Likewise, the experience gained in public construction will continue to benefit DMC and all future clients.

In Hanford, DMC has constructed the new Kings Federal Credit Union.

FINDING A NAME

"When I started this company, we needed a name," remembers McAweeney. "DMC was selected for two reasons: first, because is was easier to say than Dan McAweeney Construction, and second, because a successful company is not just one person but a team effort."

More recently, DMC has come to mean Developers, Managers, Consultants. Although not developers in the true sense of the word, DMC works for its clients as construction managers and consultants in the incredibly complex process of developing a new facility. The firm handles everything from needs assessment and land acquisition to engineering, approvals, and finally, construction. "Some of our clients build for themselves, while others are building to market," says McAweeney. "All want cost-effective, quality construction."

Over the years, the company has grown from a few fellas with pickups and power tools to 100 employees spread throughout California. DMC was named by *Inc. Magazine* as one of the top 500 fastest growing privately held companies in the United States in 1989 and again in 1990. "We are proud of our growth, but we've settled down now," says McAweeney. "We're concentrating our efforts close to home, with most of our projects right in our own backyard."

Recent contracts related to the Valley's agribusiness industry include new plants for California Citrus Pulp Producers, Faencal Chemical, and Cantisano Foods, packagers of the "Newman's Own" product line. Truly a diversified company, DMC is also managing the construction of a five-story, six-acre office building project for a major insurance company, an expansion of the Fresno Art Museum, a regional service plant for Southern California Gas Company, and a church addition.

As it looks to the future, DMC is turning its focus to private construction. "Our construction management techniques and our referral business are keeping us very busy these days," says McAweeney. "The '80s were like college for DMC, and now we are applying our education to an ever-changing, exciting industry."

FRANK B. HALL & CO.
ROLLINS HUDIG HALL

S ince 1976, dedicated local insurance professionals, aided by the resources of a leading worldwide insurance brokerage, have developed what has become the predominant insurance agent/broker in the area specializing in placing commercial property and casualty risks for its many diverse clients located throughout Central California. ◆ David F. Griffin, chief

executive officer of the Central California Division of Frank B. Hall & Co. and a native of Fresno, says Hall's corporate headquarters has, over the years, committed its financial resources and the expertise of its staff to fully developing the Fresno operation. That commitment has resulted in the formation of one of the few genuinely customer-oriented insurance brokers in Fresno. "We don't sell insurance," explains Griffin. "We purchase it for our clients. In that sense we are one of the only true insurance brokerages in town."

The firm adheres to the philosophy of risk management, an innovative approach to customer service in today's insurance industry. "We feel that the best way to manage risk is to avoid it, and we work with our clients on how to best achieve that end," says Griffin. "We do not have salesmen trying to sell as much insurance as possible to earn a commission. Our people are trained to develop an insurance package that best serves the needs of the individual client."

A DIVERSE PORTFOLIO
Although Frank B. Hall's Fresno office serves a wide range of businesses, insurance for agricultural clients comprises about 50 percent of its portfolio, while construction and development make up another 30 percent. The office maintains a staff of approximately 70 professionals and support personnel to meet the needs of its many clients.

Frank B. Hall has a particularly diverse group of agricultural clients, ranging from small mom-and-pop farming operations to some of the largest diversified agricultural companies in the United States. Located primarily in the Central Valley, these clients are engaged in everything from cattle

production and dairy farming to the growing and processing of high-value tree fruit, grapes, and row crops.

Another aspect of Frank B. Hall's risk management approach is to develop self-insurance programs, whereby a client sets aside its own funds to cover some types of losses. In recommending self-insurance programs, Frank B. Hall & Co. always has the long-term interest of its clients in mind, not the short-lived gain of selling lucrative but unnecessary coverage. "It may be less expensive in the long run for a client simply to pay for some types of losses than to pay for insurance coverage," explains Griffin.

As for the company's other major specialty, Chief Operating Officer John C. Day states, "We are as strong in construction and development as anyone in the area. We have a whole team of experts in the Fresno office devoted solely to this area of insurance coverage."

Frank B. Hall representatives work closely with local developers and contractors on public projects such as roads and highways and on commercial and residential development projects. These clients depend on Frank B. Hall for assistance in securing surety bond requirements. In the competitive construction industry, operating with a bonding capac-

Above and left: Frank B. Hall's Fresno offices are located in the Fig Garden Financial Center.

Hall's offices are the setting for meetings with clients from throughout the San Joaquin Valley.

ity can mean the difference between success and failure for a contractor who is competing for large-scale public and commercial projects. "We have negotiated and serviced insurance and surety bond coverage of $50 million and more for projects in these categories," Day says. "Our support also extends to local contractors for contract, fidelity, license, and permit bonds."

In addition to its areas of primary concentration, the Fresno office of Frank B. Hall serves clients in other industries that utilize the multi-faceted abilities of the local staff.

Aviation insurance, for example, is a highly specialized area that brokers at the Fresno office are well-qualified to handle. The firm's parent company serves more than half of the flag-carrying airlines in the western hemisphere.

Company expertise extends into the area of environmental insurance as well. The firm offers insurance planning for Central California clients with complicated toxic and hazardous material storage and disposal requirements. "Few brokerages have the expertise to counsel clients in the area of toxic waste. This is a relatively new and sophisticated industry," says Executive Vice President Larry D. Edde.

The Fresno office also develops risk management programs for many other types of businesses such as financial institutions, marketing firms, and manufacturers. The list of services also includes employee benefits and workers' compensation consulting.

Frank B. Hall's staff members attend to the daily needs of the company's diverse clientele.

CONFIDENCE IN THE FUTURE

Frank B. Hall & Co. has planned for continued success through a program of controlled growth and stability. To that end, company officials hope to build on the firm's long-term customer relationships by always keeping the client's best interest in mind and by maintaining a dedicated staff with the expertise to meet virtually every insurance need.

"We are confident in our future and our abilities," says Griffin. "We don't even mind if clients test someone else's waters, because we know they will frequently return to us for our expertise and dedication to service."

e Dig California" is the humorous but accurate slogan of All America Trenching, Inc., a Clovis-based company that does large-scale excavation and toxic waste cleanup jobs throughout California. ♦ Founded in 1976 by George Barnes, a native of Madera, California, All America Trenching, Inc. specialized during its early years in excavation projects such

as dams, bridges, tunnels, canals, pipelines, and underground tank installations and removals. Starting out with rented equipment, the company soon acquired an extensive line of its own excavation equipment and began landing a variety of jobs from the Oregon border to the deserts of Southern California.

During its 17 years in business, the company has been hired for all types of excavation projects, from removing fuel tanks at an altitude of 9,000 feet to digging up old lava flows near Chico in Northern California and trolley tracks in downtown Fresno. Other Fresno jobs have included excavations for the overpass footings for Freeway 41, the basement and foundation of the 10-story downtown Fresno jail, and the tunnel under Fresno Street that links the old and new jails.

Among its diverse projects, the company installed a methane extraction system at a local landfill.

AN EXPERT IN HAZARDOUS WASTE CLEANUPS

From the early 1970s to the mid-1980s, All America Trenching, Inc. developed an expertise in the removal and disposal of hazardous or toxic wastes. Today, cleanup projects comprise the majority of the firm's work. "Our company began doing environmental work before 'environmental' became a household word," says Barnes, who serves as president of the company. "Today we have a dedicated staff of professionals who have years of experience in cleaning up a wide range of contaminated materials."

The firm's staff of 12 employees includes geotechnical and civil engineers who provide the full spectrum of services for cleaning up hazardous waste sites, including environmental audits, master design plans, construction and supervision of cleanups, and information on compliance with local,

All America Trenching completed an emergency spill cleanup of diesel contaminated soil on Highway 99.

Since its founding, the company has completed 1,200 excavation and cleanup projects, including this large-scale cleanup of petroleum-contaminated soil.

state, and federal environmental regulations.

Much of the company's work includes removal of leaking storage tanks, pesticide cleanups at storage facilities in the San Joaquin Valley, and Superfund projects which are supported by the federal government. The company also does cleanup work for local and state governments, many Valley agribusiness concerns, and several oil companies, among many other clients. "Our biggest job to date," says Barnes, "involved removing 40,000 cubic yards of acid-contaminated soil at a cottonseed de-linting plant in the Imperial Valley."

DIVERSE STAFF EXPERTISE

Staff members in the company's environmental division are knowledgeable in diverse areas and have decades of combined experience. Vice President Steve Coldren, a 10-year veteran of the pesticide and petroleum industries, earned a bachelor of science degree from California State University, Fresno. He is an expert in cleanup techniques ranging from bioremediation, which involves utilizing genetically engineered bacteria to break down toxic materials into harmless forms, to soil binding, an innovative process that avoids the expense of removal by locking up contaminants in a cement-like material on-site, thus rendering them harmless. Coldren's project experience includes the installation of a methane/vinyl chloride vacuum system at a city landfill, site evaluation and risk assessment for closure of a pesticide drainage pit, a field study on the bioremediation of pesticides, and bioremediation of petroleum-contaminated soil.

Consulting engineer John Minney brings to the firm more than 20 years of experience in soil and groundwater investigations. Projects he has tackled include the monitoring of a Madera County landfill, soil and groundwater assessment of the Oakhurst sewage disposal facilities, and numerous diesel tank, concrete vault, and toxic pit removals.

David Charter, company geologist, is a graduate of the University of Massachusetts and has two decades of experience evaluating hazardous sites. His areas of expertise include bioremediation, soil logging, investigations of soil and groundwater contamination caused by jet fuels and waste fuel lubricants, and nuclear and explosives safety and security procedures.

MINIMIZING EXPENSE FOR CLIENTS

Barnes emphasizes the cost-conscious approach that All America Trenching, Inc. takes with each project and says he and his staff take pleasure in solving customer problems at reasonable expense. Much of the firm's business comes from repeat customers who are happy with the way All America Trenching, Inc. handled a previous cleanup job, or from new clients who learn of the company's reputation for professionalism and efficiency by word-of-mouth.

Since its founding, the company has completed a total of 1,200 excavation and cleanup projects—each with its own unique challenges. "This is an exciting business in these environmentally conscious times," adds Barnes. "No two days are the same for All America Trenching, Inc."

Barnes predicts that in the future there will be less emphasis on digging up contaminated materials and hauling them to hazardous waste disposal sites, often at substantial cost. Instead, he says, continuing scientific breakthroughs in genetically engineered bacteria will allow scientists and engineers to battle toxic waste at the scene, rendering it harmless without the expense of removal.

Although many toxic hot spots remain in California and elsewhere, Barnes is optimistic and convinced that American know-how and technological advances in monitoring equipment and bioremediation will solve many of today's environmental problems. He adds, "I hope All America Trenching, Inc. will continue to provide and be a part of those solutions."

President and Chief Executive Officer Tom Beene says California Valley Bank is steadily, and without a lot of fanfare, becoming Fresno's best kept banking secret. Founded in 1978 by local representatives of the area's agricultural industry, the firm has grown into what is now a banking enterprise with $140 million in assets. Most of the people who started the bank back then are still involved today as members of the board of directors.

The bank operates branch offices throughout the Valley, including its Shaw/Freeway 41 location in Fresno. (Bernard Boling photo)

"A lot of people haven't heard of us yet and don't know we're headquartered here in Fresno," relates Beene. That is why he wasn't surprised to find that six out of 10 customers come to California Valley Bank as referrals from satisfied existing customers. Beene explains what this means to the bank: "Word of mouth is our greatest advertisement, and it has allowed us to continue to quietly go about our business and work diligently on meeting our customers' needs."

It is this personal focus that has been the foundation upon which the bank has built its corporate philosophy. So in 1987, when Valley National Corporation of Arizona added California Valley Bank to its group of wholly owned, locally managed bank subsidiaries, it was only natural that things really started happening.

"We already had our foundation established as a locally managed community bank," says Beene. "But now, with the corporation's support and access to the products and services of our parent company with up to $10 billion in assets, we continue to offer the personal service of a local community bank coupled with the comprehensive products and experience levels offered at much larger banks."

DIVERSE, INDIVIDUALIZED BANKING SERVICES

Over the years, the bank has expanded from its agricultural origins to offer a complete line of banking services for Valley businesses, both small and large. California Valley Bank specializes in customized loans, including the financing of accounts receivable, inventory, and equipment acquisition. The bank also offers traditional deposit accounts and services such as payroll and courier pick-up service of non-cash deposits. Through Valley National Corporation, the bank also offers investment products, letters of credit, credit cards, lockboxes, and credit lines for larger businesses.

Even though its brochures have a long list of products, California Valley Bank prefers to consult with customers and tailor-make the proper combination of products and terms that fit their individual needs. "We have no cookie-cutter programs like a lot of the big banks offer," Beene says. "Our philosophy is to identify the needs of our customers and adjust our services accordingly, rather than try to fit the customers into a mold we've already made. We have a slogan all of us try to bring alive: 'We provide Solutions. Not problems.'"

California Valley Bank has never been content to rest on its laurels. "Keeping pace with growing communities means seeking new and current ways of serving those communities," Beene says. In this regard, the bank has a strategy of meeting the financial needs of its customers that are no longer being met by other financial institutions.

◄ BERNARD BOLING

"We find we can come in where someone else has left off, offer our local expertise and personalized banking service, and fill voids," continues Beene. "For example, where many lenders have had to withdraw from real estate construction lending activities, we have been able to remain active and provide a reliable source of funds for this important industry in the Fresno area."

The bank's senior officers are (from left) President Tom Beene, Ken Donahue, Mike Wyrick, Susan Good, and Ed Keith.

With an ever-expanding base of services, Beene believes the bank's future is unlimited. "We intend to maintain our community banking focus, which we believe will best serve our customers," he says. "Plus, we are growth-oriented. Our goal is to serve the entire region and add branch offices between here and Sacramento to better serve the unique needs of our fellow residents in the San Joaquin Valley."

I n 1978, Industrial Medical Group of Fresno was established as the first occupational medical care facility in Fresno. At first, the clinic provided care to worker's compensation cases only. The current owners, Dr. Theodore Johnstone of Fresno and Dr. Paul Cohen of Los Angeles, have since expanded its scope to include efficient emergency and follow-up care for

workers injured on the job, as well as all types of physical examinations geared to the individual needs and requirements of each industry.

The Industrial Medical Group opened its first facility 15 years ago in downtown Fresno at Tuolumne and "P" streets. In 1985, the clinic moved to its current location on South East Avenue in the heart of the city's Free Enterprise Zone. Over the years, the clinic has enjoyed tremendous growth in terms of number of patients and clients served, staff additions, and new services. The group has also built a solid reputation for outstanding care and continues to provide the best service available.

Today, physicians at the clinic see from 80 to 120 patients daily and serve some 1,500 employers throughout the area. Its clients are involved in virtually every kind of industry Fresno has to offer.

In addition to Cheryl King, business manager, and owners Johnstone and Cohen, the clinic employs 21 medical personnel. Its 7,000-square-foot facility houses a fully equipped X-ray department, computerized pulmonary function equipment, audiometrics testing for hearing loss, EKG testing equipment, a physical therapy department, and a complete gymnasium for therapy and conditioning purposes.

Today, physicians at the clinic see from 80 to 120 patients daily and serve some 1,500 employers throughout the area.

SPECIALIZING TO MEET LOCAL NEEDS

Industrial Medical Group offers several specialized services, which Doctors Jonhstone and Cohen expect will become even more widely used due to the passage of the Americans With Disabilities Act (ADA). This federal law, which went into effect in July of 1992, mandates significant improvements in how a business must accommodate disabled customers and employees.

One related service, pre-placement ability assessment, is designed to assist employers in their efforts to comply with the law. Because ADA explicitly outlines obligations to accommodate handicapped workers, employers now need very precise medical information on the physical abilities of workers. This procedure allows a company to evaluate the physical capabilities of applicants and employees, and enables them to make intelligent, informed decisions regarding placement of applicants into suitable positions.

The Industrial Medical Group also helps employers comply with ADA requirements concerning on-the-job injuries. For example, the clinic's staff can monitor the healing process of an employee and advise employers on the capabilities of the worker to perform various tasks. Likewise, Industrial Medical Group's outstanding therapy department works with individuals to speed the recovery process.

The group has also developed a special expertise in the complicated area of worker's compensation claims. Because Industrial Medical Group completes the forms accurately and efficiently, claims are processed much faster, which in turn benefits the injured worker and the employer.

Pre-employment drug testing is another service the group offers. More and more employers are taking advantage of this type of service to avoid employee problems associated with drug and alcohol abuse, such as lower productivity, theft, absenteeism, and job-related injuries. Industrial Medical Group follows very rigid controls in its drug testing procedures to assure accurate results and to protect the integrity of the tests.

After 15 years of service to the local business community, the Industrial Medical Group looks forward to a future of growth and expansion. The owners believe the clinic's outlook in Fresno is promising because of the staff's level of knowledge and ability, the continuing growth of the industrial medicine field, and its increasing importance in the marketplace.

In 1985, the clinic moved to its current location on South East Avenue in the heart of Fresno's Free Enterprise Zone.

*T*he story of Quickie Designs Inc. is one of determination, innovation, and a desire to reach beyond conventional wisdom. While many organizations boast a commitment to quality assurance and customer service, few can also claim revolutionary roles in their respective industries. But that's where Quickie parts company with the average business. ◆ *Marilyn Hamilton,*

one of the company's founders and current senior vice president of marketing, took a personal tragedy and turned it into a triumph for wheelchair users worldwide by spearheading the development of cutting-edge technology that addressed the needs of an untapped consumer market. In 1980, Hamilton and two friends launched their experiment from a 600-square-foot shed where they produced custom lightweight aluminum wheelchairs at the painstaking rate of one a day. The company has since soared to a worldwide leadership position in custom lightweight wheelchairs.

"From our humble beginnings just over a decade ago, Quickie Designs has developed a worldwide manufacturing and distribution system in custom wheelchairs and related equipment," says Tom O'Donnell, Quickie president.

Today, at its 140,000-square-foot manufacturing plant in Fresno, the firm employs more than 400 associates and ships more than 1,000 units a week around the world. Since it was purchased in 1986 by Sunrise Medical Inc., a public company listed on the New York Stock Exchange, Quickie has built satellite manufacturing facilities in Elyria, Ohio and Brierley Hill, U.K.

A virtually limitless number of color, size, and style combinations are available on a measure-to-fit basis in less than two weeks at prices ranging from $850 to $3,000. The business now has 36 sales representatives across the country and more than 2,000 dealers. According to company officials, product quality is a major reason for the firm's enormous success, but they consider the company's philosophy the most important ingredient. "Our primary objective," O'Donnell says, "is to provide an improved quality of life to the physically challenged individual."

DEVELOPING A GROUND-BREAKING PRODUCT

In 1979, Hamilton was paralyzed in a hang-gliding accident. She was not willing to merely accept her condition. While adapting to her new role in the world, she became frustrated at the limitations of the archaic wheelchairs then available.

In hopes of improving quality of life for herself and all other wheelchair users, Hamilton recruited two of her hang-gliding companions. Together, they created the "Quickie," the world's first custom lightweight wheelchair, now commonly seen across the globe.

The ground-breaking product shocked the country with its versatility, and the return on the wheelchair's skyrocketing popularity has been tremendous. In 1991, just over a decade since the company's inception, Quickie's annual revenues reached nearly $50 million. "Our product has definitely been well-received," O'Donnell says. "We combine advanced design methods, aesthetics, quality in manufacturing, and functionality to make a superior product."

Quickie's products, all custom-made, are manufactured only after physical therapists have worked extensively with a prospective user for maximum results.

AN EXTENSIVE AND GROWING PRODUCT LINE

The company's extensive and growing product line includes manual and power chairs made from materials such as aluminum, carbon fiber, and titanium. The simplest, least expensive power prod-

Quickie's custom lightweight wheelchairs can be designed for anyone, ranging from the everyday user to the elite athlete.

uct is the Quickie P100, while the upscale model is known as the Quickie P300. A pediatric power chair, the Zippie P500, is also available. Manual chairs weighing as little as 18 pounds are manufactured for both children and adults and can be designed for anyone, ranging from the everyday user to the elite athlete.

Thorough, up-to-date research is essential to the firm's success in this highly competitive, technical market. As a result, many current users of Quickie products have become an important part of Quickie's ongoing research program. The company meets its research needs partly by sponsoring a variety of users—both business people and athletes—through product donations and financial support. In turn, their invaluable opinions about a product's design and durability are incorporated into the ongoing evolution of Quickie products. Input from within the company is also an important part of the research process, since six associates use Quickies themselves.

Though research generally leads to a better product, Quickie has a unique way of responding to specific customer demands. All custom-made, the chairs are manufactured only after physical therapists have worked extensively with a prospective user for maximum results. Rehabilitation professionals, usually the ones who know the user's needs best, assess all environmental conditions of the client. Only then can a physically challenged person be assured of the best possible mobility device for his or her personal needs. "The rehabilitation professionals help every user to get the best fit possible," O'Donnell says. "And that's a very important part of the equation at Quickie."

FOUNDED ON A COMMITMENT TO QUALITY

Although its product line is designed for clients with physical disabilities, the company's accomplishments have not gone unnoticed outside the health care industry. In 1991, *Business Ethics Magazine* honored Quickie for its innovation and superior line of products with the magazine's Business Ethics Award. Likewise, Marilyn Hamilton has received individual recognition, including the 1992 National Victory Award presented by the President.

Quickie Designs was founded over a decade ago on the idea of providing the best possible product to a unique and growing segment of American society. Today, quality remains the company's byword: quality in design, in manufacturing, in marketing, and especially in the lives of those who use Quickie products.

*T*he building industry in Fresno has been active and lucrative for many years, and local building contractors have enjoyed a wealth of commercial and residential projects. The Schaal/Lechner Corporation, a Fresno building contractor, could have taken the less difficult path and pursued traditional building projects. Instead, the company goes after the more

challenging projects, and it has become quite successful in the process.

"Our forte is to take an unusual project and make it work," says Roy Lechner, one of the principals of the firm. "We thrive on doing the tough jobs."

The Fresno Juvenile Hall Annex is an example of the type of project the company has completed. "Working in an occupied building is tough enough," Lechner says, "but this one had special problems. We were restrained by the rules and procedures that keep inmates isolated from outsiders and visitors."

Figuring downtime in a project like this can make or break a bid, not to mention a contractor, says Lechner, but the Juvenile Hall Annex job was done within budget and on schedule. For their efforts and success on this project, the Schaal/Lechner Corporation was named "Contractor of the Year" in 1981 by the American Public Works Association.

Schaal/Lechner received an Award of Merit at the Pacific Coast Building conference for its construction of Kaiser Permanente Medical Center.

Another example of the type of project that attracts the Schaal/Lechner group was the construction of the Fresno Imaging Center, the first MRI (magnetic resonance imaging) facility to be located in Central California. "The solution to difficult logistics brought this project to a successful conclusion," says Lechner. "Imaging equipment is extremely sensitive, so the building had to be constructed so as to protect it from any outside radio interference, such as from a car phone or citizen band radio."

The company received an "Award of Merit" for this project. Other award-winning projects include the Fresno Arts Center, College Satellite Union, and Kaiser Permanente Medical Center.

A HISTORY OF PROFESSIONALISM AND EXPERTISE

James Schaal and Roy Lechner met in San Diego in 1977 while working for R.G. Fisher Corp., a building contractor. The pair decided to pool their resources, move to Fresno (Schaal's hometown), and start their own company. With Lechner at the helm of office management and Schaal in charge of field operations, the company has experienced remarkable success.

Winding up its first year in 1978 with $1.7 million in volume, the company now completes up to $40 million in projects each year. The firm has done work from Santa Rosa and Sacramento in the north to Santa Maria and Bakersfield in the south. When asked if Schaal/Lechner had any difficulty establishing itself in the Fresno market, Schaal says there were few bumps on the road to success. "When we opened our doors, things took off right away. There was more work here than there were contractors to fill the need."

Schaal attributes much of the company's success to its employees, who have high standards of professionalism. Both Schaal and Lechner began their careers as carpenters, so they interact well with their field workers and know to listen to their ideas. The same rapport exists between Schaal and Lechner and their office staff. "When we want to know the best way to do something," Schaal says, "we invite our field personnel into the discussion because their everyday experience provides valuable input."

Schaal and Lechner's commitment to quality has not been limited to their business lives. When they launched the company 15 years ago, they made a pledge to improve the quality of life in the city that would provide their living. Today, both are active as soccer coaches, and through their financial generosity, prospective Olympic athletes from the Fresno area are developing their skills by participating in international soccer competitions.

Both Schaal and Lechner believe in supporting local activities as a way of investing in the city's future. "This city really has been good to us," Lechner says. "It's our commitment to try to give something back."

sity, Fresno. After graduation in 1975, Diane went to work with Michael Ray as a chemist at a winery in Fresno; she would later entice him to join APPL in 1986. When she left the winery in 1976, Diane became a research chemist for a pesticide manufacturer, ultimately heading up its local state-certified laboratory testing division.

FROM HUMBLE BEGINNINGS

When Diane, Brad, and Pamela joined forces in 1982, they began operations in a modest 1,600-square-foot facility near the firm's current location on West Swift Avenue. The expense of simply opening the doors, especially the prohibitive cost of state-of-the-art equipment, forced the Andersons to donate their own kitchen refrigerator to cool test samples to the temperatures required by the EPA.

Their diligence and patience soon began to pay off, and by 1987 APPL had outgrown its original facility. Responding to a phenomenal 800 percent, five-year employee growth rate, the firm and its staff of 25 moved into a new 10,000-square-foot location. According to Ray, that early level of success can be attributed to hard work and word of mouth. "Promoting the company has never been a primary consideration for us," Ray says. "We are a bunch of chemists. We don't know anything about advertising!"

Nevertheless, the growth patterns continued. By

Currently, the firm has an estimated $12 million invested in laboratory equipment.

1988, the employee roster had doubled, and the firm once again had outgrown its facility. "We went back and leased our old building just a half block away," says Ray. "That additional space now serves as an annex to our Swift Avenue headquarters."

APPL has also added a significant amount of equipment during its decade of growth. Currently, the firm has an estimated $12 million invested in laboratory equipment alone. Likewise, its full-time staff has swelled to 55 employees, many of whom received their training locally. "Sixty percent of our chemists are graduates of CSUF," Ray says. "We are very proud of that."

As a leader in the environmental testing field, APPL has a great deal to be proud of, including its membership in numerous national associations. For example, the firm is a member of the Association of Analytical Chemists, the Association of Chemical Testing Laboratories, The American Institute of Chemists, and the International Association of Environmental Testing Laboratories.

Diane has also established an individual reputation for her achievements. Locally, she has been nominated twice as Fresno's "Woman of the Year," but her expertise has garnered respect far beyond the Valley. "Diane is recognized throughout the United States as a pesticide expert," says Ray.

Looking to the future, APPL is prepared for further expansion as the need for innovative environmental testing procedures continues to grow. By 1994, the firm plans to move into a new 25,000-square-foot facility, and company officials expect the workload to double.

Despite their rapid success, Diane and Brad Anderson have not forgotten APPL's humble roots. Says Ray, "We still use that old refrigerator."

APPL specializes in environmental testing procedures designed to find traces of chemicals and metals in water, wastewater, sludge, and soil.

*A*ssuring that the water supply is clean and safe—something most people take for granted—is foremost in the minds of the people at CMB Industries, makers of FEBCO Backflow Preventers and Bailey Polyjet sleeve valves. These water quality and control products are sold worldwide in the irrigation, waterworks, plumbing, fireline, and industrial markets.

Whether it is a backflow prevention assembly in a school or hospital, a 60-inch control valve releasing water from a reservoir, or a pump recirculation valve which is protecting the Fantasmic show at Disneyland, CMB Industries is a leader in the water quality and control industry.

"Because our FEBCO products are public health protectors, they must be extremely reliable and easily tested and maintained," says Chief Operating Officer John Brewer.

Worldwide, FEBCO is the second largest volume manufacturer of backflow prevention assemblies, which are designed to prevent contaminated water from entering the potable water supply by allowing water to flow in only one direction. As a result, company officials don't take the issue of water quality lightly. "Back siphonage and back pressure cause backflow of contaminated water into our potable water supply every day," explains Brewer. "People get sick and die because of water contamination problems. Our products are designed to prevent health hazards caused by contaminated water."

FEBCO began in 1924 when Fred Reinecke Sr. of Los Angeles secured the exclusive western states franchise for products manufactured by John A. Brooks Co. of Detroit. Known as Brooks of California, Reinecke's operation marketed water pressure-driven irrigation valve sequencers and spray-type lawn sprinklers throughout the western United States.

When the 25-year franchise agreement ended in 1949, Reinecke formed FEBCO, Inc. to continue the irrigation products specialty he had established. According to family lore, the name FEBCO was derived from the first-name initials of Reinecke's children: Fred Jr., Ed, Bill, Charlotte, and the "Old Man." All of the children were active in the company. In the mid-1950s, automatic sprinkler controllers were developed, allowing FEBCO to collaborate with golf course architect Robert Trent Jones to create the master/satellite golf course control system.

The mid-1960s heralded a period of consolidation throughout the irrigation industry. In 1965, Jim Coson, the owner of General Sprinkler Co., purchased FEBCO from the Reinecke family and moved its operations to his Fresno plant. The Johns-Manville Corp. purchased General Sprinkler in 1972 with the idea of creating a single, comprehensive manufacturer of irrigation products, a strategy that proved unsuccessful. In May 1980, the Charles M. Bailey Co. bought FEBCO, and both companies were sold in 1983 to the Michael Coyne family of San Francisco, who combined the two companies under the name of CMB Industries.

In 1984, CMB purchased property at 1550 North Peach Avenue in Fresno. The FEBCO division was relocated from Villa Avenue to the newer, larger Peach Avenue facility. Bailey's Emeryville operations were moved to Fresno in 1985, bringing both divisions of CMB under one roof. Since then, two expansions have tripled the plant's size to 117,000 square feet.

Top right and above: CMB's facility in Fresno employs approximately 120 people who manufacture water quality and control products for a variety of applications.

A LONG, PROUD HISTORY

CMB Industries traces its long, proud history to two predecessors, the Charles M. Bailey Company and FEBCO, which joined forces in 1980.

The Charles M. Bailey Company was established in 1923 in San Francisco by Charles M. Bailey, an industrial valve salesman. Frustrated by inadequate parts deliveries from his suppliers, Bailey set out to manufacture his own valves. In the late 1960s, Bailey developed an innovative product line known as Polyjet Sleeve Valves, which is the flagship of the Bailey product line today. These valves set the current standards for state-of-the-art flow control and energy dissipation.

Since it initiated the "team concept" in 1992, CMB has significantly improved efficiency, cutting standard assembly times in half on many items.

Today, the Fresno facility runs two shifts a day, employing approximately 120 people who manufacture water quality and control products for a variety of applications. For example, the Bailey Polyjet sleeve valve line, which is designed to control flow and pressure through water systems, can be used in water treatment plants, at the outlet from reservoirs, and for hydroelectric turbine bypass. FEBCO backflow prevention valves can be found in many applications, including hospitals, office buildings, shopping malls, municipal systems, fire protection systems, schools, manufacturing plants, and irrigation systems.

REVITALIZATION FROM WITHIN

In the late 1980s, as the backflow prevention industry became highly competitive, foreign manufacturers threatened to enter the U.S. market. In light of increased competition and to ensure CMB's industry standing, company officials decided to initiate a revitalization from within. Recognizing that employees either make or break a company, CMB initiated the "team concept" in 1992. Under this new management system, workers determine production and vacation schedules, and individual performance evaluations are done by teams of employees.

According to Brewer, this team concept has made a world of difference to the company and its employees. "It has enabled us to significantly improve efficiency," he says. "In fact, our standard assembly times have been cut in half on many items, and our products will soon be granted approval under the very prestigious Australian standards. We are now pursuing the tougher ISO 9000 industry standards as a way of improving our production efficiency and preparing us to compete in the European market."

As teamwork and communication have increased, so has accountability. "Each team is responsible for defining goals. Through a regular corporate report card, our employees can keep tabs on how the company is doing and how their efforts are paying off," says Brewer.

To achieve these sweeping changes, company officials have adopted a number of ideas from the winners of the Malcolm Baldrige National Quality Award. "We're adopting proven concepts and implementing them at CMB Industries," says Brewer.

CMB has also begun an aggressive campaign of charitable donations. Recently, the company donated more than $50,000 in backflow prevention assemblies to be used throughout the Fresno area for protection of the potable water supply in schools, parks, and the municipal system. Likewise, employees have donated their time by installing an irrigation system near the CMB plant, which enabled the Tree Fresno organization to plant several trees. A recycling program, with proceeds benefiting local needy families, has also been implemented. "We feel it is important to give something back to our Fresno community," says Brewer.

After a decade of success in the San Joaquin Valley, CMB Industries plans to perpetuate its commitment to water quality and control worldwide. With the combined resources of two longtime experts in the water quality and control industry, Bailey and FEBCO, this Fresno-based company looks forward to an exciting future of innovation and growth.

*W*ith a background as diverse as the region, Dritsas, Groom & Goya has provided quality audit, accounting, financial consulting, and tax services to a select group of privately held companies for more than a decade. The Fresno-based firm prides itself on offering attentive, personalized service to its clients, which include businesses and individuals from the

agriculture, construction, and retail sectors, as well as professionals, such as doctors, lawyers, and architects.

"The primary focal point at Dritsas, Groom & Goya is between client and partner," explains Russel Dritsas, a founding member of the firm. "Our principals are always accessible to our clients. We take phone calls, we meet with bankers, and we are personally involved in our clients' financial and accounting affairs."

*From left:
Russel J. Dritsas,
Jenny K. Chiang,
Kendall J. Groom, and
John J. Dritsas.*

FOUNDED ON DIVERSITY

A full-service certified public accounting firm, Dritsas, Groom & Goya offers areas of expertise beyond traditional accounting services, including negotiation, mergers and acquisitions, and liquidation of companies.

The firm was founded in Fresno in 1981 by brothers Russel and John Dritsas. Within the first year of operation, Kendall Groom joined the partnership. In addition to the three original partners, Dritsas, Groom & Goya today employs six certified public accountants, three bookkeepers, and support personnel.

All three principals bring a wealth of business experience to their profession and to the firm. Russel Dritsas began his professional career in sales management in the computer industry. His brother, John, operated a retail business, and Kendall Groom, who comes from a farming background, brings years of agricultural expertise to the partnership.

Such diversity broadens the firm's perspective according to Russel Dritsas. "We have dealt with

the day-to-day difficulties of owning and operating a business, and we have seen business from both sides," he says. "That kind of experience and professional depth allows us to more readily empathize with the client."

The firm puts its extensive agricultural experience to use for clients in the Valley farming community. "We have a diverse background in agriculture, covering everything from permanent and field crops to packers and shippers," says Dritsas.

COMMITTED TO QUALITY AND PROFESSIONALISM

Over the years, Dritsas, Groom & Goya has taken steps to ensure quality and the highest degree of professionalism for both its clients and employees. Most recently, the firm moved its headquarters to the Woodward Centre Complex on Fresno and Herndon avenues, allowing the staff to more efficiently serve its clients.

Likewise, the partners emphasize an atmosphere of teamwork aimed at maximizing responsiveness to clients. Those efforts are aided by the fact that many of the firm's employees have been with Dritsas, Groom & Goya for a number of years. "Our clients are not dealing with new faces every time they call on us," says Dritsas. "As a result, they enjoy a degree of continuity that is beneficial to them, as well as us."

Since Dritsas, Groom & Goya began using computer networks in 1982, the firm has been a Central Valley leader in computerized accounting. From simple word processing to complex accounting procedures, the firm's integrated computer network helps increase efficiency.

The firm sponsors regular in-house training programs for employees. It also subscribes to Quality Review, a formal peer review program in which other firms examine the Dritsas, Groom & Goya operation. Every third year, the firm engages an independent certified public accounting organization to perform a thorough audit of its practices and procedures.

"In both employee and client relations, we are committed to being as good as we can be," says Dritsas. "After more than a decade of accounting excellence in the San Joaquin Valley, we expect to be a partner in the future growth of Fresno and the surrounding communities."

FRESNO PRIVATE INDUSTRY COUNCIL

*T*he Fresno Private Industry Council has funded local employment training and placement programs for thousands of Fresnans since 1983 when the organization was established by a Joint Powers Agreement between Fresno city and county governments. Today, the Council supports approximately 60 programs with federal dollars it receives as a result of

legislation passed in 1982 by Congress to promote job training.

The mission of the Fresno Private Industry Council is to deliver employment, education, and job training services that enable the unemployed of the local labor force to obtain full, long-term employment that enhances the economic well-being of the entire community.

Deputy Director M.J. Peterson notes that approximately 178,000 county residents, or 27 percent of the population, are on some form of public assistance. "Many individuals will continue to be dependent on public assistance because of physical or mental limitations," she says. "Others, however, can be contributing members of the community if given opportunities, and that's where the Fresno Private Industry Council steps in as a funding organization."

Staff members of the Summer Youth Employment & Training Program search for potential worksites.

FUNDING A VARIETY OF PROGRAMS

With a $16 million annual budget, the Council partially or fully funds training programs and "service providers," such as Vocational Management Services, Fresno County Economic Opportunities Commission, Proteus, SER Jobs for Progress, the Older Americans Employment and Training Center, the Fresno County Probation Department Manpower Program, and the Summer Youth Employment & Training Program. The Council also offers financial assistance for training programs for qualifying private employers. In recent years, programs funded by the Council have served approximately 9,000 adults and youths annually.

The Council funds those training programs that show the most promise for fulfilling its goal of enhancing employment opportunities for program participants. Understandably, the Council is proud of its track record. For instance, the Dislocated Workers Program, which works with displaced workers, served 410 people in 1991, with 274

completing the program and 198 reentering the job market. Fresno County Economic Opportunities Commission, which serves urban adults, provided training to 307 people in the same year, with 232 completing its programs and 166 reentering the job market.

The Council's financial support goes out to many training programs that teach job skills, such as welding or computer operation, as well as programs that offer job placement services or teach job search or interview skills. Other programs, cosponsored by high schools, community colleges, and California State University, Fresno, offer remedial academic courses in English, math, and other subjects. "Although the academic programs do not usually result in immediate employment, they boost the recipient's long-term prospects for finding gainful employment," says Executive Director Charles Francis.

Those who may qualify for these services include the marginally educated, ex-offenders, unskilled adults who have lost their jobs due to company layoffs or downsizing, or virtually anyone who is facing a serious barrier to employment, including a physical handicap.

Executive Director Charles Francis (left) and Deputy Director M.J. Peterson believe the long-range benefits of Council-funded programs are incalculable.

AN EYE ON THE FUTURE

The long-range benefits for participants in Council-funded programs, as well as for the community, are incalculable. "The participants learn to help themselves and acquire marketable skills that promote employment success," says Peterson. "They also become taxpayers instead of tax consumers."

Francis adds that the Council is committed to training individuals for jobs that will be viable over the long term. "There are going to be a lot of changes in our local and national economies over the next couple of decades in terms of types of job skills that will be needed," he says. "We want to help prepare individuals for these changes by funding appropriate training programs. The present and future health of the Fresno economy are of equal importance to the Private Industry Council.

"Established businesses are growing, while other companies are relocating to the Fresno County area. As a result, there are new demands for skilled workers. We in Fresno County must offer an employable population with the skills to meet those job demands in order to be competitive in the global marketplace."

*M*auldin-Dorfmeier Construction, Inc. (MDC) has made an immense impact on the construction industry in Fresno and Central California since its founding in 1983. Pat Mauldin and Alan Dorfmeier, with 50 years of combined construction experience, have dedicated their lives to providing construction services that emphasize quality work, safety, professional management, and early completion.

Mauldin and Dorfmeier both grew up in Fresno, received degrees in civil engineering from California State University, Fresno, and worked together at another local construction firm in the 1970s and early 1980s. Mauldin's previous experience in design and construction supervision includes such diverse projects as buildings, bridges, sewer and water treatment facilities, roads, and utilities. Dorfmeier supervised construction crews on a number of projects and was chief estimator responsible for obtaining an annual work volume of $15 million.

MAJOR PROJECTS IN FRESNO AND BEYOND

The willingness to accept the challenge of difficult projects has been a source of pride since the company's inception. During its first decade of growth, MDC has tackled and successfully completed diverse projects throughout California. In 1987, MDC won a $2.5 million contract to con-

One Shaw Plaza, a 34,000-square-foot retail center at Shaw and Blackstone avenues, demanded countless hours of coordination with subcontractors, structural engineers, the architect, and the City of Fresno.

struct a maintenance facility for PG&E at the Helms Project in the High Sierra. The facility, situated at a 7,000-foot elevation, included warehouse space, offices, vehicle repair shops, sand and salt storage buildings, and mechanical buildings. When MDC was allowed on the site to start work on August 15, the winter months were just around the corner. Crews demolished an existing structural steel building, started setting new structural steel on September 1, and poured 2,000 yards of concrete in just 21 days, allowing MDC to meet the completion deadline of November 11.

After earthquakes rocked Coalinga, destroying much of the city and all of its public swimming pools, MDC was contracted to build an olympic swimming and recreation complex. From the start, the company's depth of experience, strength, and versatility were put to the test. Aftershocks of as much as 6.0 on the Richter scale hampered accuracies demanded by olympic competition standards. When the project's pool subcontractor went out of business, time constraints forced MDC to take over the pool construction. The structural steel buildings and canopies of the recreation complex proved to be an equal challenge, as the exposed connections required precise fabrication and fitting. Despite these challenges, MDC completed the job on time and within budget, and the project won the prestigious *Architectural Record* award for "Excellence in Design and Execution."

Mauldin-Dorfmeier completed the $1.2 million renovation of the Fresno Center Plaza Parking Garage in 1987. The facility had been condemned after officials investigated surface fractures and concluded the structure was damaged and unsafe. MDC, the only contractor willing to handle such a difficult task, was selected by the City of Fresno and the original builder to perform the work. With carefully planned and executed jacking and shoring, MDC safely stabilized the structure, allowing crews to substantially increase footings and structural bearing points with high-strength, cast-in-place concrete and high-pressure epoxy injection. The structurally enhanced garage was returned to the City of Fresno, and it continues to create revenue from parking.

The Tropical Rain Forest at Chaffee Zoological Gardens proved to be one of MDC's most unusual projects to date. The $2.3 million, 22,000-square-foot exhibit simulates the conditions of a South American tropical rain forest. Wood poles averaging 70 feet high are enclosed by a plastic-coated wire mesh to create an aviary structure that houses tropical and exotic creatures. Waterfalls, streams, and a misting system simulate a damp morning on the Amazon River. Careful placement of over 2,800 pressure-treated timbers and fire-retardant thatch complete the jungle canopy effect.

The innovative structure has won a number of design and construction honors, including an Award of Merit for "Excellence in Design and Execution" from the San Joaquin Chapter of the American Institute of Architects and a Constructor Award from the Associated General Contractors of California for "Meeting the Challenge of the Difficult Job."

In 1992, MDC was the first contractor in the Central Valley to receive the coveted Constructor Award for "Excellence in Client Service" from the Associated General Contractors of California.

The Bulldog Stadium project is another example of MDC's proven management abilities. The firm was awarded the $2.1 million contract to remodel and expand the stadium by 3,000 seats in early 1991. MDC's aggressive and professional approach prompted CSUF officials to consider accelerating the expansion program, thereby saving a year of construction activities. The revised contract added 7,000 more seats and enabled the Bulldog football team to enter the Western Athletic Conference in 1992. Though construction on the additional seats did not begin until April 1991, the project was completed in time for the season opener on September 7. In 1992, MDC became the first contractor in the Central Valley to receive the coveted Constructor Award for "Excellence in Client Service" from the Associated General Contractors of California for its work on Bulldog Stadium.

One Shaw Plaza, a 34,000-square-foot retail center at Shaw and Blackstone avenues, demanded a versatile and dedicated staff. MDC met the challenge head-on and commenced building on August 1 without a complete design or building permits. With a completion deadline of November 15, the project schedule was critical. Through countless hours of coordination with subcontractors, structural engineers, the architect, and the City of Fresno, the first lease space was ready for occupancy in only 107 days. The remainder of the project was completed and ready for occupancy 29 days later in time for the holiday season.

Three large projects for United Parcel Service

have been completed by MDC. The 56,647-square-foot addition to the UPS/Fresno Distribution Facility was the first project undertaken. Tilt-up concrete walls and a structural steel framework house tons of sorting and distribution equipment. The second project, a 30,000-square-foot facility in Ceres (Stanislaus County), was completed in 105 days (two weeks ahead of schedule) and was operational for the holiday season. The third project, a 28,000-square-foot facility in Santa Cruz, was completed in November 1991, 10 days prior to the contract completion date.

COMMITTED TO EXTENSIVE PLANNING AND SAFETY

One reason for MDC's success is a belief in extensive planning. The firm uses the latest proven technology to the advantage of its clients, including a state-of-the-art computerized scheduling system and an impressive computer software package allowing unparalleled precision in estimating and monitoring job costs.

With more than 100 craftsmen, safety is a primary concern of everyone at MDC. The company is proud of its commitment to safety and its employee-supported policy for a drug-free workplace, which MDC believes is an essential element of its outstanding safety program. In 1989 and 1991, the firm won "Safety Excellence" awards from the Associated General Contractors of California.

Pat Mauldin and Alan Dorfmeier believe they hold the key to establishing a first-rate reputation in the construction business: bring every project in on time and within budget, and do it safely and professionally. It's this combination that has produced some of Fresno's most visible and impressive construction projects. It's also the reason that MDC has received numerous industry honors, including the 1991 Contractor of the Year award from the Associated General Contractors of California-San Joaquin District. With these commitments and proven success, Mauldin-Dorfmeier Construction is poised for another decade of success in Fresno and beyond.

In 1990, the firm completed a building project for the Fresno Metropolitan Flood Control District.

or the weekend warrior who overdoes it in a neighborhood game of football, the skier who makes a wrong turn down the slope, the factory worker who throws his back out, or the avid golfer and sportsman, the California Orthopedic and Medical Clinic-Fresno provides expert medical care. Dr. John Janda, an orthopedic surgeon and sports medicine specialist, treats

everything from minor injuries and runner's knee to major trauma. Dr. Janda's state-of-the-art medical practice encompasses reconstructive surgery on knees, hips, fingers, toes, and other joints, as well as general orthopedic surgery, including lumbar laminectomy, commonly known as back surgery.

A FULL-SERVICE CLINIC

The California Orthopedic and Medical Clinic in Fresno is considered a full-service clinic, with a comprehensive list of services offered under one roof. Dr. Pam Janda specializes in internal medicine. Family care facilities, orthopedic surgical and sports medicine treatment, a laboratory for various blood tests, radiological capabilities, and treadmill examinations are available as well. The facility also offers a wellness and rehabilitation program supervised by a registered physical therapist, a weight loss clinic with a registered dietitian, and a smoking cessation clinic.

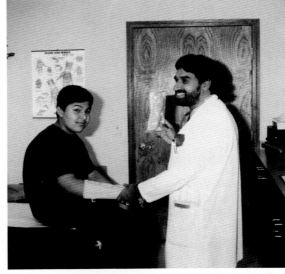

Dr. John Janda specializes in sports medicine and orthopedic surgery for patients of all ages throughout the community.

The clinic offers a comprehensive array of programs and services: internal medicine/family practice, laboratory services, orthopedic surgery and sports medicine, physical therapy, radiology, rehabilitation services, cardiovascular rehabilitation, a smoking cessation program, and a weight loss program.

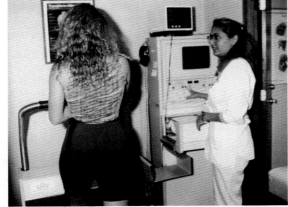

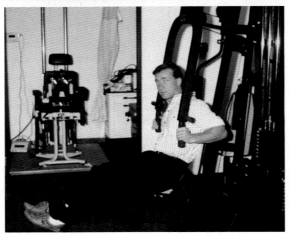

In July of 1975, Dr. Janda received his medical degree from the University of Aberdeen in Aberdeen, Scotland. He practiced general medicine and surgery in Scotland and England from 1975 to 1977. Dr. Janda later completed his residency and training in orthopedic surgery at Thomas Jefferson University Hospital in Philadelphia, which offers one of the country's top orthopedic surgical programs.

Dr. Janda began his medical and surgical practice in the San Joaquin Valley in January of 1983. He opened a second office in Madera in 1985. Today, Dr. Janda divides his time among offices in Fresno, Madera, and Sanger.

The bulk of Dr. Janda's practice today is devoted to sports medicine and orthopedic surgery related to trauma in the sports arena. He also treats general trauma and chronic disabling conditions.

Adjoining the clinic is Healthfirst Physical Therapy, which boasts up-to-date equipment and a registered physical therapist who provides excellent care for patients. Located in the same building, Advanced Orthopedic and Rehabilitation Associates (A.O.R.A.) is dedicated to the treatment of occupational injuries and the rehabilitation of injured workers.

According to Dr. Janda, he has enjoyed a very satisfying and rewarding 10 years of practice in the Valley. He says, "I hope to be of service for many, many more years."

GRISANTI & ASSOCIATES, INC.

L ocated in Kingsburg, 30 miles south of Fresno, Grisanti & Associates, Inc. is an environmental engineering firm that specializes in hazardous waste assessment and remediation in the San Joaquin Valley. Since 1984, the husband-and-wife team of Jack and Debby Grisanti, both registered environmental assessors, have built a company that is today an integral part of Fresno County's business community.

Grisanti & Associates serves a diverse client base, ranging from tire manufacturers, oil companies, printers, and service stations to farmers, bankers, and the U.S. Department of Defense. The company specializes in hazardous waste management, property assessment, contamination assessment, and site cleanups. It is this diversity of experience that allows the consultant to find the client's way through the environmental regulatory morass that exists today.

"Our number one objective is to make our clients feel they have a handle on their potential environmental problems," says President Jack Grisanti. "To do that, we must not only be on top of the ever-changing regulatory environment, but also have cost-effective solutions for our clients to comply with them. Often this entails setting up a preventive environmental program to minimize future environmental liability. When the client calls with an existing problem, coming up with effective solutions must take into consideration the client's needs and particular circumstances. It is this customizing of programs that we feel is our greatest asset."

COMPANY BEGINNINGS

The Grisantis, who began their consulting business in their Kingsburg home in 1984, were among the first of about 100 registered environmental assessors in California, a professional group which now numbers more than 6,000. They occupied their current office on Draper Street in downtown Kingsburg in 1986, and today have 11 employees, five of whom are either registered geologists, engineers, or environmental assessors. Their business volume has grown rapidly, averaging about 30 percent annually since the company's founding.

Jack Grisanti's academic background and work experience gave the couple the confidence to start their own business. Grisanti graduated in 1974 from CSU, Northridge, with B.S. and M.S. degrees in Environmental Health Science. He has conducted two years of post-graduate work at the University of California, Berkeley. Grisanti is also certified by the Hazardous Materials Management Program of the University of California, Davis. From 1977 to 1979, he worked for the Kings County Division of Environmental Health Services as an assistant air pollution control officer. He then joined Beacon Oil Company of Hanford, California, where he served as an environmental and safety engineer until 1982. From 1982 to 1984, he was president and CEO of Cal-Alga Resources, Inc., a high-tech aquacultural company.

Debby Grisanti, who earned a bachelor of arts from CSU, Northridge, has over the past eight years gained extensive knowledge of hazardous waste management and consulting through on-the-job experience. She completed the Environmental Auditing Certificate Program of the University of California, Davis, and in 1992 received her California Environmental Assessor Registration. She now serves as the corporation's secretary and treasurer.

PROFESSIONAL SERVICES

Grisanti & Associates offers a broad range of environmental services, including industrial and agricultural environmental auditing, property assessment, soil and groundwater contamination investigations, hazardous substance management, and safety and emergency response training. Remedial services range from underground tank removal and facility decontamination to soil cleanup of waste, such as petroleum, pesticides, paints, solvents, metal plating, and heavy metals. Grisanti & Associates also provides assistance in obtaining difficult wastewater, solid waste, and air pollution control permits. Sometimes the company just helps clients understand and cope with the myriad of environmental regulations facing them.

Since 1984, Jack and Debby Grisanti have built an environmental engineering firm that is today an integral part of Fresno County's business community.

The company that the Grisantis started in their home nearly a decade ago is a thriving business, which has grown by referrals from the company's many clients. "Ninety-nine percent of our business comes from word-of-mouth advertising," says Jack Grisanti. "In a business that lives and dies by referral, customer satisfaction is the only path to success."

He adds, "We had a vision to provide a full-service environmental program at a reasonable cost—one that would be a positive influence on a company, not just another overhead expense. We believe we have achieved that goal, and we are very proud of that."

FRESNO SURGERY AND RECOVERY CARE CENTER

*I*t doesn't look like a hospital. It doesn't feel like a hospital. And in a hundred ways—some obvious, some less so—it doesn't function like any hospital that has come before it. The Fresno Surgery and Recovery Care Center is a short-stay surgery facility for people who are seeking an alternative to the traditional acute-care hospital. ♦ The Fresno Surgery and

Recovery Care Center was the nation's first freestanding outpatient surgery and recovery care center. Designed specifically to meet the needs of the elective surgery patient, it is currently sparking a revolution among health care providers to change the delivery of post-surgical care. The center is considered to be the premier facility of its kind in the nation and receives more than 20 site visits per year from health care professionals interested in learning more about the center's success.

NEARLY A DECADE OF GROWTH

In 1984, 75 physicians established the Fresno Surgery and Recovery Care Center as strictly an outpatient surgery center. Its original 12,000-square-foot facility housed five operating rooms. Soon after the center's opening, founder Alan Pierrot, M.D. and a group of physicians began lobbying the state legislature to expand the facility to include overnight stay.

In light of the center's initial success, California Senator Ken Maddy believed the state was ready for an alternative method of treating surgery patients. Senator Maddy spearheaded the passage of State Senate Bill 1953, which approved the establishment of 12 post-surgical recovery care centers throughout California. The Fresno Surgery and Recovery Care Center is the first center in the nation to integrate outpatient surgery with post-surgical overnight care.

Established in 1984, the Fresno Surgery and Recovery Care Center was the nation's first freestanding outpatient surgery and recovery care center.

Since opening, the center has consistently ranked in the top 5 percent nationwide in case volume. Over 40,000 patients have used the facility. To accommodate the expanding patient load, the staff has grown as well. Today, approximately 130 employees assist the 250 practicing physicians who are associated with the center.

In recognition of its commitment to quality and innovation, the Fresno Surgery and Recovery Care Center has received the "Award of Merit" from the

Healthcare Forum and the "Innovator of the Year Award" from the Society for Healthcare Planning and Marketing. Several national publications have also lauded the center's efforts, including the *Wall Street Journal*, the *New York Times*, *Modern Healthcare, Hospitals Magazine, OR Manager*, and *American Medical News*.

MINIMIZING EXPENSE, MAXIMIZING QUALITY
According to Chief Executive Tony Carr, nearly 70 percent of all surgery can be performed in an outpatient and recovery care environment. As a result, the Fresno Surgery and Recovery Care Center strives to provide its patients with more affordable, personalized care without sacrificing quality.

From the first step into the lobby, a patient encounters all the grace and welcome of a small hotel.

Since its inception, the center has endeavored to minimize patient expense primarily by keeping overhead costs down. For example, the facility does not support 24-hour emergency rooms and intensive care services. These unique advantages translate into a savings of approximately 15 to 30 percent over traditional hospital care for the same services.

Despite the focus on reduced costs, the center has not sacrificed quality. From the first step into the lobby, a patient encounters all the grace and welcome of a small hotel. Each of the 20 state-of-the-art patient rooms is private and includes several home-like amenities, such as a television, VCR, artwork, books, and a private refrigerator. Unsightly oxygen and suction panels are tastefully hidden behind artwork. Throughout the facility, emphasis is placed on privacy and comfort.

Crucial to the center's commitment to overall

The center's 20 state-of-the-art patient rooms are private and include several home-like amenities, such as a television, VCR, artwork, books, and a private refrigerator.

quality is the expertise of its personnel. The nursing staff at the Recovery Care Center is made up exclusively of registered nurses, all of whom are certified in Advanced Cardiac Life Support. The center's nurse-to-patient ratio of one to three approaches that of a hospital intensive care unit. No other hospital in California can boast that achievement.

The staff of registered nurses has helped the center meet its quality goals, maintain its commitment to innovation, and improve the overall cost-effectiveness of the institution. The all-registered nurse staff is also an important statement about the value the institution places on the role of the nurse. The center's management believes that by hiring extraordinary people, listening to them, and implementing their ideas, something wonderful happens. Employees acquire a sense of pride and ownership through their jobs. As a result, patients are treated as people, not numbers.

Even the food at the center is superior. Chef Chrissy Steele-Dillard is a graduate of the Culinary Academy of San Francisco, and the center's employees say her menus are second to none. As guests, family and friends are encouraged to join patients at mealtime at no additional charge.

"Unique," "revolutionary," and "wonderful" are but a few of the words patients have used to describe their experience at the center. All patients are given a survey, and what they maintain again and again is that comfort and privacy do make a

difference. One patient remarked, "I was treated like royalty and felt very secure and in capable hands."

As it prepares to enter a second decade of service, the Fresno Surgery and Recovery Care Center faces the challenge of keeping pace with the rapidly changing health care industry. Through its innovations, the center has set in motion a tide of change that is slowly transforming the way an industry thinks about healing.

The nursing staff at the Recovery Care Center is made up exclusively of registered nurses, all of whom are certified in Advanced Cardiac Life Support.

FRESNO
California's Heartland

1 9 8 5 - 1 9 9 3

With each new arrival, Fresno is transformed from a farming village into a regional urban center. As the city spreads further out toward the horizon, it remains a place where the quality of life is high and the cost of living is reasonable.

1985	CELLULAR ONE
1985	COMMUNITY PHYSICIANS OF CENTRAL CALIFORNIA
1985	FRESNO IMAGING CENTER
1985	KMSG, CHANNEL 59
1986	DeBAS CHOCOLATE, INC.
1986	EMCON ASSOCIATES
1987	CEDAR VISTA COMPREHENSIVE PSYCHIATRIC SERVICES
1987	VALLEY YELLOW PAGES
1988	BRIGHTON PROPERTIES
1988	CHOICE TV
1988	PHILLIPS JUNIOR COLLEGE
1989	COCOLA BROADCASTING COMPANIES
1991	SAN JOAQUIN VALLEY REHABILITATION HOSPITAL

*T*he earliest reactions to the Fresno Imaging Center were a combination of amazement and a little skepticism. When the facility opened in 1985, its equipment was so advanced that doctors from throughout the nation, as well as from Japan and France, traveled to Fresno to see the new center. They found equipment and a building so sophisticated that many felt the

start-up costs were too high to see a return on the considerable investment. Adding to that concern was the fact that the center was charting unknown waters: In 1985, it was the only local freestanding health care facility in the Central San Joaquin Valley to provide a complete spectrum of major imaging services.

As it turned out, it was the inspired physicians, not the skeptics, who were clearly on the right track. The Fresno Imaging Center has achieved enormous success in its seven years of operation, enjoying growth in terms of patient visits and widespread recognition for outstanding service. Says Dr. Leo Shishmanian, one of three Fresno radiologists who founded the facility, "The Fresno Imaging Center was conceived and developed to provide outpatient medical imaging that represents the cutting edge of technology, and to do so at lower costs and with a level of service not known before. We have achieved our goal."

GEORGE O'BRIEN

NEARLY A DECADE OF INNOVATION

The state-of-the-art technology that initially drew the most attention to the center was its equipment for magnetic resonance imaging (MRI). The Fresno Imaging Center was the first health care institution in the community to offer this diagnostic procedure, which generates a three-dimensional anatomical view of any portion of the body through a process involving a high-strength field magnet. "MRI can provide very detailed images," says Dr. Hagop Tookoian, who today serves along with Dr. Shishmanian as a managing partner, "and this enables us to diagnose certain problems earlier than before, such as multiple sclerosis."

In addition, the 15,000-square-foot Fresno Imaging Center offers ultrasound imaging, computed tomography (CT scan), nuclear medicine, angiography, biopsy, general radiology, and fluoroscopy. The physicians and staff of the center see 180 to 200 patients daily, a remarkable statistic considering that in its first year the center averaged only 60 patients each day. The center's staff has grown accordingly; originally employing 35 people, it now has a staff of 80.

A CARING ENVIRONMENT

Recognizing that technology is only one aspect of superior medical care, the physicians and staff emphasize quality of service. Creating and maintaining a genuine, caring environment for patients has

been a priority at the center since its inception. To that end, a consultant experienced in this area conducts regular employee seminars to help staff members understand patients' needs and respond accordingly. "We have seen positive results from these training courses," explains Dr. Tookoian. "Our employees understand that all of our patients deserve special consideration, and they've developed sensitive ways to help patients deal with their unique situations."

The center's 80 staff members see 180 to 200 patients daily.

Efficiency is another important aspect of quality service at the Fresno Imaging Center. The average waiting room period is six minutes, and the average time spent at the center is less than one hour, even when accounting for procedures that require up to five hours. This level of efficiency can be attributed, in part, to the fact that the center assigns a hostess to each patient to escort him or her through all testing procedures, to answer any questions, and to oversee the patient's visit from beginning to end.

The third major ingredient in the center's success is careful cost containment. When it opened seven years ago, the Fresno Imaging Center was able to offer all diagnostic imaging services at a significant savings over other comparable local providers. As more private imaging centers have been established in Fresno, competition has increased, but the Fresno Imaging Center continues to grow. The center can still offer the same services for 20 to 70

Since 1985, the Fresno Imaging Center has provided a complete spectrum of major imaging services from its main building on North Thesta Avenue.

percent less than local comparable imaging facilities. "We believe that supplying our advanced imaging services at lower costs has been a significant benefit to the community," says Dr. Tookoian.

MILESTONES FOR THE FUTURE

With the center's success have come opportunities, and in 1991 an important one was realized when Fresno Imaging Center formed a partnership with Saint Agnes Medical Center, a leader in the Fresno medical community. The relationship is beneficial to the center because it can contract for managed care and has access to the superior purchasing power of a major institution. Saint Agnes benefits by broadening its services to the community and avoiding duplication of services, which would result in increased costs. The success of the partnership is based on the fact that patients have new access to efficient, low-cost imaging services, especially those whose employers engage in managed care contracts.

In response to the continuing growth of the center's existing mammography service, the Fresno Imaging Center opened the community's first free-standing mammography center in early 1992. With six radiologists on staff, the center sees from 60 to 80 mammography patients daily, which is more than the volume of any other medical facility in Fresno, according to Dr. Shishmanian. The new 4,000-square-foot facility, located at 6181 North Thesta, is staffed exclusively by women and is decorated and dedicated to serve the needs of women.

AN EMPLOYEE-ORIENTED COMPANY

Known throughout the community for superior service and concern for its patients, the Fresno Imaging Center also considers employee satisfaction a top priority. The center promotes a family atmosphere and pleasant work environment that have resulted in low employee turnover. The center sponsors outside activities such as volleyball and baseball leagues, and the counseling services used to improve patient relations are also employed to promote inter-departmental relations. Additionally, the center is involved in numerous educational programs and charitable causes benefiting the community.

"Patients tend to respond positively to their visits here when they are in the hands of staff who are well trained, caring, and obviously enjoy their jobs," says Dr. Shishmanian.

Since its founding seven years ago, Fresno Imaging Center has earned its place as a leading provider of imaging services throughout Fresno and the Central Valley. Advanced technology, outstanding service, and efficient management have joined forces to give the local community indispensable life-enhancing and life-saving medical services.

According to the managing physicians, "Our slogan is 'Caring through Technology,' and we spare no effort in providing both. The success of our physicians and staff continue to exemplify our dedication."

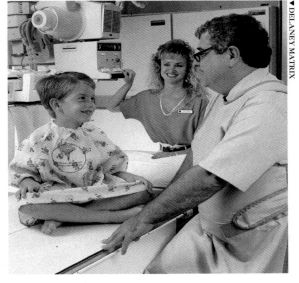

Dr. Hagop Tookoian and a radiologic technologist prepare a patient for a CT scan.

I magine working in a regulated industry that has no rules, only because they are changing every day. Or working in a high-tech field where the newest technology routinely becomes obsolete. Shelley Ehlers, director of marketing at Cellular One in Fresno, remembers those early days of cellular communication. "In the beginning, everything was very intense," she

says. "The technology was so new that it was changing faster than anyone could keep up. There was no manual to follow. We were writing the textbook as we went."

SERVING FRESNO SINCE 1986

On October 4, 1986, Cellular One received its license to sell in Fresno. Less than 48 hours later, the firm was already working from a booth at the Fresno Fair. Cellular One built an initial customer base using the competitor's system while constructing its own. On November 5, 1987, the firm completed construction of its first four cell sites and literally "turned on the switch," providing cellular service to all Cellular One customers. Meanwhile, parent company McCaw Cellular Communications, Inc. was actively improving coverage and clarity by adding cell sites and making agreements with other cities, as well as building and purchasing systems throughout California.

Many of Cellular One's original staff members are still with the company today, indicative of its strong commitment to employees. They remember when Cellular One moved into its permanent location in the Fig Garden Financial Center and the immediate need for additional employees to service a growing customer base. Because of the industry's fast pace, Cellular One emphasized adding people who would take on the personal challenge to excel in such an environment. Today, most of Cellular One's 100-plus employees consider their jobs a lifetime commitment, and the team atmosphere is unmistakable.

CUSTOMER COMMITMENT

Cellular One attributes its past, present, and future success to its primary focus—customer commitment. This concept is most notable in Cellular One's many innovations: high-tech switches, increased cell sites, a 24-hour customer care line, and a Customer Convenience Center. The company is also building the North American Cellular Network, the first and only seamless cellular network to go from coast to coast, allowing customers to place calls and easily receive them from practically anywhere in North America.

Cellular One always strives to simplify the communication process for the customer, to improve service, and to make the customer feel like part of the decision-making process. It's not uncommon for Cellular One to host customer luncheons to

see if their needs are being met and to discover ways to improve service. "Customer commitment goes beyond just servicing customers' daily needs," says Ehlers. "It extends to the community, of which Cellular One has strived to become an integral part."

Cellular One operates a Customer Convenience Center in Fresno's Fig Garden Financial Center.

To that end, Cellular One is involved with many charitable organizations: Easter Seals, Valley Children's Hospital, American Lung Association, United Cerebral Palsy, the Metropolitan Museum, the San Joaquin River Parkway, the Bulldog Foundation, CSUF Business Association, and the San Joaquin Crackdown. The company has developed a "Fog Program" with the California Highway Patrol to prevent fog-related accidents on Fresno's surrounding highways. Likewise, Cellular One plays an important role in maintaining communication between sheriff, police, and fire authorities in such disaster situations as the 1991 San Francisco earthquake and the 1990 Yosemite fires.

Many believe that the future of communication is held in cellular technology. With the help of McCaw Cellular Communications, Cellular One will maintain its position as the nation's largest cellular provider. According to Ehlers, "The future holds many exciting new innovations for Cellular One and its customers—innovations that will make our company strong and our customers' lives easier."

Zig Fischer had a lifelong ambition to begin his own business. While working as an executive in the telephone directory division of Pacific Bell in San Francisco, he developed the idea of a business directory that would do much more than provide names and phone numbers. It would be an invaluable resource for all types of information, and it would serve as an

effective vehicle for advertising. His idea, however, did not find a receptive audience at the company.

In 1985, after 20 years of service, Fischer left Pacific Bell, and along with him went two co-workers, Doris Engelmann and Larry Cheng. After publishing a directory designed as a resource for the automotive industry, the three entrepreneurs decided to publish a complete business telephone directory that would compete with the traditional Pacific Bell yellow pages directory. After much research they chose Fresno, and in February 1987 established an office in cramped 600-square-foot quarters. With a 12-member staff, the company started on its mission to convince local merchants that David could beat Goliath.

President Zig Fischer cites lower prices, more information, and better service as reasons for the rapid growth of Valley Yellow Pages.

"It was an uphill battle, but with a dedicated, resourceful staff working 18 hours a day, we published a very good first directory," says Fischer. "Free enterprise is the best way of ensuring that the customer is getting the best possible product at the best possible price. I firmly believe that."

The company has since begun publishing Valley Yellow Pages directories for Bakersfield-Kern County, Sacramento, Stockton, and Stanislaus County. Today, Fischer serves as president of the company, overseeing 140 employees. Always a prudent planner, he sees the company's explosive growth carrying it into other Valley areas.

A POPULAR, AWARD-WINNING DIRECTORY

One important reason for the popularity of Valley Yellow Pages with local businesses is its reasonable advertising rates. "Advertisers know that with Valley Yellow Pages they are spending about half

what they would with the phone company," says Fischer.

Another of the directory's appealing features, particularly with consumers, is the Community Information Blue Pages, a unique innovation that Fischer envisioned during his telephone company career. The Blue Pages include such features as Telephone Related Services, a ZIP Code Street Index, Pro Teams and Local Sports schedules, an AT&T 800 Number directory, Senior Services, a community Calendar of Events, and names, addresses, and photos of federal, state, and local elected officials, plus much more.

From left: Vice presidents Larry Cheng and Doris Englemann joined Zig Fischer in making Valley Yellow Pages the largest independent directory publisher in Central California.

The Valley Yellow Pages was one of the first publications to include such a section. Since then, directories throughout the state published by other companies, including Pacific Bell, have copied Fischer's innovative idea. Also, only Valley Yellow Pages includes ZIP codes in all of its yellow pages listings for easier reference. "We're pretty proud that we started all of this," says Fischer.

Not only popular, the company's directories are award winners. In 1992, Valley Yellow Pages was given the prized Gold Book Award from the Association of Directory Publishers for "Best Civic Information" among directories across North America. A 1992 study by Verified Audit Circulation, an independent research company based in Marina Del Ray, California, found that Valley Yellow Pages was number one in possession, usage, and preference in many of the communities it serves.

With such an emphasis on community information, it's not surprising the company is so active with community charities and events. Valley Yellow Pages supports many local organizations, such as the Blood Bank, Partnership for a Drug Free America, Valley Children's Hospital, Valley Public Television, the Special Olympics, the Muscular Dystrophy Association, the Fresno Rotary Club, and the Chaffee Zoological Gardens.

By bringing competition to the local yellow pages market, Zig Fischer has proved that free enterprise, vision, and persistence can lead to prosperity. Valley Yellow Pages has become not only an important corporate citizen in Fresno, but also a valuable contributor to the community.

I n recent years, visionary business leaders in California's San Joaquin Valley have begun to recognize the potential of what has long been the fastest growing segment of Valley society. The Hispanic market, which comprises nearly 35 percent of the total Valley population, today wields formidable economic power and has become a dominant force in the community.

KMSG, Channel 59 is among the few Hispanic-oriented, Fresno-based firms to embrace this under-served market, and the 19-employee company has become an integral part of Hispanic life in the process. The television station's six-county service area, representing the 12th largest Hispanic market in the United States, is home to 542,000 Spanish surname residents. According to KMSG marketing data, 70 percent of those area Hispanics prefer to speak only Spanish at home.

KMSG's six-county service area, representing the 12th largest Hispanic market in the United States, is home to 542,000 Spanish surname residents.

"Statistics show that Spanish people, even though acculturated into local society, still enjoy programming in their own language," says Maria Rodriguez, station manager. "We give our audience an alternative to other local programming."

Broadcasting with 1.35 million watts of power, KMSG boasts a service area that covers more than 8,035 square miles, including Merced, Mariposa, Madera, Fresno, Kings, and Tulare counties. The station is also carried by Continental, Consolidated, Falcon, Northland, Coalinga, and Warner cable services.

Sports, drama, cartoons, and music are all part of KMSG's diverse format. "We provide information to the community, in addition to educational and entertainment opportunities," Rodriguez says. "We also have a very broad viewer focus, ranging from older, more established residents to the youngest groups."

AN INCREASING HISPANIC FOCUS

KMSG, Channel 59 went on the air in 1985 after a patient five-year wait for an FCC license. Owned by Sanger Telecasters, Inc.—a partnership between James Zahn, who serves as program director and operations manager, and Diane Dostinich, company president—KMSG originally offered a Christian format. It was also the first television station in Fresno to broadcast in stereo and later added a home shopping program in 1986.

KMSG moved toward its current Hispanic focus on March 7, 1988 through an association with Telemundo Group, Inc. of New York City. Telemundo not only owns and operates Spanish-language television stations across the United States, but also produces and syndicates Spanish-language programming and sells advertising time on

behalf of its stations and affiliates.

Though KMSG initially scheduled just three hours of Telemundo programing each weekday, the community response was so enthusiastic that Hispanic offerings have since edged out the other facets of the original format. In fact, Spanish-language programs are now broadcast from 7 a.m. to 11 p.m. Monday through Friday, and from 1 a.m. to 12 midnight Saturday and Sunday.

This relationship has also boosted the quality and diversity of KMSG's programming, allowing the local station access to popular shows such as "Cine en su Casa" (Mexican Cinema Classics), "Cara a Cara" (prime-time discussion), "Ocurrio asi" (cutting-edge broadcast journalism), and "Futbol y Boxeo" (soccer and boxing). Likewise, viewers can enjoy Spanish-language versions of CNN, "Million Dollar Movies," game shows, and entertainment variety shows. KMSG also offers a Spanish version of MTV, Music Television Internacional, which produces a contemporary, bi-lingual music video format exclusively for Spanish-language stations.

Although KMSG's primary focus is on the Hispanic community, company officials are proud of the station's flexibility. English-language religious programming and Iranian television help round out KMSG's viewing opportunities. "We think our programming is among the best and broadest in the Valley," says Zahn. "We recognize the diversity of the Fresno population, and we are currently working on programming agreements with the local Hmong, Filipino, and Indian communities."

COMMUNITY LEADERSHIP

According to company officials, KMSG is dedicated to providing leadership throughout the Hispanic community. For example, the station sponsors an annual Hispanic Health Day, which offers information and services on health and nutrition issues. Approximately 10,000 local residents attend the one-day event held each March at Fresno's Manchester Center shopping mall, where they can take advantage of free blood-pressure and cholesterol tests, eye exams, and dental and chiropractic examinations.

"Nearly 30 different display booths are available," Rodriguez says. "Hispanic people have a

Broadcasting with 1.35 million watts of power, KMSG boasts a service area that covers more than 8,035 square miles, including Merced, Mariposa, Madera, Fresno, Kings, and Tulare counties.

chance to get free health screening, attend health and nutrition seminars, and pick up complimentary literature and product samples related to health care. Information about social issues such as teen pregnancy and gang activity is also available."

KMSG's two-day Cinco de Mayo celebration, held at Fulton Mall in downtown Fresno, is another important Hispanic event in the Valley. Each year, up to 35,000 people join in the festivities to honor the Mexican national holiday, and KMSG is on hand to broadcast the excitement to its viewers.

Since 1989, KMSG has been the official sponsor of the Mexican Independence Day Parade, held annually in mid-September to celebrate Mexico's independence from Spain in 1810. Parade crowds of 35,000 to 40,000 people make this event the biggest celebration of its kind in the San Joaquin Valley.

Each fall, KMSG also participates in the Big Fresno Fair, broadcasting live from the fairgrounds during the two-week October program. "We offer a

profile of fair events on a daily basis and on-the-spot television coverage of different activities," says Rodriguez.

PREPARED FOR GROWTH

While KMSG has already become an important resource for the Valley's Hispanic community, plans are on the table to expand the station's services even further. "My dream is to start our own news division," Rodriguez says. "We want to include local, Spanish-language news coverage in our format as soon as possible."

With an eye on expansion and a track record of success, company officials have not forgotten that the Hispanic community is still perhaps the most under-served aspect of Fresno's population. "There is a lot of growth expected in the Hispanic community," Rodriguez says, "and we intend to harness its potential and make a positive contribution to the future of that important population segment."

Established in Fresno in 1985, Community Physicians of Central California is a managed care and business management association of San Joaquin Valley doctors who have joined with health care insurers to reduce medical costs without sacrificing service quality. ◆ *Today, more than 400 physician members from Fresno, Kings, and Madera counties have pooled their*

resources and centralized many of their administrative activities through Community Physicians. From a 7,000-square-foot office on East Shaw Avenue in the heart of northern Fresno, the organization and its 56 employees are working to increase efficiency, lower overhead costs, and pass the savings on to patients—sometimes as much as 30 percent.

"This approach to health care service frequently results in more affordable insurance premiums, reduced share-of-cost payments, and lower deductibles," says Constantine Michas, M.D., president of Community Physicians of Central California. "In an era of soaring medical costs, we feel our organization is making a positive impact on the communities we serve."

SERVING PHYSICIANS, INSURERS, AND PATIENTS

Representatives of Community Physicians meet with prospective health care insurers—including insurance companies, health maintenance organizations (HMOs), preferred provider organizations (PPOs), and privately funded corporate programs—to negotiate contracts for medical services. For example, preset fees are established with a PPO for each service, while a monthly, per patient flat rate is negotiated with an HMO to cover all medical services a patient might require.

"For the HMO patients, these rates remain constant whether patients are treated for flu symptoms or need brain surgery," Michas explains. "It is then up to us to manage our program so we can cover actual expenses."

Though fees for member physicians are reduced to make a service contract attractive to insurers, there is adequate incentive for local doctors to join the group. Those new to the community or new to private practice can use the system to help them establish a patient base. Likewise, a physician who acknowledges the importance of reducing overall health care costs also joins.

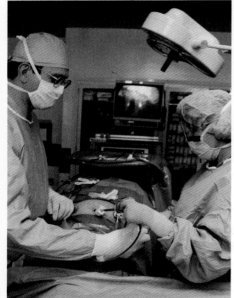

Through Community Physicians, Valley residents have access to modern medical procedures, such as laparoscopic cholecystectomy, at more affordable rates.

Regardless of the circumstances, the benefits of membership are numerous, says Michas: "Even an established physician would be interested in Community Physicians of Central California. Our affiliation with literally hundreds of insurers provides access to approximately 100,000 patients within our PPO business and an additional 35,000 within our HMO contracts. Approximately 90 percent of Fresno County residents belong to a medical plan that includes a reduced fee-for-service structure."

Another major benefit to member physicians is access to the group's administrative services. Community Physicians, in conjunction with Community Hospitals of Central California, has the ability to manage all or part of a physician's practice, from furnishing an office to everyday business management, including hiring employees and paying rent and utilities. "We feel our administrative services not only make the physician's practice more efficient, but they also reduce physician stress and increase the time devoted to direct patient care," says Michas.

Another example of the organization's strides toward greater efficiency is its in-house claims processing. Through contractual agreements requiring insurers to pay a predetermined monthly payment, Community Physicians has established its own pool of financial resources for processing and paying member physician service claims. This simplifies the process for both patient and doctor by essentially removing the insurer from the loop.

Community Physicians also manages medical services for all members of the network. By controlling the use of unnecessary procedures, acting as a centralized referral agency, and targeting the appropriate doctor for specialized services, the organization can help keep costs down.

In addition, Community Physicians is seeking ways to further improve its administrative methods. For example, the group is developing a new computer system that will enable each of its physician members to access mainframe computer storage banks. Scheduled to be fully operational by 1995, the system will make a wealth of necessary information, including patient medical records and account status, available at the touch of a button.

Full computerization will also allow Community Physicians to convert to electronic billing. "Paperwork is one of our major headaches," Michas says. "In the next five years, we hope to go to a paperless

The board of directors and staff of Community Physicians of Central California are dedicated to increasing efficiency, lowering overhead costs, and passing the savings on to patients.

system that will streamline the operations of individual physicians, as well as our own."

Another service offered by Community Physicians as a cost-saving measure is its Wellness Program. In operation since 1990, the preventive medicine program offers seminars for insurers and other organizations on topics such as early cancer detection, cholesterol checks, general nutrition, and the hazards of smoking. Seminars are free to physician members and affiliated organizations and open to the general public for a nominal fee of $5. "The Wellness Program has been embraced throughout the Fresno area," Michas says. "Organizations such as the City of Clovis utilize the service."

Community Physicians also offers a training program for its physician members which focuses on methods of keeping costs down. Information on the best way to submit claims and updates on changing Medicare laws are typical topics of discussion. A monthly Community Physicians newsletter, *Traditional Medicine Today*, is distributed to more than 1,000 local hospitals and health care providers, attorneys, insurance companies, and other organizations.

"Our patrons frequently call on us for details on new technology, legal issues, and improved medical practices," Michas says. "The industry is evolving so rapidly, we feel it is necessary to keep the information flowing."

NEARLY A DECADE OF GROWTH
Since its founding nearly a decade ago, Community Physicians has experienced significant growth. Community Hospitals of Central California, the

organization's primary hospital affiliate, initiated the formation of Community Physicians in 1985. From a one-room office at Community Hospital and Medical Center in downtown Fresno, the organization has expanded rapidly to meet the ever-changing health care needs of the San Joaquin Valley.

Founding CEO William H. Rowe became Community Physicians' first executive director, supported by one employee, Diane Bissonnette. When Rowe retired in 1988, Don Kanesaki joined the organization to succeed him. That same year, Community Physicians acquired Foundation Health Care Administrators, a competing organization, and its employee roster jumped to eight. By then, the physician membership had grown to nearly 300 shareholders and more than 50 contracted physicians. In July 1990, Community Physicians moved into a 5,800-square-foot office on Bulldog Lane in northern Fresno, within blocks of its current West Shaw location.

Along with this growth in size, revenues have increased significantly. Net cash on hand at the end of 1985 was $61,416. In 1991, Community Physicians reported $12 million in revenue, and company officials see more of the same for the future.

"There are probably 100 or so organizations of this kind in California, but we are among the 10 or 15 largest," says Michas. "I don't see how an individual physician can continue to function outside this kind of system for much longer. We believe Community Physicians is a model of things to come."

Environmental engineering is among the newest, most exciting areas of specialization within the engineering field, combining the study of both biological and physical sciences. Since its Fresno branch opened in 1986, EMCON Associates has worked with local public and private businesses to meet the environmental engineering challenges of the 21st century.

A publicly held, full-service environmental consulting firm with nearly 40 offices nationwide, EMCON was founded in San Jose, California in 1971 by a group of landfill engineers who got their start designing waste management units. "In the old days, we just called them dumps," says Herman Schymiczek, manager of the Fresno office. "Now they are generically referred to as waste management units, which includes facilities ranging from municipal solid waste landfills to hazardous waste disposal sites."

DIVERSE ENVIRONMENTAL EXPERTISE

Today, EMCON offers one of the most comprehensive environmental programs available anywhere, including underground tank services, soil and groundwater investigations, property transfer assessments, environmental services for agriculture, groundwater resource services, environmental and health risk assessments, and air quality monitoring and modeling services. "Because the different facets of our environment are so interdependent," Schymiczek says, "it would be difficult for a company like EMCON not to address all of these areas."

EMCON's wide range of services for underground storage tanks includes installation of exploratory borings and monitoring wells, soil sampling and analysis, laboratory testing, remedial action planning, and treatment. Since 1971, the firm has successfully completed more than 1,000 storage tank projects throughout the United States. EMCON employs state-of-the-art hydrogeologic inspection techniques to determine the soundness of a tank and the extent of contamination, if any. "We use a multi-disciplinary approach to our investigation," Schymiczek explains. "We are also experienced in overseeing tank removal and soil excavation and disposal."

In the area of groundwater investigation, EMCON provides consulting, analysis, and monitoring services for identifying contamination. The company uses a combination of surface and subsur-

EMCON's comprehensive training program prepares employees to handle hazardous waste.

"Water is a very important issue throughout the Valley," says Herman Schymiczek, "especially in an area like ours that has competing industrial, agricultural, and residential interests."

face exploratory methods to evaluate the geologic characteristics of an area and predict potential contaminant migration. Over the years, EMCON has conducted more than 500 non-storage tank investigations of this type, including studies to assess the physical and chemical character of groundwater, soil, and rock.

EMCON also puts its testing expertise to work when conducting property transfer assessments for buyers, sellers, developers, and lending institutions. The accurate assessment of contamination levels is critical in evaluating property value and owner responsibilities when a property changes hands. "If you buy a contaminated site," Schymiczek warns, "you could be liable for cleaning it up, whether you are an independent purchaser, a bank, or a broker, and the cost can be substantially greater than the value of the property."

In the desert-like environment of the San Joaquin Valley, EMCON has also become an important player in the effort to ensure an adequate and clean water supply. Its services in that field include resource studies, well design and location, operational evaluations, aquifer testing, and supervision of drilling. Nationwide, EMCON has investigated water resource supplies for purity and volume in more than 350 locations, enabling municipalities across the United States to set long-term growth goals and ensure a safe, plentiful water supply.

These services are particularly important in Fresno, one of the fastest growing cities in the country. "Water is a very important issue throughout the Valley," Schymiczek says, "especially in an area like ours that has competing industrial, agricultural, and residential interests."

A REPUTATION IN SOLID WASTE DISPOSAL

Since its founding, EMCON Associates has built its strongest reputation for innovation in solid waste disposal. The phenomenal surge in California's population, which totaled approximately 30 million in the 1990 U.S. census, has forced many of the state's disposal sites to the point of overflow. Each year, Californians discard more than 50 million tons of solid waste, or 1.5 tons of garbage per person. At least 100 of the state's 350 landfills are

expected to reach capacity and close by 1994.

Similar patterns can be seen in Fresno. In 1992, Fresnans discarded an estimated 291,000 tons of solid waste—1.6 million pounds per day. By the year 2000, a projected 620,000 tons of trash will leave Fresno for disposal sites around the area. "That's a lot of trash," Schymiczek says. "It's amazing. It makes you wonder what the numbers must be like in the Los Angeles basin."

But amid tougher state regulations, EMCON Associates is taking steps to address the growing solid waste disposal problem. The firm not only has the capability to monitor existing sites, it also is on the cutting edge of developing and implementing new disposal methods. While incineration has been used recently as an alternative in other parts of the country, air quality has come under severe scrutiny in California. As a result, composting is gaining popularity as a safe and effective alternative for relieving some pressure on landfills, and EMCON is a leader in this expanding technology.

Paper, together with yard waste (mostly leaves and grass clippings), comprises over 50 percent of the solid waste destined for landfills. This material, along with sewage sludge and food waste accounts for nearly all of the organic fraction of the solid waste stream. Composting is one way of reusing this organic material by converting it into useful products such as mulch for landscaping and high-quality compost as a soil amendment. Explains Schymiczek, "The basic rule is that if it was once alive, it can be composted."

EMCON assists clients—such as golf courses, school districts, and city and county governments—in choosing the best composting methods for their operation. The firm also recommends the combination of special equipment—shredders, grinders, front-end loaders, and turning equipment—that will meet the individual client's composting needs. Likewise, EMCON recommends mitigation measures to control dust, odor, and litter and assists clients in complying with federal, state, and local regulations. EMCON can also estimate start-up costs and operational expenses for various composting programs. "Alleviating our solid waste problem is more than just desirable," Schymiczek says. "It is now mandated by California state law."

Passed in 1989, the California Integrated Waste Management Act has set targets for decreasing solid waste across the state. "Every municipality in California must reduce its solid waste volume by 25 percent by 1995," Schymiczek explains. "And by the year 2000, we need to cut our waste in half. I see this as our biggest challenge for the immediate future, both as a community and as an environmental consulting firm."

Working toward this goal in the Fresno area, EMCON holds seminars and workshops on solid waste management. The firm recently cosponsored a Fresno County Public Works seminar on composting for managing organic wastes ranging from yard waste to municipal solid waste. EMCON also works closely with elected officials and business leaders. "We are very active locally as members of the Chamber of Commerce Environmental Issues and Water Resources committees," Schymiczek says, "and we serve as advisors to the Chamber's Environmental Advocacy Committee."

As to the future of Fresno's environment, Schymiczek sees a need for a comprehensive, integrated approach to waste management. Placing too much emphasis on a single aspect of the overall problem is not the answer.

"I would personally like to get involved in an integrated waste management program," says Schymiczek. "For example, it seems like the folks who handle trash hardly ever talk to the people who work with sewage. It seems to me there is a potential for solving both problems at the same time, and EMCON plans to be a part of that process."

DeBas Chocolate, Inc.

With wine- and champagne-filled chocolates, cappuccino bars, and truffles packaged in elegant tapestry boxes, DeBas Chocolate, Inc. has been setting trends in the gourmet chocolate industry since its founding in 1986. ◆ President Guy DeBas, who eats a pound and a half of chocolate a day, prides himself on making the finest gourmet chocolate on the market. He uses only the highest quality Swiss, Belgian, and German chocolate available, and his 20 employees lovingly handcraft the unique confections in a 6,000-square-foot plant in southeast Fresno. His wife, Wendy, assists with marketing efforts and the design of the elegant packaging.

"We are the Rolls Royce of the chocolate industry," says DeBas. "If somebody comes to me and says 'I tasted a better chocolate,' I will work harder. We are committed to being number one."

In keeping with that philosophy, the company introduces a new chocolate product every six months. "It keeps the customer and the retailers happy," explains DeBas. "Chocolate lovers everywhere look forward to seeing and tasting what we're going to do next."

A Long List of Chocolate Delicacies

A partial list of the company's products would impress any chocolate lover: Irish cream, creme de menthe, raspberry, amaretto, and peanut butter truffles, as well as numerous wine-filled chocolates, which DeBas makes for 72 different wineries in the Napa and Sonoma valleys.

DeBas was the first chocolate manufacturer to produce espresso and cappuccino chocolates, six varieties of sugar-free truffles, and the signature wine-filled chocolates, which are carefully blended to be compatible with the individual winery's vintage. In all, the company makes 15 different kinds of truffles, including a sake-filled version for a Japanese sake company.

The company's handmade chocolates are sold under private labels in distinguished department stores across the country, including Gottschalk's, Neiman Marcus, Broadway, Emporium, and Liberty House. DeBas also makes private label truffles for Disneyland and Knotts Berry Farm. In Fresno, DeBas products are available at Sauce for the Goose, Candy Time, the Sierra Nut House, Gottschalk's, Cabbages and King, and Gourmet Delight.

The company also produces 2,000 pounds of high quality chocolate bars each day to be used by schools, churches, and hospitals in fund-raising drives. "The nice thing about our bars is that the superior quality of our high-end products is maintained in everything we make," says DeBas.

A Legacy of Quality

While other companies have cut costs in the face of economic downturns, DeBas Chocolate has done just the opposite, a strategy that clearly sets the company and its owner apart from the competition. "When times were tough, we increased quality and improved packaging," says DeBas. "Despite the added expense, our efforts have definitely paid off."

But quality has always been important to Guy DeBas, who came to the United States from Lebanon. For 20 years, his family owned a chocolate factory near Beirut, called Chantilly Chocolatier International. In 1978, DeBas immigrated to California to finish his studies in agriculture at CSU, Fresno. During that time, he imported chocolate directly from the family factory in Lebanon for sale to U.S. customers until the facility was bombed in 1982.

DeBas decided to start his own wholesale chocolate operation in 1986. With only two sample truffles in hand, he attended the International Fancy Food Show in San Francisco where he secured a $35,000 contract with Trader Joe's, a Los Angeles-based gourmet food chain. That single contract launched the company on a road to success that appears to have no end.

Today, the commitment to quality continues. With over 2,600 accounts nationwide, DeBas Chocolate reported more than $1 million dollars in gross sales in 1992. After just eight years in operation, the company has carved a significant niche in the nation's gourmet candy industry. From its home base in Fresno, DeBas Chocolate looks forward to a prosperous, chocolate-filled future.

Offering such delicacies as truffles packaged in elegant tapestry boxes, DeBas Chocolate has become a trendsetter in the gourmet chocolate industry.

CEDAR VISTA
COMPREHENSIVE PSYCHIATRIC SERVICES

edar Vista, founded in 1987, is a relatively new psychiatric care and treatment facility. But it has rapidly taken its place as a leading member of the local health care community, serving a seven-county area around Fresno. The list of local organizations receiving funding or benefiting from Cedar Vista's free community services is lengthy; it includes such organizations as the

Mental Health Association, Alcoholism Council, Fresno and Clovis Unified School Districts, California State University, Child Abuse Prevention Network, and Rape Counseling.

"We have tried very hard to become part of the community by looking for ways to fill real needs," says Nancy Lucinian, director of marketing and community relations. "Another important goal of Cedar Vista is to help educate the community about mental illness. The profession and this facility have very effective ways of treating all types of mental or emotional disorders. Our greatest obstacle is that people do not seek help because of a fear of how they will be perceived or their lack of understanding that life could be better."

Cedar Vista opened in 1987 as an inpatient treatment facility for adults and adolescents suffering from all types of psychiatric disorders, from depression to multiple personality disorder. In its second year of operation, the hospital began offering an inpatient program for children. Most recently, Cedar Vista has expanded its services to include partial hospitalization outpatient programs for all age groups. This newest offering provides intensive treatment but allows the patient to return home at the end of the day. The service will be expanded in the near future to include an evening program, allowing people to go to work during the day while benefiting from intensive outpatient treatment in the evening. Currently, the 60-bed facility and its 173 doctors and other staff members serve approximately 1,000 patients yearly.

PROMOTING MENTAL HEALTH
IN THE COMMUNITY

Cedar Vista has recently established several innovative outpatient programs for promoting mental health among adults and children. The Odyssey program, developed to help adults learn to work together more effectively, focuses on communication, leadership, and problem-solving skills. Offered to businesses and groups, the program is particularly effective when the entire staff of a business completes the course together. "Many employees have found this course to be very helpful because it teaches the benefits and the skills of team effort," Lucinian says.

Group activities include overcoming physical obstacles such as ropes, cables, and logs. Class members may be asked to traverse a cable line suspended in midair or climb a wall 14 feet high. One popular exercise involves challenging a team

Group activities at Cedar Vista include overcoming physical obstacles such as ropes, cables, and logs.

member to fall backwards off an elevated platform into the waiting arms of colleagues. Adds Lucinian, "Participants learn to trust others and to find courage within themselves that many never realized they had."

A summer camp program to help children develop problem-solving and decision-making skills was recently developed by the Cedar Vista staff. The program, which includes many typical summer camp activities, is staffed by hospital employees who specialize in working with children. "A child with low self-esteem can be helped in this type of program," says Lucinian, "but it is designed so that every child can benefit from participation."

After five years of service, Cedar Vista is striving to provide the best in treatment aimed at encouraging, promoting, and teaching mentally healthful lifestyles. With the finest in personnel and programs, Cedar Vista looks forward to meeting the psychiatric care needs of the growing Fresno community.

Residential areas at Brighton Crest have been carefully planned so that 40 to 45 percent of the homes front the golf course.

estled in the gently rolling foothills north of Fresno, a dynamic master-planned community called "Brighton" is springing up near Millerton Lake, in the heart of the San Joaquin Valley. The master project, being developed by Brighton Properties, is slated for completion around the year 2000. This new community will boast hiking and biking trails, tennis courts, a modern sports/exercise facility, wildlife preserves, and a mixture of restaurants, retail stores, and office spaces surrounded by tastefully built homes, villas, and apartments. When all five phases are completed, the community will contain approximately 4,350 residences and 9,000 to 11,000 people.

Brighton Crest, the first phase of the community currently being built, offers its residents custom homes with stunning views of the San Joaquin Valley and the Sierra-Nevada Mountains, as well as championship golf. Brighton Crest is the beginning of what will become a self-contained "New Town" as originally approved by Fresno County.

In all, over 2,000 acres will be developed under the Brighton master plan, including five separate communities all drawing on the Brighton theme. The first, a 488-acre community known as Brighton Crest, earned approval of its tentative tract map in 1988. Construction on Brighton Lakes is slated to begin in 1993, with Brighton Fields, Brighton Meadows, and Brighton Hills to follow. The visionary of the Brighton community is A. Ben Ewell Jr., president and CEO of Brighton Properties. The vision, which began in the early 1980s, is named after Ewell's boyhood home of Brighton, Ohio. One of California's preeminent water rights attorneys, Ewell envisioned a pioneer development carefully integrated into the natural environment. To that end, the original terrain and topography of the land have been preserved to the greatest extent possible, retaining native California plants and Blue Oaks, a tree found only in the California foothills. Each spring, residents enjoy a profusion of wildflowers which carpet the foothills.

Protection and preservation of the natural environment and implementation of conservation measures are an important part of the Brighton community. As a result, the development was selected as the winner of the Gold Nugget Grand Award by the Pacific Coast Builders Conference in 1990 as the "Best Master-Planned Community in the 14 Western States." A six-acre bird sanctuary has been set aside within the initial development as a further commitment to the environment.

Adding to the Brighton community's appeal is its proximity to Fresno, only a 15-minute drive away. The Brighton development is also a 45-minute drive from the Sierra-Nevada Mountains and a short distance from Millerton Lake State Park, making it a natural for the sports-minded resident. "A person can go skiing in the morning, play a challenging round of golf in the afternoon, and finish the day watching the sun set while sailing on Millerton Lake," says Toni Breadmont, executive office director of Brighton Properties.

UNIQUE IN THE SAN JOAQUIN VALLEY

Though still in its early stages of development, the award-winning Brighton community is already on its way to becoming the San Joaquin Valley's premier planned community. The focal point of Brighton Crest is the Brighton Crest Country Club and its 18-hole championship golf course. Designed by PGA golf professional and celebrity Johnny Miller, the course is rapidly gaining a reputation as one the most challenging in the region. In 1992, *California Golf Magazine* named the course "One of the Top 10 Private Courses in the State," an honor that no other course in

the San Joaquin Valley has earned. The Brighton Crest Country Club is a private facility which currently has a program for non-member golf play and an active tournament and social schedule.

PGA golf professional and celebrity Johnny Miller designed the 18-hole championship course at Brighton Crest.

During construction on the course in 1989, Johnny Miller personally visited the project site every few weeks to ensure that every detail of his stunning design was followed. Since its dedication in September 1990, Miller has played the course several times and has given it his stamp of approval.

According to Ewell, the 6,821-yard, 18-hole course is full of challenges. "The course receives tremendous compliments," he says. "There is no other course like it in the San Joaquin Valley. It provides a very unique and exciting golfing experience."

In keeping with the overall community design, the course was constructed with sensitivity to the surrounding environment. On the seventh hole, a dramatic view of the Valley opens up. Other holes are flanked by majestic oaks, which were preserved as part of the natural terrain and add to the course's appeal. "With emphasis on the natural terrain, it was designed so very few trees were removed," says Ewell.

Championship golf is not the only amenity drawing people to Brighton Crest. Residents can dine at Harland's Cafe, an informal eatery operated by Brighton Properties in conjunction with famed restauranteur, Roy Harland. Likewise, a spacious Signature Room for members and special guests is available, as well as a full pro shop carrying a line of signature and monogrammed clothing. Outdoor patios and deck areas together with a lap pool and spa have already been completed. The Brighton Crest golf course is host to many Fresno-area charity golf tournaments.

Construction is also under way on single-family custom homes at Brighton Crest. Lot sizes range from 10,000 square feet to more than one acre. The residential areas have been carefully planned so that 40 to 45 percent of the homes front the golf course, while many of the remaining homesites offer an excellent view of the course or the surrounding hills. Since the first subdivision map was recorded in December 1989, several single-family homes have been completed at Brighton Crest. Construction is ready to begin on the first single-family detached villas. Developed by BDC Development of Fresno and Pismo Beach, the 2,400- to 2,800-square-foot homes are located along the 18th fairway. When the entire Brighton Crest phase is complete, there will be 320 single-family homes and 100 villas.

Brighton Crest has been designed so that residents will never have the feeling of being in a large development with hundreds of homes. "Thanks to the gently rolling terrain, there is a sense of

In 1992, California Golf Magazine *named the course "One of the Top 10 Private Courses in the State," an honor that no other course in the San Joaquin Valley has earned. (Ken E. May photos)*

privacy," explains J.P. Leviste, a principal and chief financial officer of Brighton Properties, "but residents have the security of knowing there are neighbors close by."

PERSEVERANCE AND COMMITMENT: COMPANY WATCHWORDS

From a championship golf course to the finest in residential construction, the first community being built is unlike anything else in the San Joaquin Valley and is rapidly becoming the model for other communities.

Creating an entirely new town is a tremendous challenge. It takes more than time and a strong commitment. Brighton Properties, through its principals and staff, has coordinated the efforts of a multiplicity of local, state, and federal agencies, as well as numerous community and environmental groups. Taking on and meeting this challenge has made the Brighton Crest project an unparalleled success and has set the stage for Fresno's future.

THE CHALLENGE CONTINUES

Planning is well under way for Brighton Lakes, the next Brighton community. While different from Brighton Crest in that densities are higher and the development is intended for a broader market appeal, all of the commitments to environment and community are being carried forward.

t Phillips Junior College in Fresno, students address teachers by their first names and often drop by faculty offices just to say hello. It's all part of the friendly and relaxed atmosphere that characterizes this small but growing junior college. ◆ Making students feel comfortable and instilling a sense of professionalism are important to the mission of the faculty and staff at

this private, two-year college. With a total enrollment of approximately 450, Phillips offers six associate of arts and sciences degrees, as well as a number of diploma programs.

"The thing we do best here is care about our students," says Herman Whitaker, director of high school admissions. "We offer an alternative for students who don't think they could survive in a larger college atmosphere. Ours is a professional, caring environment, but one that is also relaxed. We become a mentor and friend to every student."

In a society that has become highly technical, Phillips Junior College is dedicated to providing the specialized education needed for individuals to enter and advance in today's workplace. Graduates pursue careers in such fields as business management, accounting, travel and tourism, computer programming, electronics, and retail management. They also hold clerical positions, some specializing in medical and legal office administration. "We teach our students how to market themselves to employers," says Whitaker, adding that Phillips students come from virtually every age group and all walks of life.

Electronics technology is the college's largest program, with more than 100 students currently enrolled.

THE ROAD TO FRESNO

Phillips Colleges, Inc. has a proud history that began in 1946 when Ary and Bess Phillips purchased their first vocational school in Mississippi. Gerald Phillips, son of the founder and current president, joined the company in 1961 and began an expansion program concentrating primarily on growth in the South. By 1972, Phillips Colleges had grown to encompass three campuses. By the late 1980s, Phillips Colleges, Inc. had acquired several schools throughout the country including the prestigious Katharine Gibbs secretarial schools on the East Coast.

Headquartered today in Gulfport, Mississippi, Phillips Colleges operates 58 schools in 25 states. The company entered the Fresno market in 1988

with the purchase of National College, a career college that had existed in the area for more than 10 years under different ownership. A diverse student population now attends the Fresno location, a 19,000-square-foot modern facility which houses nine classrooms, four laboratories, faculty and administrative offices, a library, and a student lounge.

Associate of Arts degrees are offered in business management and computerized office administration. Associate of Science degrees are available in computer information systems and computerized accounting. Two of the college's most popular programs are electronics technology (the largest program, with more than 100 students) and travel and tourism.

A UNIQUE LEARNING ATMOSPHERE

Students at Phillips enjoy many benefits not always available to their counterparts enrolled in public colleges and universities. According to Whitaker, classes are readily available and most programs can be completed in 18 months. Likewise, the college offers a comprehensive career development program, which helps students develop resumes and make employer contacts. It also provides refresher courses in all subjects at no additional cost. Job placement services from any of the 58 Phillips schools nationwide are available throughout each graduate's working career.

Phillips Junior College takes a unique approach to course scheduling as well. During each 12-week term, classes are held four days a week, and faculty members are available on Fridays for student conferences and to give individualized instruction.

The college is also concerned with developing, in all students, the appreciation for knowledge and the skills necessary for lifelong learning in their chosen field. To that end, Phillips offers a variety of instructional programs and academic counseling services. "We are very career-oriented. There are no lines to wait in and no overcrowded classrooms," says Whitaker. "We are giving students specific marketable skills."

As part of the college's emphasis on hands-on training, students are taught by professionals with experience in their individual fields. "We're a school that cares about our students," says Whitaker. "We're the best kept secret in the San Joaquin Valley."

SAN JOAQUIN VALLEY REHABILITATION HOSPITAL

San Joaquin Valley Rehabilitation Hospital views physical rehabilitation as opportunity. Its staff members work together to maximize patients' capabilities, striving to restore purpose and quality of life to each individual. ◆ A freestanding, comprehensive rehabilitation facility, the hospital is owned and managed by Continental Medical Systems, Inc.

(Mechanicsburg, Pennsylvania), the nation's leading independent provider of comprehensive medical rehabilitation. The Fresno hospital is the first hospital in the Central Valley with a staff dedicated to providing diagnosis and treatment exclusively in physical rehabilitation. Prior to its inception, the same sort of care was available locally only in general acute-care hospitals.

"This hospital marks another milestone in the development of specialized facilities which focus solely on a specific aspect of medicine, thus offering a high level of skill and attention," says administrator Betsy Guthrie. "The people who work here, from physicians to specially trained staff, have devoted themselves to the betterment of individuals who need their very special skills."

San Joaquin Valley Rehabilitation Hospital is committed to helping each patient reach his or her potential through customized programs.

The 60-bed, 80,000-square-foot modern facility is designed to meet the needs of individuals who have experienced a disabling injury or illness—and also to help their families. With an ambulation course, indoor therapeutic pool, transitional living apartment, and specialized brain-injury units, the facility is equipped to suit the unique needs of its patients. More importantly, the team of physicians, nurses, psychologists, social workers, and physical, recreational, speech, and occupational therapists offers a dynamic approach to therapy and education.

The path to independence starts with an interdisciplinary team strategy. Medical and health care professionals combine individual expertise and training to treat the whole person. Instead of dividing therapy procedures by areas of specialization, treatments are grouped logically. For instance, speech and mobility are addressed simultaneously, since patient communication usually enhances and accelerates physical and emotional recovery. "We see the interdisciplinary rehabilitation process as vital to the patient's long-term success. Our facility, by design, supports this approach," Guthrie explains.

MAXIMIZING POTENTIAL

The hospital's commitment is to help each patient reach his or her potential through customized programs. Upon admission, every patient is carefully evaluated by a licensed team of rehabilitation professionals to determine the patient's particular strengths and weaknesses. This initial assessment serves as the foundation for the development of an encouraging, highly individualized treatment plan.

Working closely with family members, the hospital staff prepares a set of progressive goals, and intensive therapy begins. A thorough case management system ensures that these goals, the treatment program, and discharge plans are reviewed and adjusted as necessary. The intent is to provide optimum care while assisting insurance companies in controlling escalating health care costs.

Referring physicians can guide their patients in a smooth transition from an acute-care facility to San Joaquin Valley Rehabilitation Hospital. The physician can participate in the rehabilitation programs with the support of the hospital's specialized staff and modern medical equipment. Outpatient services are also available, with van transportation provided to patients and family members.

UNIQUE REHABILITATION PROGRAMS

At San Joaquin Valley Rehabilitation Hospital, a physiatrist (a physician trained in physical medicine and rehabilitation) leads an experienced team of rehabilitation specialists in a variety of customized programs. The hospital's Hydro Conditioning classes, for example, consist

of water exercises and aerobics aimed at cardiovascular conditioning, strengthening muscle tone, and improving flexibility. The Therapeutic Pool Program, conducted in the facility's indoor swimming pool, has been adapted for wheelchair users and offers individual sessions of low-intensity conditioning and exercises modified for individuals with physical limitations.

The 60-bed, 80,000-square-foot modern facility is designed to meet the needs of individuals who have experienced a disabling injury or illness.

Perhaps the most unique program at the hospital is the Transitional Living Unit, which includes a fully furnished studio apartment used for reentry education. The unit is designed to help patients recapture the ordinary skills they had before their injury or illness. Because cooking, dressing, and personal hygiene—activities most people take for granted—frequently pose obstacles to individuals with physical limitations, the unit allows patients to regain the personal freedom and independence they need to live in a typical home environment. And that's the ultimate goal of every program at San Joaquin Valley Rehabilitation Hospital.

Founded in Fresno in 1989, Cocola Broadcasting Companies is a conglomerate of local independent television stations that provides a broad selection of viewing options, including home shopping, pay-per-view music videos, and locally produced formats. ◆ This growing broadcasting enterprise is the brainchild of owner and founder Gary Cocola. Housed in 8,000 square feet

of space at Morris Cocola Broadcast Center in north Fresno, the company offers 24-hour programming through three individual stations: channels 34, 43, and 66.

BUILDING A DREAM

Cocola's personal story is intimately linked to the history of his business. Throughout his college days, he worked hard to learn the broadcasting field and continued along that career path after graduation. His early experience included hosting his own programs on KFRE-TV, KAIL-TV, and KFRE Radio, all in Fresno. He also worked with KERO-TV in Bakersfield and KMBY-Radio in Monterey.

"I have always dreamed of being in broadcasting," says Cocola. "That's why I studied it in college. I discovered, however, that the road to your dreams is not always a straight line."

In 1964, Cocola set his dream of a broadcasting career aside to join his father in the family produce business in Fresno. For more than two decades, he remained at Cocola Fruit Corporation, a shipper and distributor of fresh California fruits and vegetables, eventually serving as company president.

In 1977, he renewed his quest for a broadcasting career with hopes of establishing his own station. Despite his unwavering determination, the road to success was not easy. "We struggled for seven years to obtain an FCC license and get permission to build," Cocola remembers. "There were times when I doubted if we would ever get off the ground."

Along with Diane Dostinich and friend James Zahn, a broadcasting engineer from San Francisco, Cocola founded Sanger Telecasters, Inc. in 1985. With significant radio and television experience

Cocola Broadcasting is headquartered in the 8,000-square-foot Morris Cocola Broadcast Center in north Fresno.

already under his belt, Cocola and his partners envisioned an innovative format that combined the capabilities of both media. Their plan called for all-music video programming, a relatively new concept at the time, supported by stereo sound, which had never before been used in Fresno. Unfortunately, advertising support for the untried format was virtually nonexistent. "I don't think advertisers had fully realized the potential of the teenage dollar yet," Cocola says, "so our plans seemed to fall apart before our eyes."

With a $1.5 million investment on the line, the partners launched a comprehensive search for alternative programming ideas and found strong interest from a growing industry segment. "I discovered that Christian broadcasters didn't need advertisers," Cocola says. "They were prepared to pay for their own time. This was the break I had been looking for, and we began operations."

In 1985, KMSG, Channel 59 began broadcasting 18 hours a day of Christian programming with the support of two full-time and three part-time employees. The station quickly became Fresno's number one source for religious broadcasting, bringing such well-known evangelists as Jim Baker, Jimmy Swaggart, Pat Robertson, and Oral and Richard Roberts into local homes.

In 1986, Sanger Telecasters seized an opportunity to broaden its focus by becoming an affiliate of the Home Shopping Network. In 1989, Cocola left KMSG to start Cocola Broadcasting Companies under an agreement that allowed him to take the Home Shopping Network contract with him. "KHST-TV, Channel 66 was launched in 1989," Cocola says. "It exceeded my wildest expectations. Home Shopping Network viewers spent more than $150,000 during our first week of operation."

RAPID GROWTH IN FRESNO

KHST-TV, Channel 66 soon expanded to a 24-hour-a-day format and exceeded $500,000 in monthly sales. That pattern of growth has continued at Cocola Broadcasting. In January 1992, the company reintroduced a "classic" form of television to Fresno: locally produced programming. By purchasing KGMC, Channel 34, Cocola revived the broadcasting concept he had enjoyed so much as a child.

The company has opened up prime-time programming opportunities to Fresno's general public, offering locally produced programs from 6 p.m. to 11 p.m., seven days a week. For $75 a half hour or

Gary Cocola's personal story is intimately linked to the history of his business. "I have always dreamed of being in broadcasting," he says. "That's why I studied it in college. I discovered, however, that the road to your dreams is not always a straight line."

$125 an hour, virtually any individual or organization can air its own television programs. Budding entertainers, bands, comics, and talk show hosts are among the many locals who regularly use the service. Ethnic programming, such as "Awaaz-E-Waatan," a cultural Punjab Indian program, and "Hmong TV Live," are also offered on Channel 34. "The only requirement," Cocola says, "is that the program must be in good taste. We want to promote serious local producers, not those interested in distasteful subject matter."

An example of the unique programs currently offered is the Jefferson News Network, produced by local school children from Clovis Elementary School in the nearby town of Clovis. The 30-minute, monthly segments focus on local issues and events of interest to school-age children. An estimated 30 youngsters participate in the show through writing, reporting, and on-air responsibilities at a cost of about $90 per show. The program is underwritten by advertisers, so that no student or school funds are used. "It's the kind of programming stations used to offer 30 years ago," Cocola says, "before they turned into giant network organizations. Sometimes I really miss those days."

On the heels of this new programming addition, Cocola Broadcasting has continued to build on the owner's dream. In September 1992, the company reached an agreement with San Joaquin Television Improvement Corp. to broadcast pay-per-view music videos, a programming format similar to Cocola's original vision for KMSG in 1985. For $2.50 per call, local viewers may dial a "900" number and select among country, contemporary, Hispanic, and classic rock music videos from on-screen television menus.

Cocola himself has enjoyed the format so much that he is currently purchasing KSDI-TV, Channel 43, and he expects approval from the FCC soon. "I guess you could say I have come full circle," Cocola muses. "If you stick with your dreams, they really can come true."

Cocola Broadcasting Companies is also negotiating for a fourth station to be located in Omaha, Nebraska. The new organization, which will carry Cocola's tried and true Home Shopping Network, is expected to be on the air by 1993.

But despite the company's potential growth beyond its San Joaquin Valley base, Cocola does not plan to leave Fresno—his home for more than 40 years. "I was born and raised here," he says. "This city has been very good to me, and I can't imagine living anywhere else."

ounded in September 1988, Choice TV has brought the latest in technological advances in cable television broadcasting to Fresno area residents. One of only four companies of its kind in California, Choice TV offers residents of the central San Joaquin Valley diverse cable television programming via a microwave system of broadcasting, rather than the more common hardwired cable transmission.

The company's transmitting tower, located atop Owens Mountain 18 miles northeast of Fresno, receives television satellite signals and broadcasts them to a 4,000-square-mile service area that extends north of Fresno to Chowchilla and south to Visalia. Choice TV's primary advantage over the many competing cable television companies in the same service area is its ability to broadcast a signal that is consistently clear and strong and unaffected by weather. "The system operates without an extensive network of cables that require repair and maintenance," explains Terry Holmes, general manager. "Choice TV has a 99.9 percent dependability rating. There are only two sources of potential failure in the system—the transmitter and the equipment at a customer's home. That's the beauty of it—very simplistic, very reliable."

This combination of product quality and an extraordinary level of dependability has resulted in a tremendous growth rate for the wireless television industry. "It is the fastest growing segment of the media industry today," says Holmes.

Choice TV of Fresno has been part of this exciting growth phenomenon. After three years of intense market research and development, the company launched its operation in August 1991. Just one year later, Choice TV had built a customer list of nearly 5,000, at an average rate of 100 new customers weekly. Likewise, its staff grew from five employees to 16. The company is owned by Fresno MMDS Associates, a partnership of 40 investors from across the country.

SUPERIOR SERVICE

"I think the company's success is partly due to our outstanding customer service program," Holmes says. The simple installation procedure takes about an hour and is handled by one of many Fresno area independent contractors. A technician erects a small antenna on the customer's roof and then connects it to an addressable convertor that is usually placed on top of the television set.

"Every installation job or service request is followed up with a call from a Choice TV representative to ask about the quality of the service. Surveys have shown that our customer satisfaction

Choice TV backs its superior product with an outstanding customer service program.

Managing Director Robert Hostetler and General Manager Terry Holmes take part in Choice TV's grand opening festivities with the Fresno Chamber of Commerce.

rate is 94 to 99 percent. We are very proud of that," says Holmes.

To remain competitive, Choice TV officials also keep abreast of innovations in the wireless broadcasting industry. One such advance is digital transmission, which will enhance the quality of broadcasting significantly. Compression, another process currently being tested, will allow wireless broadcasting companies to increase tremendously the number of channels they can broadcast compared to the number that are currently available through the Federal Communications Commission. When this process is perfected, Choice TV will be able to expand channel selection from its current number of 23 to more than 150. Both digital transmission and the compression process are expected to be introduced to the Fresno market during the mid-1990s.

Choice TV is also committed to using its technology to service the needs of the greater community— specifically, the local education community. The company is in the process of establishing a broadcasting facility to meet the classroom and professional needs of the Fresno County School District, Fresno City College, and California State University, Fresno. Expected to be fully operational by spring of 1994, the facility will enable the three institutions to share programming with one another at various educational receiving sites, as well as with all Choice TV subscribers.

With the substantial foothold of drawing 5,000 customers in its first year of operation, Choice TV looks forward to the challenge of attracting many more new customers in a service area that includes more than 1 million residents. "Our objective," Holmes says, "is to provide a superior product at a fair price, backed by excellent service. We are also committed to keeping pace with every technological innovation that could enhance our product."

PHOTOGRAPHERS

PHOTO EDITOR TIM FLEMING, a graduate of Fresno City College, owns and operates Flash Foto, a leading professional and commercial photography lab with two locations in Fresno. Prior to opening Flash Foto in 1982, he was a fine art and commercial photographer exhibiting throughout the western states and accepting commercial and corporate assignments. Fleming is now studying electronic- and computer-manipulated photography and producing a library of stock photos of Fresno and the Valley area. He has combined his hobby of hang gliding with photography to produce beautiful aerials of the Sierra. Fleming lives in Fresno with his dog, cat, and his two children.

POINT ANDERSON, a resident of Fresno, has traveled and photographed extensively the American West, including Alaska. He operates Point's Unknown Photography, a library of artful medium- and large-format images of scenic landscapes of the West. Anderson also works as an audio engineer and union stage hand.

DAVID ASHCRAFT has been a free-lance photographer for 12 years, doing wedding, portrait, and commercial work while continuing fine art photography. He works as the official photographer for Summit Adventure, a Christian mountaineering organization. Ashcraft's photos have been published in *National Geographic World Magazine* and on album and book covers.

RICHARD DARBY, a native of Fresno, has worked as a staff photographer for the *Fresno Bee* for more than 30 years, focusing on editorial, wildlife, and military and high-performance aviation photography. Darby has received several state and national awards for his wildlife photography.

OSCAR DeLEON has been a professional photographer for 20 years, specializing in television news and special events. He has been instrumental in producing annual media events and recently started his own business in television production. Employed as photo chief at the local Univision Station (Channel 21), DeLeon cofounded the local chapter of the Chicano Media Association.

GEORGE FLINT JR., a graduate of Bucknell University, moved to Fresno in 1956 after serving in the U.S. Marine Corps Reserve and taught in the Fresno Unified School District for 27 years. A free-lance photographer since 1980, Flint now concentrates on landscapes and photographic close-ups, exhibiting locally and in McCall, Idaho. He is a charter board member of Central California Photographers' Guild.

RUBEN FLORES, a native of Fresno, attended Kings River Community College in Reedley, California, and opened Ruben Flores Photography in 1989. His work has been published in *Hispanic Profiles Magazine, Lifestyles Magazine*, and *Passion Hair Magazine* of Japan. His most recent project was the United Way's local poster campaign.

DAVE FULTZ has been a free-lance photographer for 10 years and has exhibited both locally and internationally. A native of Fresno, he received a Bachelor of Arts degree in journalism from CSU, Fresno, and an Associate Science degree from Fresno City College. Fultz's areas of specialty include sports, theater, architecture, and commercial tabletop photography. He is currently helping develop new marketing techniques for the real estate market.

RODNEY KACHE GAVROIAN, born and raised in the San Joaquin Valley, is a free-lance photographer who has turned his long-term interest in photography into a business, Kach A Memory Photography. He specializes in scenic, nature, agricultural, and local interest stock imagery, as well as action sports and team photography. Gavroian's work has been published on the cover of a national sporting magazine and has been used in postcards, brochures, and newsletters.

RICHARD HAAS, a life-long resident of Fresno, graduated from UCLA with a Bachelor of Arts degree in 1950, a Master of Arts degree in 1958, and a Ph.D. in 1969 in zoology. He retired as professor of biology at CSU, Fresno, in 1992. Haas specializes in nature photography—scenics, animals, and flowers.

SHAWN JEZERINAC is an advertising/corporate photographer specializing in location lighting. Though his reputation has been built on photographing people for the past 13 years, he now performs product illustration and architectural photography as well. Jezerinac is represented internationally by Custom Medical Stock Photography in Chicago.

MICHAEL KARIBIAN, a native of the San Joaquin Valley, has worked in Fresno as a commercial photographer and graphic designer since 1977. He has produced a range of work for print media assignments, including editorial, advertising, corporate, public relations, and medical photography. In 1990, Karibian produced a documentary exhibit featuring oral histories and photography of elderly Armenian immigrants.

BOB KEMPEN JR. is owner of Data-Central Collection Bureau in Fresno. His photography focuses on landscapes, seascapes, and all types of sports, particularly motor sports and kite festivals. Kempen's Indy 500 car images have been used in various magazines, calendars, posters, and program covers.

PAUL J. RUTIGLIANO, born in Rochester, New York, opened Ros-Lynn Studios in Fresno in 1973, specializing in wedding, portrait, and stock photography. He has been an instructor of photography at State Center Community College since 1986, and his work has been published in magazines and journals in over 45 countries.

TAMELA RYATT, originally of Kingsburg, California, received a Bachelor of Arts degree from CSU, Fresno, in 1989. Her company, Ryatt Photography, focuses primarily on producing black-and-white portraiture, interiors for designers, and artists' portfolios. Ryatt received the Golden Oak Award for photography in advertising in 1992 and is currently working on her first book of photography.

KEITH SEAMAN received his training in advertising photography at Art Center College of Design in Los Angeles and later apprenticed with three Los Angeles advertising photographers. He and his wife now own and operate CAMERAD, INC, located in downtown Fresno. The Seamans coordinate and execute major location and studio productions as well as simple studio product shots. Seaman is a member of the Los Angeles chapter of Advertising Photographers of America.

E.Z. SMITH, a sixth-generation Fresnan, has owned and operated E.Z. Smith Photography for 12 years. His work ranges from his photography services for artists to fine art images. Smith has exhibited his work nationally and internationally and has organized and judged many photography competitions. His most recent show, *Naked Fascists on the Grapevine,* was held in Fresno in June 1992.

LOUISE STULL, a Fresno native, is a retired university librarian, after 40 combined years of service at the University of Illinois and CSU, Fresno. She has traveled widely, taking photographs on all seven continents. Stull is a current member in and former officer of many photographic organizations, including the Photographic Society of America, the Fresno Camera Club, and the San Joaquin Valley Camera Club Council.

DONN R. WESTMORELAND is an advertising and print media photographer who has lived in Fresno since 1976. He is also the publisher of *Going Out* magazine, a local tourist guide. Westmoreland works with the Fresno Chamber of Commerce and the Fresno Historical Society in collecting, recording, and preserving images of the San Joaquin Valley. A specialist in black-and-white photography, he is currently expanding his studio in the historic warehouse district to include portraiture.

The daring young man and his flying machine landed after the pioneer flight into Yosemite Valley to be greeted by park superintendent W. B. Lewis (right) in 1923. Seventy years later, not only are planes forbidden on the valley floor, but automobiles may soon be as well.

NICK P. MARMOLEJO has been a part-time free-lance photographer since 1987 specializing in stock and wedding photography. Marmolejo has been a member of Central Valley Professional Photographers since his move to Fresno in 1980. He is also a member of Spectrum Gallery in Fresno.

MEGAN A. MICKEL, a professional free-lancer for over 12 years, is a native of Fresno and the owner/operator of Multi-Media Advantage. A 1987 graduate of CSU, Fresno, she has produced numerous promotional pieces for CSUF Athletics, as well as coordinated their sports photography. Mickel specializes in advertising, publicity, special events, environmental portrait, and stock photography. Her work has been published in *The Sporting News* and in numerous local publications.

BRENT OLIPHANT is a San Joaquin Valley native who graduated from CSU, Fresno, in 1973. He has been a free-lance photographer and designer for 12 years, and his award-winning work has appeared in annual reports and agricultural publications. Oliphant lives in Fresno with his wife and two daughters.

MICHAEL PENN, originally of Hanford, California, graduated from CSU, Fresno, in 1984. Penn worked for three and a half years at the *Anchorage Daily News* before joining the staff at the *Fresno Bee* as an editorial photographer in May of 1988.

RICK PRESTON, a full-time fine art photographer since 1972, specializes in large-format landscape images. Before turning to photography, he worked as a white-water river guide and also served as a fighter pilot in the U.S. Navy. Preston's photographs have been exhibited in 24 states and two Canadian provinces, including *Dreams of Stone,* a one-man show at the Fresno Art Museum in 1992. Currently, eight galleries and agents carry his work coast to coast.

Some of Fresno's finest proudly demonstrate the fire department's first hook and ladder truck in 1889 on Fulton Street next to the old Barton Opera House (left). In the distance stands the Fresno Water Tower.

INDEX TO PATRONS

The past and future of
Fresno are solidly repre-
sented in the old Water
Tower and the new City
Hall, constructed nearly
a century apart.